DEMOGRAPHY, DEMOCRACY, AND DEVELOPMENT: PACIFIC RIM EXPERIENCES

Proceedings of the Second Annual
University of Victoria–National Sun Yat-sen
University Social Sciences Symposium
held at National Sun Yat-sen University,
Kaoshiung, Taiwan, April 24-25, 2000

DEMOGRAPHY, DEMOCRACY, AND DEVELOPMENT: PACIFIC RIM EXPERIENCES

edited by

Robert E. Bedeski and John A. Schofield

Canadian Western Geographical Series

Volume 38

Copyright 2002

Western Geographical Press

DEPARTMENT OF GEOGRAPHY, UNIVERSITY OF VICTORIA
P.O. BOX 3050, VICTORIA, BC, CANADA V8W 3P5
PHONE: (250)721-7331   FAX: (250)721-6216
EMAIL: HFOSTER@OFFICE.GEOG.UVIC.CA

Canadian Western Geographical Series

editorial address

Harold D. Foster, Ph.D.
Department of Geography
University of Victoria
Victoria, British Columbia
Canada

Since publication began in 1970 the Western Geographical Series (now the Canadian and the International Western Geographical Series) has been generously supported by the Leon and Thea Koerner Foundation, the Social Science Federation of Canada, the National Centre for Atmospheric Research, the International Geographical Union Congress, the University of Victoria, the Natural Sciences Engineering Research Council of Canada, the Institute of the North American West, the University of Regina, the Potash and Phosphate Institute of Canada, the Saskatchewan Agriculture and Food Department, and the BC Ministry of Health and Ministry Responsible for Seniors.

DEMOGRAPHY, DEMOCRACY, AND DEVELOPMENT:
PACIFIC RIM EXPERIENCES

(Canadian western geographical series; 1203-1178; v. 38)
ISBN 0-919838-28-6

1. Pacific Area—Economic conditions—Congresses. 2. Pacific Area—Social conditions—Congresses. 3. East Asia—Economic conditions—Congresses. 4. East Asia—Social conditions—Congresses. I. Bedeski, Robert E. II. Schofield, John A. III. Title. IV. Series.

HC460.5.U54 2000   330.95   C2002-911357-1

Series Editor's Acknowledgements

Several members of the Department of Geography, University of Victoria co-operated to ensure the successful publication of this volume of the Canadian Western Geographical Series. Special thanks are due to the Technical Services Division. Diane Braithwaite undertook the very demanding tasks of typesetting and layout, while cartography and cover design was in the expert hands of Ken Josephson. Their dedication and hard work is greatly appreciated.

University of Victoria
Victoria, British Columbia
November, 2002

Harold D. Foster
Series Editor

Acknowledgements

We are grateful to the participants in the symposium who made this volume possible. We are also grateful to Professor Peter Lin, coordinator of the symposium, and to Vice-President Chou Chang-hung and former Dean Don Hong of National Sun Yat-sen University for the wonderful hospitality provided to the visitors from the University of Victoria during their visit to Kaohsiung. Presenters from the University of Victoria were supported through the Faculty Travel Grant Fund of their university.

For extensive initial editing and preparation of the papers in a consistent word processing format, we are indebted to the professional assistance of Ms. Darby Carswell. Without her contribution in collaboration with Professor Lin, the task of final editing would have been significantly greater.

Technical production was in the capable hands of the team at the Technical Services Division of the Department of Geography at the University of Victoria that has been responsible for so many of the previous volumes in the Canadian Western Geographical Series: Ms. Diane Braithwaite, Mr. Ken Josephson, and Professor Harold Foster, Series Editor.

Robert E. Bedeski
University of Victoria

John A. Schofield
University of Victoria

This volume is dedicated to the memory of Dr. Daniel J. Koenig,
one of the contributors, who passed away tragically in November 2001.
His energy, insightfulness, laughter, and bravery are
remembered by all who had the privilege of knowing him.

CONTENTS

SECTION I: DEMOGRAPHY

List of Figures

LIST OF TABLES

LIST OF PLATES

all photos by David Chuenyan Lai

Introduction

Robert E. Bedeski
Professor, Department of Political Science, University of Victoria

John A. Schofield
Dean, Faculty of Social Sciences, University of Victoria

This volume consists of papers presented at a joint University of Victoria-National Sun Yat-sen University Social Sciences Symposium in April, 2000 at National Sun Yat-sen University in Kaohsiung, Taiwan. The first joint Social Sciences symposium involving the two universities was held at the University of Victoria the previous year.

The three themes of demography, democracy, and development provided an organizing framework for the 2000 symposium with a primary focus on issues pertaining to Taiwan and Canada. Papers dealing with demographic matters are included as the chapters in the first section of the volume. Papers comprising the second section relate to economic and social development as well as to political relations across the Taiwan Straits and hence the status of Taiwanese sovereignty and democratic governance.

SECTION ONE: DEMOGRAPHY

The theme of demography is richly explored in the context of Sino-Taiwan society with emphasis on migration to Canada. At the centre of several papers is the centrality of the Chinese family as a core structure. The nuclear family is a universal structure of society, and has undergone considerable transformation and erosion in the industrial countries of the West, most recently with legal judgments on same-sex marriage. In the Confucian societies of Asia—Taiwan, Japan, and South Korea—the traditional family remains the undisputed core structure of society, and even in post-Mao mainland China, Confucian family values remain dominant. Migration of individuals within or outside China tests the viability of the family, and as centuries of Overseas Chinese experience have demonstrated, both nuclear and extended family structures reinforce adaptation to new environments while preserving a core of Chinese cultural values.

Continuous family support therefore facilitates survival and prosperity in the new surroundings, but also hinders assimilation in the new society, a factor that reinforces the formation of Chinatowns throughout the world. In a manner of speaking, the subtext of the articles in Section One is "globalization" meets the "clash of civilizations." The Chinese diaspora has been a continuous outflow of migrants to most parts of the world, dispersing key components of Chinese culture on a global scale, though rarely having an impact on host cultures. Similar to the Jewish diaspora, the Chinese outmigration has produced ghettos, and sometimes experienced backlash as in Indonesia or Vietnam.

David Lai examines Chinese immigration into Canada, and the obstacles placed by government. In an about-face from the so-called "Exclusion Act" of the 1920s, Canada established an Immigrant Investor Program to attract wealthier immigrants, which has resulted in an upsurge from Taiwan (as well as a large number of alleged bogus applications).

Fong Woon describes how Chinese family values affect young single women and their migrations to industrial employment in the marketizing economy of contemporary China—the "Filial Daughter Model." Proponents see the model as a household strategy to assist the family's economic conditions, while Woon looks at how the operation of the system tends to keep women in a subordinate position within patriarchal rural society.

Robert Bedeski's essay examines some of the dangers of rapid and massive immigration. Since the reforms in the People's Republic of China (PRC) starting in 1978, emigration has become easier, and during the past decade, mainland Chinese have become the largest national category of immigration into Canada. The operations of "snakeheads" and organized crime has cast suspicion on the advisability of open immigration, while the rapid increase in Chinese immigration may also challenge the appeal of multiculturalism as a viable future in Canada.

The next three chapters focus on aged immigrants, with the common theme of the role of the family as caregiver and main source of support. This contrasts with the increasing importance of the role of the Canadian state in the domain of elderly care. Zheng Wu and Randy Hart remark that "research indicates that immigrants tend to 'chain migrate' with their immediate families, and thus the main components of their support structures remain intact.... Furthermore, immigrants to Canada establish support networks within their ethnic-cultural communities, and may well receive support from the broader communities of the host society." The Wu-Hart research examines the variables of social support, with emphasis on subjective perceptions as a key factor.

Tru-Gin Liu considers three modes of care-giving for the elderly: Mode A – independent family support and cohabitation; Mode B – caregiving centres for the elderly with co-residence of immediate family; and Mode C – professional residence centres with full-time residence of the elderly. Traditionally, Chinese wives have looked after the elder parents or parents-in-laws, but in

Taiwan, as more women go into the workforce, considerations of efficient care for the aged prompt professional care-givers to argue for Mode C. Liu examines preferences between men and women using an infra-marginal analysis approach, as well as efficiency as the key factor, with several possible outcomes.

Neena Chappell surveys a sample of elderly Chinese in the Victoria- Greater Vancouver area, looking for differences in attitudes of Chinese from Hong Kong, mainland China, and Taiwan. She starts from recognition of the deference and respect generally accorded the elderly in Chinese society, and the contrasted lowering of esteem in Canadian society. In general, Chappell finds elderly from Taiwan fare better than those from either Hong Kong or China. A major factor may be, as she suggests, the continuity of filial piety as a virtue in Taiwan. One could also suggest that the aggressive and competitive commercialism of Hong Kong, and the chaotic interruptions and interventions of radical social experiments of Maoist China deprived the now-elderly of reliable expectation for a peaceful old age.

Finally, the late Dan Koenig, to whom this volume is dedicated, examines some of the social factors that have influenced demographic change in general, and particularly aging populations. He sees a "cultural globalization" occurring which has been accelerated by consolidation of telecommunications and other modes of technology. He concludes with a set of questions about the future.

SECTION TWO: DEMOCRACY AND DEVELOPMENT

To the extent that political systems can influence the process of development, the themes of democracy and development overlap. Although he touches on the importance of good governance, Peter Lin only hints at the democracy-development connection, preferring to focus on the economic dimensions of development. He contrasts the experience and development strategies of East Asia and Latin America. East Asian economies have pursued export and market-oriented strategies, have invested heavily in education and training, and have encouraged entrepreneurship and private initiative. The result has for the most part been macroeconomic stability and rapid economic development in a reasonably equitable manner. By contrast, Latin America has looked inward with tariffs and other forms of protection in pursuit of import substitution as the basis for industrialization, has differed from East Asia in terms of other strategies, and results have been less successful. He concludes that, while there can be no single panacea for successful development, private sector development, especially around small- and medium-sized enterprises, together with the other strategies adopted in East Asia, must surely be instructive.

Alan Hedley provides the contextual framework for a research project still in process. He postulates four scenarios for the potential effects of access to the internet on the process of development. He then proposes a questionnaire survey of non-governmental organizations in India, Malaysia, and Japan to assess the impact of internet access on development objectives in these countries. The research design will allow him to speculate about which of the four development scenarios is most descriptive of the experience in each of the countries.

One of the pre-conditions of sustainable development is a relatively stable exchange rate. Reflecting particularly on the Asian currency crises of 1997, Shan-non Chin uses a game-theoretic approach to gauge the appropriate policy responses to speculative pressures on currencies. Three strategies are identified: benign neglect designed to deny speculators a fixed target, the so-called 'Caesar's wife' strategy whereby the authorities maintain a firm and credible commitment to a fixed exchange rate, and exchange controls. The analysis confirms the view that speculation can certainly destabilize currencies and that, different as they are, each of the three strategies can help to deter speculation against a fixed peg.

The final three chapters in the volume deal with the central political issue in Taiwan, namely relations with the People's Republic of China across the Taiwan Straits, an issue that is key to the maintenance of democracy and the preferred mode of development in Taiwan.

Gerard S.H. Chow analyses the state of cross-straits relations immediately before and after the 2000 Taiwanese presidential election. Each of the leading tickets in the election took a nuanced stance on Mainland policy, trying to reflect in slightly different ways the strong interest in independence that exists in Taiwan without provoking the PRC to military action. Before the election Beijing had adopted a belligerent attitude exemplified in its white paper of 21 February, 2000 in which it threatened military force if the island declared independence, fell into foreign hands or attempted to put off unification discussions indefinitely. With the election of Chen Shui-bian, the candidate most disliked by Beijing, the situation clearly involved some tension. Chow's advice is to proceed cautiously, a policy that to date the new president has in general pursued with the notable exception of statements in early August 2002 affirming Taiwanese sovereignty and the democratic right of people to choose their own political status through referendum.

Jou-juo Chu looks at the economic and political implications of the substantial outflow of Taiwanese capital to Mainland China, and the increase in social interaction across the Straits, that has occurred since the 1980s. The drive for comparative trading advantage has been behind the capital flows. A key question is: will the expansion of economic and social linkage contribute to a lessening of political tension across the Straits? It is the hope of the PRC and the fear of the ROC that it will facilitate eventual reunification, hardly a recipe for rapprochement. For Chu, on the other hand, enhanced economic and social integration should increase the potential costs of escalated political conflict and could hence stimulate attempts to find negotiated solutions to the differences that exist between the two sides.

Finally, Marion Chyun-yang Wang provides a complementary perspective on cross-Straits relations, focusing on China's role in regional cooperation. The PRC is striving for economic and socio-political advantage in the Asia-Pacific region. An important part of its strategy is to bring Hong Kong-Macau and Taiwan increasingly within its economic orbit. Based on the concept of 'Greater China' as an economic, cultural, and political entity, Beijing's approach to development and eventual reunification involves market reforms and an opening-up to foreign investment with particular emphasis, through favourable tax and other inducements, on Hong Kong-Macau and Taiwanese investment in coastal provinces. The challenge for Taiwan is to take commercial advantage of these opportunities without surrendering its political identity.

Concluding Comments

This second symposium represented a further step in international scholarly cooperation and mutual understanding, building on the experience of the first symposium. Lively discussions and commentaries made the inter-cultural project more than an academic exercise, and scholars from the two universities enhanced knowledge and broadened horizons, while stimulating further joint research. The two symposia also contributed to the broadening and deepening of intellectual exchange between Canada and Taiwan, complementing the already significant economic relations between the two societies. Canadians tend to have more knowledge and concern over mainland China and Japan, while being relatively uninformed about the remarkable progress of Taiwan under its difficult circumstances. Likewise, most Taiwanese, while well-informed about the US, tend to have little interest in Canada. The dialogue of ideas conveyed in these papers signifies an increasing determination of scholars to bridge this Pacific gap, and to build more partnerships of individuals and institutions which bring North America and East Asia closer together.

SECTION 1
Demography

Demographic Changes to Overseas Chinese in Canada after the Exclusion Act

David Chuenyan Lai

Professor, Department of Geography, University of Victoria

INTRODUCTION

In 1923, the Canadian government passed the Chinese Immigration Act, which came into force on 1 January 1924.[1] Chinese immigrants usually called it an Exclusion Act as it prohibited the entry of Chinese to Canada. For 24 years, married Chinese men in Canada were separated from their wives and children and could not lead conjugal family lives. Their families were allowed to join them only after the Act was repealed in 1947, after which Chinese immigrants to Canada increased gradually for two decades. In 1967, the Canadian government introduced a non-discriminatory immigration policy, which resulted in the arrival of Chinese immigrants from many lands and cultures, with varying educational backgrounds and occupational skills. Hence, the history of Chinese migration to Canada can be divided into three periods: the period of exclusion (1924-1946), the period of selective entry (1947-1966), and the period of non-discrimination (1967- present). Each period differs in the demographic characteristics of the Chinese population in terms of size, distribution, and components.

THE PERIOD OF EXCLUSION, 1924-1946

During this period, many Chinese residents in Canada saw themselves as "sojourners;" they eventually had to return to China if they wanted to reunite with their families. As there were very few Chinese women in Canada, marriage was rare (and intermarriage even rarer). Chinese people were not replaced by natural growth after they left Canada and returned to China. As a result, the Chinese population in Canada, which reached a record high of 46,519 in 1931, began to decline after the 1930s, decreasing to 34,627 in 1941, and 32,528 in 1951.[2]

Most Chinese confined themselves to Chinatowns in bigger cities. In 1941, for example, one-fifth of Canada's total Chinese population was concentrated in Vancouver's Chinatowns, another fifth in Chinatowns in Victoria, Toronto, and Montreal, and 10% in Chinatowns in Calgary, Winnipeg, New Westminster, Edmonton, Nanaimo, Kamloops, and Ottawa (Table 2.1). In other words, these 11 Chinatowns held about half the Chinese population in Canada.

Table 2.1   Distributions of Chinese population by city in Canada, 1941

City	Number of Persons	Percentage of Total
Vancouver	7,174	20.72
Victoria	3,037	8.77
Toronto	2,326	6.72
Montreal	1,703	4.92
Calgary	799	2.31
Winnipeg	719	2.08
New Westminster	400	1.16
Edmonton	384	1.11
Nanaimo	298	0.86
Kamloops	281	0.81
Ottawa	272	0.79
Moose Jaw	261	0.75
Windsor	259	0.75
Lethbridge	248	0.72
Regina	247	0.71
Hamilton	236	0.68
Saskatoon	206	0.59
Port Alberni	137	0.40
Quebec City	130	0.38
Halifax	127	0.37
Other towns	15,383	44.42
Total	**34,627**	**100.00**

Source: Census of Canada, 1941

Although there are no official data on which parts of China the immigrants had come from, the Chinese Consolidated Benevolent Association in Victoria keeps a record of the purchasers of Chinese Government Bonds in 1938-1939, which can be used to deduce their home county origins. An analysis of the names and home counties of 2,548 purchasers reveal that about 54% had come from *Siyi* (the Four Counties), 17% from *Sanyi* (the Three Counties), and 29% from other counties in Guangdong Province (Table 2.2). It can be deduced that most of the early Chinese emigrants originated in counties on the Zhujiang delta since these counties are located around the estuary of the Zhujiang.

Table 2.2   Classification of purchasers of government bonds by county origin, 1938-39

Home County	Number of Persons		Percentage of Total	
SIYI	1,385		54.4	
Taishan		629		24.7
Xinhui		460		18.1
Kaiping		237		9.3
Enping		59		2.3
SANYI	420		16.5	
Panyu		367		14.4
Shunde		40		1.6
Nanahi		13		0.5
OTHER COUNTIES	743		29.1	
Zhongshan		570		22.4
Zengcheng		76		3.0
Dongguan		5		0.2
Baoan		4		0.2
Heshan		2		0.1
Huaxian		1		0.0
Others		10		0.4
Unidentified		75		2.9
Total	**2,548**		**100.0**	

Source: Record of Purchasers of Chinese Government Bonds, 1938-1939, the Chinese Consolidated Benevolent Association, Victoria.

THE PERIOD OF SELECTIVE ENTRY, 1947-1966

After World War II, Chinese residents in Canada, especially veterans, lobbied the Canadian Parliament to end the exclusion, and eventually the notorious Exclusion Act of 1923 was repealed on 14 May 1947.[3] Naturalized Chinese

Canadians were permitted to sponsor their wives and children for admission to Canada, and subsequently they were also allowed to sponsor parents, fiancés or fiancées, and children of previous marriages. Although regulations were gradually broadened further to include sons-in-law, daughters-in law, and grandparents, some immigration policies still discriminated against Asians. For example, they were not permitted to sponsor their brothers and sisters, a restriction that did not apply to Canadians of European extraction.

During this selective entry period, the number of Chinese immigrants increased rapidly. For example, between 1956 and 1965, a total of 22,193 Chinese immigrants entered Canada, 66% of whom came from Hong Kong (including Mainland China), and 22% from Taiwan.[4] This era marked the beginning of many Mandarin-speaking Chinese entering Canada. Most of these Chinese immigrants went to large cities and helped rehabilitate the Chinatowns, while Chinatowns in smaller cities were depopulated and became extinct. In 1961, half the Chinese population lived in five cities: Vancouver, Toronto, Montreal, Calgary, and Victoria, where Chinatowns still had a large number of Chinese residents (Table 2.3).

Table 2.3   Distribution of Chinese population by cities in Canada, 1961

City	Number of Persons	Percentage of Total
Vancouver	15,223	26.2
Toronto	6,715	11.5
Montréal	3,330	5.7
Calgary	2,232	3.8
Victoria	2,137	3.7
Edmonton	1,805	3.1
Winnipeg	1,194	2.1
Ottawa	970	1.7
Regina	584	1.0
Hamilton	554	1.0
Saskatoon	499	0.9
Moose Jaw	467	0.8
Lethbridge	413	0.7
Other Cities	22,074	37.9
Total	**58,197**	**100.0**

Source: Census of Canada, 1961

THE PERIOD OF NON-DISCRIMINATION, 1967-PRESENT

On 1 October 1967, the Canadian government introduced a new immigration policy under which the selection of immigrants was based on a non-discriminatory and universal policy.[5] This policy allows prospective immigrants from all parts of the world, irrespective of their ethnic origin or country of residence, to be considered equally for admission to Canada, chosen according to a "100-points" system in which points are allotted for different selection criteria. For example, an "independent immigrant" could receive a maximum of 15 points if he/she is a librarian and if there is a great demand for librarians in Canada at the time of application. An "independent immigrant" would get no points for being unable to speak either of Canada's two official languages (English and French), 4 points for speaking fluently and reading well either of them, and a maximum of 10 points for fluently writing and speaking both of them. Any prospective immigrant can be admitted to Canada as long as he/she has at least 70 out of 100 points.

The new immigration policy also encourages family reunion and helps alleviate the plight of refugees through humanitarian programs. In July 1979, for example, Canada opened its door to Indochinese refugees.[6] Thus, from Vietnam alone nearly 46,000 refugees landed in Canada in 1979 and 1980. Throughout the early 1980s thousands of refugees from Indochina, of whom many were ethnic Chinese, were admitted to Canada.

In January 1986, the Canadian government implemented an Immigrant Investor Program designed to attract investors and experienced business people to Canada who would create jobs and help alleviate the country's unemployment problem.[7] This program nearly coincided with the removal of capital controls in Taiwan in 1987; hence the investment program has attracted many Chinese entrepreneurs and investors from Hong Kong and Taiwan to migrate to Canada. In 1991, for example, a total of 40,743 landed immigrants, mostly Chinese, came from Hong Kong, Taiwan, and China (Table 2.4). Nearly 69% of the Taiwan immigrants and 37% of the Hong Kong immigrants entered Canada under the two categories of investors or entrepreneurs, whereas 60% of the immigrants from China entered as teachers, engineers, technicians, artists, etc. under the category of independent immigrants. An analysis of the intended destination of the Chinese immigrants reveals that most of the immigrants from Hong Kong and China preferred Ontario, where job opportunities were greater, whereas over half of the immigrants from Taiwan preferred BC, partly because it is closer to Taiwan and partly because most of these immigrants are either investors or self-employed (Table 2.5). During this period of non-discrimination, the Chinese population in Canada has increased rapidly from 118,815 in 1971 to 921,585 in 1996 (Table 2.6). Ontario overtook BC in having the largest concentration of Chinese population, and the Toronto area replaced Vancouver as the city having the largest number of Chinese residents.

Table 2.4 Classification of immigrants from Hong Kong, Taiwan, and China, 1991

	Hong Kong		Taiwan		China	
	Number of persons	%	Number of persons	%	Number of persons	%
Investors	2,474	11.0	2,068	46.0	23	0.2
Entrepreneurs	3,602	16.0	1,017	23.0	43	0.3
Independents	5,248	24.0	758	17.0	8,409	60.0
Family	8,332	37.0	475	11.0	4,231	30.0
Assisted relative	2,321	10.0	103	2.3	347	2.5
Self-employed	304	1.4	61	1.4	36	0.3
Refugees	59	0.3	6	0.1	826	5.9
Total	**22,340**	**100.0**	**4,488**	**100.0**	**13,915**	**100.0**

Source: Census of Canada, 1991

Table 2.5 Intended destination of immigrants from Hong Kong, Taiwan and China, 1991

	Hong Kong		Taiwan		China	
Intended Destination	Number of persons	%	Number of persons	%	Number of persons	%
Ontario	11,220	50.2	1,090	24.3	5,910	42.5
British Columbia	6,301	28.2	2,617	58.3	3,544	25.5
Quebec	2,304	10.3	546	12.2	2,161	15.5
Alberta	1,829	8.2	125	2.8	1,261	9.1
Manitoba	314	1.4	44	1.0	323	2.3
Saskatchewan	207	0.9	35	0.8	429	3.1
Nova Scotia	77	0.3	21	0.5	154	1.1
New Brunswick	52	0.2	3	0.1	63	0.5
Newfoundland	14	0.1	-	-	51	0.4
Prince Edward Is.	4	0.0	7	0.1	12	0.1
N.W. Territories	18	0.1	-	-	1	0.0
Yukon	-	-	-	-	6	0.0
Total	**22,340**	**100.0**	**4,488**	**100.0**	**13,915**	**100.0**

Table 2.6   Distribution of Chinese population by province/territory in
Canada, 1971 and 1996

| | 1971 Census | | 1996 Census | |
Province/Territory	Number of persons	%	Number of persons	%
Ontario	39,325	33.10	422,770	45.87
British Columbia	44,315	37.30	312,330	33.89
Alberta	12,905	10.86	98,135	10.65
Quebec	11,905	10.02	55,870	6.06
Manitoba	3,430	2.89	14,485	1.57
Saskatchewan	4,605	3.88	9,970	1.08
Nova Scotia	935	0.79	3,675	0.40
New Brunswick	570	0.48	1,830	0.20
Newfoundland	610	0.50	1,415	0.15
Northwest Territories	110	0.09	455	0.05
Yukon Territory	80	0.07	410	0.04
Prince Edward Island	25	0.02	235	0.03
Total	**118,815**	**100.00**	**921,585**	**100.00**

Source: Census of Canada, 1971 and 1996.

Since many Vietnamese refugees choose to live in cheaper residential areas around old Chinatowns, some investors establish small malls to meet their needs. For example, the Hing Yip Plaza in Toronto's Chinatown consists of small stores selling Vietnamese products (Figure 2.1), and the store signs are written in English as well as Vietnamese and Chinese characters (Figure 2.2). On the other hand, many new immigrants from Hong Kong and Taiwan prefer living in the suburbs to living in the inner city and this has resulted in the development of many shopping plazas in the suburbs of large metropolitan cities, catering to Chinese and other Asian customers. For example, by January 2000, Hong Kong and Taiwan investors had built eight shopping plazas in Mississauga, a suburban municipality of the Greater Toronto Area (Figure 2.3).

These plazas are commonly called "Chinese Malls" or "Asian Malls" because of their distinctive Chinese characteristics, such as a predominance of Chinese customers, and billboards written in Chinese characters (Figure 2.4). The Mississauga Chinese Centre is elaborately designed like a Chinese classical garden with a bridge, a pond, a pavilion, a covered walkway, and a huge Chinese arch (Figure 2.5). The Centre's investors try to develop this Chinese shopping plaza as a tourist destination, to attract local customers and tourists alike.

Figure 2.1   A small Asian-themed mall in Toronto's Chinatown

Figure 2.2   Small retailing units in the Hing Yip Plaza in Toronto's Chinatown

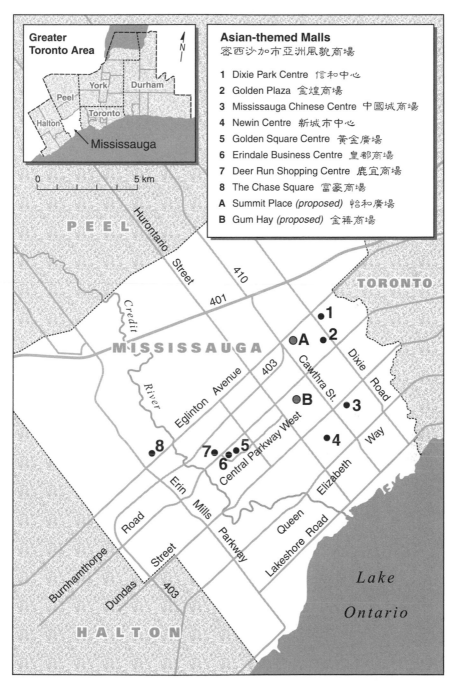

Figure 2.3   Asian-themed malls in Mississauga, January 2000

Figure 2.4   The Chase Square, an Asian-themed mall in Mississauga

Figure 2.5   The Mississauga Chinese Centre

Summary

Canada's immigration policies have had great influence on the demographic characteristics of Chinese in Canada. Before the introduction of the non-discriminatory immigration policy in 1967, most Chinese immigrants came to Canada from the Zhujiang delta of Guangdong Province and a large proportion of them were labourers. Most of them confined themselves in Chinatowns. After 1967, Hong Kong, Taiwan, Southeast Asia, and other countries replaced the traditional source areas of Chinese emigrants. Many of these immigrants were professional people and tended to live in the suburbs. The introduction of the investor program in 1986 resulted in the influx of many wealthy entrepreneurs and developers from Hong Kong, Taiwan, and other places. Hence, changes in the characteristics of Chinese immigrants have resulted in great changes in the function and form of commercial developments both in the inner city and the suburban areas of metropolitan cities. The socioeconomic characteristics of Chinatowns across Canada are being transformed: old Chinatowns in downtown cores are no longer homogeneous, while new Chinatowns or Asian-themed shopping malls and plazas have been developed in suburbs.

Endnotes

1 Canada, *Statute of Canada,* An Act Respecting Chinese Immigration, 1923, Ottawa: 13-14 George V, Chap. 38, pp. 301-315.

2 Canada. Censuses of Canada, 1931-1951.

3 Canada, *Statutes of Canada,* An Act to Amend the Immigration Act and to Repeal the Chinese Immigration Act, 1947 Ottawa: 11 George VI, Chap. 19, pp. 107-109.

4 Canada, Department of Citizenship and Immigration, Immigration Statistics, 1956-1965.

5 Canada, Order in Council, P.C. 1967-1615m 16 August 1967.

6 Canada, Ministry of Industry, Trade and Commerce, *Canada Year Book,* Ottawa, 1980-1, p.125.

7 Canada, Employment and Immigration Commission, *Immigration,* 1986, p.2.

Acknowledgement

The author is grateful to the Vancouver Centre of Excellence for Research on Immigration and Integration in the Metropolis for funding this research.

Filial or Rebellious Daughters? *Dagongmei* (Unmarried Female Migrant Workers) in the Pearl River Delta Region, South China, in the 1990s

Yuen Fong Woon

Professor, Department of Pacific and Asian Studies, University of Victoria

INTRODUCTION

On 19 November 1993, a major fire broke out in Shenzhen, leaving 82 dead and 40 suffering from serious burns. The victims were young single women from out of province. Heavy metal bars across the windows and doors securely locked from the outside—the usual deterrents to theft by employees—had sealed off any chances of escape (*Nanfang Ribao*, 2 December 1993).

This incident represents only the tip of an iceberg that has drawn international attention. Working conditions in privately-owned, collectively-owned, and foreign or jointly-owned factories in the Pearl River Delta region (hereafter "the Delta") in the 1990s are extremely oppressive and life-threatening. Intolerably high noise levels, the use of inflammable or poisonous substances, and the lack of ventilation or any protective facilities often lead to mass poisonings, widespread occupational diseases, and industrial accidents. Few factories purchase industrial accident insurance policies or offer medical subsidies to their employees. In fact, in some cases, injured workers are simply fired (He and Chen, 1997-8; *Nanfang Ribao*, 11 January 1992: 1, 2 September 1994: 1, 15 January 1995: 2; Liu, 1993a; Daming, 1996; Sun, 1996).

Despite a Labor Law passed in 1992 and made more stringent in 1994, unmarried female migrant workers (hereafter "dagongmei") are still exposed to extremely long work hours and forced to work extra night shifts. Further, despite all their hard work, they are often cheated of their pay through various fines, deductions, or other means. They are humiliated, insulted, strip-searched, beaten, tortured, and fired for the slightest infringement of factory rules, or even for daring to ask for their rightful wages (*Nanfang Ribao*, 31 March 1995: 1; Sun, 1996; He and Chen, 1997-8; Zheng and Hong, 1995; Lee, 1995).

Living conditions are equally bad. The *dagongmei* must pay rent to live in overcrowded dormitories that lack toilet and bathing facilities and have unsanitary conditions that often lead to eye infections and epidemics of skin disease. Their food, for which they pay one *yuan* a meal, is meagre in quantity and entirely lacking in nutritious value (Sun, 1996; *Nanfang Ribao*, 31 March 1995: 1).

Why do these young, single women travel long distances to endure such horrid working and living conditions? What sort of identity do they construct for themselves, slaving in alien and oppressive factory environments in the Delta?

To answer these questions, I shall first give a brief account of the local, national, and global forces that prompt the migration of these women to the Pearl River Delta region of South China. Next, I shall use media reports, my own field data and those of other researchers to examine the behaviour patterns and life-plans of these young female migrant workers, focusing especially on their relationship with their family of origin. In the last section, I shall place my findings in the context of the current academic debate on whether the *dagongmei* are "filial" or "rebellious" daughters.

MACRO CAUSES FOR FEMALE LABOUR MIGRATION IN THE PEARL RIVER DELTA REGION

Since the mid 1980s, the Delta has become a major recipient of long-distance female labour migrants, a situation resulting from the interaction of national, local, and global forces. Economic decisions by the national government in the late 1970s led to China's incorporation into the international division of labour. Between 1979 and 1988, coastal China increasingly opened to direct foreign investment for production of export-only goods. In Guangdong Province, this export-orientation strategy resulted in the creation of Shenzhen, Zhuhai, and Santou as special economic zones in 1979 and the designation of the Pearl River Delta as an "open economic region" in 1985. County leaders were given the same leeway as those in big cities and special economic zones to offer flexible terms to foreign investors, including the right to hire migrant workers for short-term contracts (Xu, Qi, and Xiangzhang, 1988a, 1988b; Vogel, 1989; Yang, 1990, 1991; Tzeng, 1991).

Internationally, intense competition with East and Southeast Asian countries, along with rising production costs, has led Hong Kong capitalists to search for cheap labour and land to relocate their assembly-line industries. Due to geographical proximity, and pre-existing kinship and district ties, many look to the Delta for factory sites. This situation in turn leads to equally fierce competition among county governments in the Delta, each trying to lure Hong Kong investors by offering the cheapest labour and production costs (Vogel, 1989; Xu, Qi, and Xiangzhang, 1988b; Xu and Li, 1990; Smart and Smart, 1991; Sung, 1991; Johnson, 1989).

Both Hong Kong investors and local cadres in the Delta prefer hiring long-distance female migrants to local ones. The former are perceived to be insecure, naive, ignorant of local pay scales, less ambitious, and therefore much more exploitable. This employer preference has encouraged female migrants to come to this part of China to earn wages working in factories that are often slave-like and inhumane.

THE HOUSEHOLD REGISTRATION SYSTEM

The process of migration and the terrible conditions endured by the *dagongmei* in the Delta result not only from the confluence of international, national, and local forces discussed above, but also because of an outmoded household registration system established by the central government that deprives them of legal protection or any social entitlements (Dai, 1998).

Since the 1960s, the household registration system was a major barrier to labor migration among peasants. In 1985, however, in the wake of post-Mao economic reforms, the system was slightly relaxed: geographic mobility was allowed provided that migrants applied for temporary residence permits (*zanzhuzheng* or *jizhuzheng*) in the destination community (Roberts, 1997; Wong, 1994; Solinger, 1993; Chan, 1996; Davin, 1999). This modification facilitated long-distance migration to the Delta, but offered outside workers little protection from exploitation. Not being permanent residents, they had absolutely no control over the terms of their contracts and were at the mercy of their employers and supervisors (Goldstein and Goldstein, 1984, 1987-8, 1990a; Dutton, 1988; Yang and Goldstein, 1990; Oshima, 1990; Christiansen, 1990; Lin, 1988; Lo, 1989; Prybyla, 1989). Under these circumstances, the *dagongmei* were doubly jeopardized, being disadvantaged first as women and second as non-holders of permanent local household registration papers (Fan and Huang, 1998; He and Chen, 1997-8).

Since the early 1990s, the household registration system has been further relaxed through marketization. Migrants working in small towns in coastal China can now purchase local household papers known as "blue cards" (*lanka*) to become permanent residents. Currently, county governments in Guangdong Province set relatively liberal terms for the purchase of these blue cards. In some counties, the Labour Office sets a quota, and any migrant with a valid temporary residence permit can apply. In other counties, female migrants are able to purchase a blue card after 5 years of marriage to a local man (*Nanfang Ribao*, 15 June 1995: 2).

Despite the liberality of these terms, blue cards are still a considerable expense for migrants. In the small towns of Guangdong, the fee ranges from 3,000 to 10,000 *yuan*, and can be waived or reduced only if employers apply on behalf of their highly skilled employees (Zhou, 1996; Wong, 1994; *Nanfang Ribao*, 15 June 1995: 2; Zhou, 1992). This does not benefit the *dagongmei*, who are often given unskilled jobs. Further, given their meagre wages, many cannot afford the fee for a blue card. For them, exploitation by factory owners continues until they leave the factory system, either by returning to their native community or by finding a local husband who purchases a blue card on their behalf.

REVIEW OF EXISTING LITERATURE

This chapter focuses on the behaviour patterns and life-plans of a sample of *dagongmei* in the Delta in the 1990s. The purpose is to add to the body of literature on the effects of labor migration on women in the People's Republic of China (hereafter PRC), and beyond that, to make a contribution to the field of women and development. Existing literature, which focuses on the micro-process of female labor migration, usually takes the woman's role and status in the household as a starting point. As these scholars rightfully point out, the family socializes women according to the prevailing cultural norms of the local community. It is within the family that a woman's subordination to male authority is generally obvious and immediate. It is the family that decides whether or not to support a daughters' education and for how long. It is the family from which a woman derives her land or inheritance rights. More importantly, the family provides the frame of reference that influences a woman's decision to migrate and her behaviour patterns at the place of destination.

The focus on the family does not mean that these scholars depict women only as passive victims and never as active agents. Indeed, surveying the literature on the relationship between migrant women and their family of origin, I discovered that scholars present two types of behaviour patterns, which, for want of better terms, I call "filial daughter model," and "rebellious daughter model."

The Filial Daughter Model

Proponents of the filial daughter model regard female labour migration as part of a household strategy, driven by economic hardship or the low likelihood of upward mobility for the family in the home community. The patriarch supports his daughters through junior high school in order to qualify them for factory employment in export processing zones. Daughters, at the bottom of the two power hierarchies of age and gender, have no choice but to migrate (Riley and Gardner, 1993; Guest, 1993; Lim, 1993; Rodenburg, 1993; Chant and Radcliffe, 1992; Huang, 1984).

Travelling with relatives or other villagers, female migrant workers often make use of trustworthy family contacts in their places of destination. Once they secure employment, they tend to send home a larger percentage of their earnings than male migrant factory workers. They internalize the belief that they are "useless daughters" who will be married off to benefit another family.

As a result, they regard factory work not as an opportunity for self-actualization, but as a filial obligation to repay their parents for raising and educating them (Riley and Gardner, 1993; Guest, 1993; Chant and Radcliffe, 1992; Ferree, 1979; Pedraza, 1991; Rodenburg, 1993; Lim, 1993).

The destination factory environment is such that the *dagongmei* have no sense of gaining liberation from their migration. They are hired for their "feminine virtues": obedience to authority, discipline, and self-denial, virtues that are continually encouraged and reinforced by the male-dominated factory management to maintain and increase productivity. In addition, female migrant workers are often segregated from the larger local community, and must abide by strict rules governing their free time. Indeed, many have merely exchanged subordination within the household for subordination in the workplace (Rodenburg, 1993).

Moreover, the occupational opportunities open to female migrant workers are generally not conducive to attaining long-term economic independence. Paltry earnings and the obligation to contribute to the family budget preclude any personal savings for their own future. They know that when their short-term contract ends, or if they are laid off during business contractions, they must return home. As a result they cannot cut ties with their family of origin (Rodenburg, 1993; Guest, 1993).

The Rebellious Daughter Model

Proponents of the rebellious daughter model argue that the migration of single women is, in fact, an act of individual rebellion against the patriarchal family for the attainment of personal autonomy, improved life-chances and increased marriage prospects. Rebellious daughters leave home for factory work even when the family objects or has no pressing need for the supplemental income. In fact, the greater these women's subordination to male authority in their family, and the more disadvantaged they are in terms of inheritance or land rights or non-agricultural employment opportunities in their home community, the stronger is their motivation to migrate (Thandani and Todaro, 1984; Chant and Radcliffe, 1992; Ariffin, 1984; Lim, 1993; Jones, 1993; Riley and Gardner, 1993; Guest, 1993; Rodenburg, 1993).

This rebelliousness is particularly prevalent among rural women who have attained high school education. They are exposed to new ideas, have relatively high employment aspirations, and are able to evaluate outside information with regards to migration. They are likely to have their own independent network outside of family connections. Their classmates and friends, for example, are often able to provide job leads and logistical assistance at the place of destination (Riley and Gardner, 1993; Guest, 1993; Rodenburg, 1993; Jones, 1993).

Despite severe exploitation, factory employment offers female migrant workers independent wage-earning opportunities. Living away from home distances them from constant surveillance by the family patriarch. They are able to keep their earnings for building their own independent future (Rodenburg, 1993; Riley and Gardner, 1993). Although these women may be laid off or resign due to harsh working conditions, they are often able to make use of new social contacts to find another job and as a result, are not compelled to return home (Rodenburg, 1993).

In fact, many decide not to return to their villages, and struggle to maintain the gains in personal autonomy that migration and employment have brought them. They dislike the prospect of returning to patriarchal domination or submitting to arranged marriages. Instead, they prefer the alternatives: overcrowded living conditions, air pollution, a faster pace of life, and intense pressure from work (Huang, 1984; Ariffin, 1984).

Pedraza (1991) sums up the tenets of the "rebellious daughter model" clearly. According to her, gender is not only at the centre of the decision to migrate, but is also at the centre of the reluctance to return. Male migrants are eager to return after years of frugal, austere living in order to regain their status and privilege in the home community. Female migrants, by contrast, tend to postpone or avoid returning because they realize it would entail retirement from work and the loss of their newly found freedom.

Sources of Data and Research Questions

Are the *dagongmei* in the Pearl River Delta region "filial daughters" or "rebellious daughters"? To debate this question, I examine their behaviour patterns and life-plans in comparison with their male counterparts.

Using data drawn from in-depth interviews of 130 factory workers in six different locations of the Delta between December, 1993 and December, 1994, I shall compare male and female subjects according to the following parameters: family background; educational attainment; reasons for migration; the way in which first and subsequent jobs in the Delta were secured; treatment in the workplace; relationship with family of origin; future plans; and marriage prospects.

Because of possible biases of my sample, I shall supplement the interview data with the results of my comprehensive newspaper scan. In addition, I shall put my findings in the context of other scholarly research on the Delta in the 1990s.

Backgrounds of Subjects

Before examining my subjects' self-declared reasons for migration, I find it important to look at their family background, education level, and work experience prior to departure.

Table 3.1 shows that the *dagongmei*, much like their male counterparts, originate from relatively affluent families. Self-reported household income per capita (prior to migration) indicates that 77.3% of female and 85.5% of male subjects come from families with incomes above the provincial average stated by the Chinese Statistics Bureau for the same year.

Table 3.1   Per capita household income by provincial standard (%)

	Male	Female
Household Income	n=55	n=75
Lower than average	7.3	18.7
Average	7.3	4.0
Higher than average	85.5	77.3
N=130	**100.0**	**100.0**

Table 3.2 shows that 57.3% of the female subjects completed junior high school while 17.3% completed senior high school. Although the educational standard is much lower than that of the male subjects, in a country in which the majority of rural women are illiterate, the *dagongmei* can be considered highly educated.

Table 3.2   Education level (%)

	Male	Female
Education Level	n=55	n=75
Primary	9.1	25.3
Junior high	52.7	57.3
Senior high and above	38.2	17.3
N=130	**100.0**	**100.0**

Table 3.3 shows that prior to departure, 44.0% of the female subjects, compared to 25.5% of the male subjects, were engaged in farming. In addition, a much lower proportion of females than males were engaged in wage earning or *getihu* (small private business) activities. It is clear from these statistics that, prior to departure, the *dagongmei* in the sample were not working in jobs commensurate with their relatively high education levels.

Table 3.3   Subject's occupation before migration (%)

	Male	Female
Occupation	n=55	n=75
Farmer	25.5	44.0
Student	20.0	29.3
Wage earner	40.0	20.0
Getihu*	14.5	6.7
N=130	**100.0**	**100.0**

* small private business operator

Motives for Migration

Table 3.4 shows that only a small percentage of my female and male subjects (17.3% and 18.2%) left home for "self-improvement." About half (49.3% of females and 52.7% of males) stated that they came to the Delta to make money.

These findings directly differ from Dai's research on female migrants in Guangzhou (1998) in which 64.2% said that they left home to experience the outside world. One possible explanation for the discrepancy is that my field sites were small rural towns rather than major cities like Guangzhou. No subjects, female or male, expected to see the "outside world" by working in small factories surrounded by paddy fields.

Table 3.4   Reasons for leaving home (%)

	Male	Female
Reasons	n=55	n=75
Difficulties at home	23.6	20.0
Self improvement	18.2	17.3
Make money	52.7	49.3
Join relatives in delta	5.5	13.3
N=130	**100.0**	**100.0**

This difference should not distract us from the fact that most of my subjects moved to the Delta on their own initiative. Table 3.5 shows that only 32.0% of the female and 29.1% of the male subjects were encouraged by their family to leave. Most either decided to migrate on their own, or were persuaded by villagers, classmates, or friends.

Table 3.5   Who encouraged subject to leave (%)

	Male	Female
Source of Encouragement	n=55	n=75
Self	34.5	38.7
Family/relatives	29.1	32.0
Friends	32.8	28.0
Others	3.6	1.3
N=130	**100.0**	**100.0**

Travelling Companions and Job Hunting Methods

No matter how independent in the decision-making stage, the *dagongmei* in my sample did not show much independence in long-distance travel. Table 3.6 indicates that 45.3% of the female, compared to 21.8% of the male subjects, travelled to the Delta in the company of family members or close relatives. Only 16.0% of females, compared to 36.4% of male subjects, made the trip alone. These statistics show that, regardless of education levels, the *dagongmei* accommodated the Chinese rural tradition condemning unchaperoned long-distance travel by women (Wan, 1995; Davin, 1999).

Table 3.6   Traveling companions (%)

	Male	Female
Travel Companions	n=55	n=75
No one	36.4	16.0
Family/relatives	21.8	45.3
Other villagers	40.0	36.0
Labour group	1.8	2.7
N=130	**100.0**	**100.0**

Upon arrival in the Delta, female subjects with senior high school education were as reliant as their less educated sisters on relatives and people of the same provincial origin (*tongxiang*) for job leads. By contrast, of the 21 male senior high graduates in my sample, 13 left home alone, and secured their first jobs in the Delta themselves, by going through formal application processes.

This gender difference does not apply to subsequent job searches, however. As can be seen from Table 7.3, 34.6% of the female and 38.1% of the male

subjects found their present job by applying on their own. Only a small minority relied on their family network. The existence of a dynamic non-state labor
market in the Delta provides a variety of opportunities. Being in the Delta for a
prolonged period, the majority of my subjects have learnt to make use of a
number of channels to find new jobs.

Table 3.7   How present job was found (%)

	Male	*Female*
Job Leads	n=55	n=75
Self	38.1	34.6
Family/relatives	12.7	29.3
Tongxiang/friends	49.1	36.0
N=130	**100.0**	**100.0**

*People from same community of origin

Working Conditions in the Pearl River Delta Region

Similar to other *dagongmei* in this region (Sun, 1996; He and Chen, 1997-8), my
female subjects endured long hours of work, which normally included 12-hour
shifts, and extra shifts for rushed orders. Except for the Spring Festival, most
were not given any time off for statutory holidays.

    Again, similar to other *dagongmei* in the Delta (Sun, 1996), my female sub-
jects are lower paid than males. Table 3.8 shows that only 16.0% of the females,
compared to 38.2% of the males, earn more than 500 *yuan* per month. Most
earn about 300 *yuan* a month (including overtime shifts). Out of this, they pay
an average of 90 *yuan* a month (3 *yuan* per day) for food, and 60 to 90 *yuan* for
their dormitory space. Apart from personal necessary items of expense, my
subjects calculated that they have a net savings of about 100-150 *yuan* per month.

Table 3.8   Monthly earnings in the Delta (%)

	Male	*Female*
Earnings (in Yuan)	n=55	n=75
Below 300	16.4	34.7
300 - 499	45.5	49.3
500 and above	38.2	16.0
N=130	**100.0**	**100.0**

That the *dagongmei* are given fewer responsibilities than their male counterparts can be seen from a detailed look at the way senior high graduates in my sample have been treated by management. Managers favoured the 13 male senior high school graduates soon after they commenced employment. Recognizing their work experience in past white collar or skilled jobs, managers gave these male subjects a short orientation period and promptly promoted them to section chiefs. They now eat separately and live in rental units away from the workers' dormitories. In contrast, none of my female subjects with senior high school education and appropriate work experience were treated any differently from other women. Like female workers elsewhere in China, they were not highly regarded by factory management (Goldstein and Goldstein, 1996; Fan and Huang, 1998; Davin, 1996; Lan, 1996; Sun, 1996; Knight and Song, 1995; Lee, 1995).

In general, the *dagongmei* in my sample feel that they receive less consideration from employers than men. Table 3.9 shows that only 26.7% of the females, compared with 50.9% of the male subjects would dare approach company management for assistance.

Table 3.9   Sources of assistance in the Delta (%)

Sources	Male n=55	Female n=75
Family/relatives	3.6	26.7
*Tongxiang**	40.0	44.0
Locals	5.5	2.7
Company management	50.9	26.7
N=130	**100.0**	**100.0**

*People from same community of origin

Other studies in the 1990s confirm that the *dagongmei* in the Delta commonly work and live in a discriminatory and segregated environment. In addition, management often uses kinship and district ties to induce submission. Lee (1995) and Ngai (1999) who observed factory life in Shenzhen in the 1990s both note that the management plays one group of workers against another, so there is no socializing or cooperation across dialect or provincial lines even on the same factory floor. Language differences and social prejudice also prevent the *dagongmei* from merging into the larger society. In addition, the factory is managed like a huge patriarchal family: the *dagongmei* are reminded frequently that they are female and therefore must be obedient, hard working, and filial (Ngai, 1999; Lee, 1995).

Dai's study (1998) in the Delta supports these observations. She finds that of all types of female migrants in her sample, factory workers are the least assimilated into the larger society because they are the most confined. Their social circle consists of relatives and friends from the same hometown. However, they are usually too busy and too far away from each other to meet these contacts on a regular basis. Generally, the *dagongmei*'s only contact outside of their immediate co-workers is with their home family. They write letters, phone, return for visits, and remit their savings home.

Financial Contributions to Family of Origin

Both Ngai and Dai's research leads to the conclusion that the segregation and discrimination faced by the *dagongmei* in the Delta only strengthen their emotional attachment to their family of origin. This conclusion is confirmed by my data.

Table 3.10 shows that 24.0% of the female, compared to only 9.1% of the male subjects, regularly remit over 60% of their savings home. Furthermore, the 13 male senior high school graduates consistently remit less than 40% of their net income to relatives at home despite having achieved section chief positions. They put aside the remainder of their savings to purchase blue cards for permanent residency in the Delta.

Table 3.10   Income remitted home (%)

| | *Male* | *Female* |
Income Remitted Home	n=55	n=75
Under 20%	29.1	28.0
20-39%	29.1	21.3
40-59%	32.7	26.7
Over 60%	9.1	24.0
N=130	**100.0**	**100.0**

Guangdong's media in the 1990s gives considerable coverage to stories of "filial daughters" amongst the *dagongmei* in the Delta. These stories are derived from interviews conducted by reporters at major bus stops and railway stations during the 2 weeks of the Spring Festival. One article, for example, features a *dagongmei* telling the reporter proudly that she is the only one in her family earning a wage, and that she feels gratified to be able to give money to grandma, parents, and younger brother on her trip home (*Nanfang Nongcunbao*, 6 February 1994). Another article features a happy *dagongmei* telling reporters that she is taking a lot of expensive gifts home. In the past year, she has brought her sister to work with her in the same factory and helped her brother pay for vocational school and dormitory fees. As a result, she has won the affection of both her siblings and parents (*Nanfang Ribao*, 23 December 1994: 3).

The *Nanfang Ribao* (Southern Daily) dated 3 March 1995 carried a 1-page feature article depicting the filial acts of a *dagongmei* from a mountain village. Three years ago, she gave up her senior high school studies and came to Dongguan to work in a factory. The family needs her to support her second brother's higher education while the eldest brother stays home to farm. Her wages are very low even though she works long hours. To save money for her family members, she has not returned home for the Spring Festival in the past 3 years.

Future Plans

Although many migrant workers regularly remit a large portion of their hard-earned wages to support their family and annually bring expensive gifts home during the Spring Festival, they may not plan to return home permanently. Indeed, out of the 130 subjects in my factory worker sample, only 35 (or 26.9%) indicated that they plan to return home in 5 years' time.

Table 3.11 shows, interestingly, that a larger percentage of male (74.5%) than female subjects (56.0%) plan to stay in the Delta on a long-term basis. This is in direct contrast to Pedraza's claims that male migrants are eager to return to regain their prior social status in the home community, while female migrants are eager to stay behind to protect the autonomy they have gained.

Table 3.11   Future plans (%)

Future Plan	Male n=55	Female n=75
Stay in Pearl River Delta	74.5	56.0
Return home	16.4	34.7
Undecided	9.1	9.3
N=130	**100.0**	**100.0**

The reason for the discrepancy between my findings and Pedraza's lies in the opportunity structure in the Delta. Despite the harsh working and living conditions in the factory compound, even the most unskilled migrant workers earn much more in the Delta than they can at home. This is particularly true for male subjects: the longer they stay, the more likely they are to achieve a relatively good position. By contrast, the *dagongmei* suffer consistently from job discrimination. Even those with senior high school education find it difficult to secure a well-paid and high-status job, regardless of how long they stay in the Delta to accumulate work experience.

Nevertheless, over half of the female subjects in my sample do plan to prolong their stay. They want to earn as much as they can, even though they have little chance for a high-status job. Their asset is their cheap labour and there are numerous labour-intensive manufacturing industries in this part of China to offer them employment.

The *dagongmei* who plan to return home in 5 years' time do so because they can no longer stand the oppressive and life-threatening factory regime in the Delta. However, they do not aspire to return to farming. Similar to their male counterparts, 65.4% of the possible returnees among the *dagongmei* said they plan to operate a small-scale private business at home (see Table 3.12). This ambition to become a small entrepreneur is also prevalent among the *dagongmei* in Shenzhen studied by Lee (1995).

Table 3.12   Intended occupation for returnees (%)

Intended Occupation	Male n=9	Female n=26
Farmer	11.1	19.2
*Getihu**	66.7	65.4
Wage earner	22.2	15.4
N=35	**100.0**	**100.0**

*small private business operator

Marriage Prospects

Most factories in the Delta do not hire older or married women: the *dagongmei* who decide to remain cannot forever rely on their labour for a living. They must develop an alternate life-plan. Many, therefore, look to the prospect of marrying a local man as a solution, since this would qualify them for the blue card necessary for permanent residency in the Delta (Zheng and Hong, 1995; Lee, 1995; *Guangzhou Ribao,* 17 February 1992: 2; *Guangzhou Shehui,* 3 February 1993).

Finding a local marriage partner is very difficult for the *dagongmei.* Factory compounds are usually full of non-local female workers. Long working hours, factory restrictions on free time activities, language and psychological barriers, and social prejudice all present problems for any *dagongmei* trying to break into the local social circle (Davin, 1999).

Despite all these difficulties, however, 11 out of my 75 female subjects (14.7%) eventually married local men, and they do not represent isolated cases in the Delta. According to the 1994 marriage registry record in Zhongshan County, of the 539 newly wedded couples, one-third consisted of migrant women marrying local men. In a village in Dongguan where migrants out-number local workers, many *dagongmei* married locals, while local women complained that they cannot find husbands (*Nanfang Ribao*, 15 June 1995: 2).

Wong (1994), who studied migrant workers in 1989, calculated that eight to ten thousand female migrants have already married local men in the Delta. She explains: "From my interviews with cadres and local residents, outsiders are actually preferred over indigenous women for a number of reasons. First, many men find northern girls physically attractive. Second, some migrants are better educated than local women. Finally newcomers are not as demanding about such things as nuptial gifts" (Wong, 1994).

Existing literature offers contradictory answers as to whether the *dagongmei* who are determined to marry local men are filial or rebellious daughters. On the one hand, Wong's findings seem to indicate that such marriages are a part of the *dagongmei*'s family strategy. According to her, the newly-wedded migrant wives are filial daughters who often exert pressure on their husbands to remit money to their natal family, send for kith and kin later on, and assist them in settling down in the Delta (Wong, 1994).

On the other hand, other scholars have found that the *dagongmei* in the Delta are rebellious daughters who strongly resist marriages arranged by their parents. Gao (1994), for example, notes that some *dagongmei* would rather commit suicide than go home to be married. Similarly, the media reports many cases of *dagongmei* rejecting the fiancé arranged by their parents in favour of a local man, largely because they do not want to return home to be confined again (*Foshan Ribao*, 14 March 1992: 2; 12 September 1992: 2).

PORTRAIT OF A REBELLIOUS DAGONGMEI IN THE DELTA

A media report written by Liu (1993b), which features the life story of a young migrant woman from Hunan Province, best captures the defiance and rebelliousness of the *dagongmei* in the Delta. I briefly summarize below.

Ms. B., aged 16, had just graduated from junior high school. Her father refused to let her continue in school, saying that education was not for girls. He had already arranged for her to marry a boy in the next village. That very night, Ms. B. ran away from home. She had heard from many of her village friends who were already in the Delta that it was easy to make money there, so she took a southbound train to look up a classmate. Through the latter's introduction, she landed her first job in a toy factory in Dongguan.

She recalled having to work 24 hours a day for 10 consecutive days whenever there was an urgent order from Hong Kong buyers. There was a lot of scolding and sexual harassment in the factory compound, but no one dared to complain. The rules were extremely harsh. For example, a total of 5 minutes were set aside for a "bathroom break" for all the *dagongmei* on the same factory floor. Anyone who stayed in the toilet too long would be beaten or fined.

Ms. B's father somehow found out where she was, and appeared suddenly on the factory floor one day. He slapped her across the face, shouting "only prostitutes work in the Delta." He dragged her along, forcing her to go home and marry the boy he had chosen for her. She sneaked away at the train station.

She looked for work in Guangzhou by herself, and became a telephone operator in a small privately owned company. But Ms. B. was fired after a short while, because the boss' wife suspected her of seducing him. She found a third job working in an earplug factory. The conditions were so bad that she decided to quit.

The reporter found her loitering on the streets of Guangzhou. When asked why she did not intend to go home, Ms. B replied,

"I am only 20 years old, and am in no mood to settle down with a husband and children, doing heavy agricultural work in mountainous Hunan. Besides," she added, "I love to wear skirts, apply makeup, and wiggle my hips when I walk, I cannot do those things in my home community...."

CONCLUSION

Among scholars doing research on female labour migration in China, Zhang (1999), who completed fieldwork in Tianjin in 1994, is the strongest proponent of the "rebellious daughter" model. Based on in-depth interviews of female subjects working in domestic, catering, and manufacturing sectors, she argues that migrant women are a catalyst to a radical redefinition of gender roles in the PRC. According to her, rural women in post-liberation China are still bound to their home villages by patriarchal traditions and by the state, which defines them as peasants holding agricultural household registration papers. By out-migration, and through active pursuit of their own income and marriage goals, these rebellious daughters are able to break the control of their parents over their movements and life-plans, and the state's restrictions over their geographical mobility (Zhang, 1999; Davin, 1999; Lee, 1995).

The design of my study is different from that of Zhang's in three ways. First, my field sites are small towns, not major cities. Second, while Zhang's subjects are engaged in different types of jobs, my subjects are all factory workers. They all work in the Pearl River Delta region: the part of China most notorious for the poor treatment of female migrant workers. Third, I derive my conclusions from direct comparisons between female and male subjects.

For these reasons, my findings produce a more mixed picture than do Zhang's. Like hers, my female subjects are from relatively affluent families by provincial standards. Many are educated but have been confined to agricultural work at home, and most have made their own decision to go to the Delta. To them, migrating to the Delta may not have been a matter of survival. Unlike Zhang's subjects, however, few *dagongmei* in my sample declared that they left home for "self-improvement" or "to see the world." Their primary goal was to earn more income than they could at home. Many followed the traditional method of travelling with relatives and family members and relied on personal connections to obtain their first jobs in the Delta. Nevertheless, as time passed, they, like Zhang's subjects, have become more self-reliant and applied for their own jobs.

In the Delta, the behaviour patterns of my female subjects again emulate in some ways, and differ in some ways from those of Zhang's subjects. Unlike Zhang's subjects, the *dagongmei* in my sample follow the "obedient daughter" model in providing considerable financial resources for their family of origin. Compared to their male counterparts, they remit a higher percentage of their net income to support their parents and male siblings. However, like Zhang's subjects, many *dagongmei* in my sample do not want to return home. They would rather endure the slave-like, inhumane, and life-threatening working conditions in the Delta. Those who want to return home, plan to operate small businesses instead of going back to agriculture. When it comes to marriage, many *dagongmei* in the Delta refuse to marry partners arranged by their parents. Despite all social and institutionally-imposed barriers, they actively seek out local men to marry in order to change the agricultural household status imposed on them by the Central State. Nevertheless, existing literature is unclear whether marrying local men constitutes rebelliousness on the part of the *dagongmei*, or whether it is part of a family strategy to help parents or siblings settle in the Delta.

This mixed picture leads me to question whether there can be a definitive answer to whether female migrants are "filial" or "rebellious" daughters, or whether this question is too simplistic and needs refining. The fact is that these labels are imposed on migrant women by researchers: they may or may not have meaning for the subjects themselves. As a result, the same female migrant can be "rebellious" and "filial" at the same time, or at different stages of her life, with no apparent contradictions. Let me give three concrete illustrations from this study.

First, rural daughters may decide to leave home for self-actualization, but at the same time, their decision to migrate might win the whole-hearted approval of the head of the household. The very fact that their parents have supported them through junior high school to enable them to qualify for factory jobs in the Delta indicates that their migration may also be part of a family strategy.

Second, many may have been "filial" daughters at the time of departure, and then turn "somewhat rebellious" after a few years when they develop more self-confidence. They may not want to return to their home community or to marry the boy chosen by their parents. However, at the same time, they are still filial daughters who send a large percentage of their hard-earned wages home. Segregated life within the factory compound, and constant patriarchal domination and indoctrination from employers and supervisors must reinforce their self-identity as "worthless daughters" who must redeem themselves by supporting their family before their marriage.

Finally, the *dagongmei* may want to marry locally in order to secure a future for themselves. At the same time, however, they may also have the future of their family of origin in mind. Marrying a local man enables them to settle permanently in the Delta and serve as a bridgehead for siblings and parents.

Given the complex ways in which the behaviour patterns and life-plans of female migrants can be interpreted, we should refrain from trying to label individuals as totally "filial" or "rebellious." Instead, it might be more meaningful to focus on understanding the tension faced by migrant women as individual actors and as part of the patriarchal structures within both family and workplace. It is likely that the *dagongmei* both internalize the sense of family obligation and develop a growing sense of individualism.

Nevertheless, "filial daughter" and "rebellious daughter" labels can still serve as a useful heuristic device for researchers. These ideal types can be seen as opposite sides of the same continuum by which to measure reality. As an indication of social change, it can be intellectually enlightening to re-examine the behaviour patterns and life-plans of female migrants at different time intervals, to see if there has been a progressive shift from one side of the continuum to the other.

However, substantive problems of what constitute "filial" or "rebellious" behaviours remain unsolved. As time passes and with the increasing magnitude of long-distance out-migration among rural women from interior China, the prevailing cultural norms of the local community are likely to change. What present researchers define as "rebellious" behaviour of female migrants may become so commonplace and acceptable by the subjects' home community that concepts like "filial" and "rebellious" will have to be redefined by future researchers.

REFERENCES

Ariffin, J. (1984). Migration of women workers in Peninsular Malaysia: Impact and implications. In J.T. Fawcett, S-E. Koo, and P.C. Smith (Eds.), *Women in the cities of Asia: Migration and urban adaptation* (pp. 221-226). Boulder, CO: Westview Press.

Banister, J. (1987). *China's changing population.* Stanford, CA: Stanford University Press.

Boyd, M. (1989). Family and personal network in international migration: Recent developments and new agendas. *International Migration Review*, 23(3), 630-680.

Caldwell, J.C. (1976). Towards a restatement of demographic transition theory. *Population and Development Review*, 2, 321-366.

Cao, J. (1996). Thoughts provoked by the registration with blue cover and blue stamp. *Chinese Sociology and Anthropology*, 29(1), 86-102.

Chan, K-W. (1996). Post-Mao China: A two class urban society in the making. *International Journal of Urban and Regional Research*, 20(1), 134-150.

Chan, R.C.K. (1992). Challenges to urban areas: The floating population. In K. Hsin-Chi and M. Brosseau (Eds.), *China Review* (pp. 1-21). Hong Kong: Chinese University of Hong Kong.

Chant, S., and Radcliffe, S.A. (1992). Migration and development: The importance of gender. In S. Chant (Ed.), *Gender and migration in developing countries* (pp. 1-29). New York: Belhaven Press.

Chen, Z., and Juntao, W. (1996). *Diffusing China's bomb*. Missisauga, ON: Mirror Books.

Cheng, T., and Selden, M. (1994). The origins and social consequences of China's Hukou System. *China Quarterly*, 139, 644-668.

Christianson, F. (1990). Social division in peasant mobility in Mainland China: The implications of the Hu-k'ou System. *Issues and Studies*, 26(4), 23-42.

Connell, J., Dasgupta, B., Laishley, R., and Lipton, M. (1976). *Migration from rural areas: The evidence from village studies*. Delhi: Oxford University Press.

Dai, F. (1998). The feminization of migration in the Pearl River Delta. *The Journal of Geography*, 8(2), 101-115.

Davin, D. (1996). Migration and rural women in China: A look at the gendered impact of large-scale migration. *Journal of International Development*, 8(5), 655-665.

Davin, D. (1999). *Internal migration in contemporary China*. Cambridge: McMillan Press Ltd.

Dutton, M. (1988). Introduction: Basic facts on the household registration system. *Chinese Economic Studies*, 22(1), 3-21.

Fan, C.C. (1999). Migration in a socialist transitional economy: Heterogeneity, socioeconomic and spatial characteristics of migrants in China and Guangdong Province. *International Migration Review*, 33(4), 954-987.

Fan, C.C., and Youqin, H. (1998). Waves of rural brides: Female marriage migration in China. *Annals of the Association of American Geographers*, 88(2), 227-251.

Ferree, M.M. (1979). Employment without liberation: Cuban women in the United States. *Social Science Quarterly*, 60, 35-50.

Foshan Ribao (Foshan Daily). 1992-1995.

Gao, M. (1994). Migrant workers from rural China: Their conditions and some social implications for economic development in South China. In D. Schak (Ed.), *Entrepreneurship, economic growth and social change* (pp. 21-38). Queensland: Griffith University Centre for the Study of Australia-Asia Relations.

Gilpin, R. (1987). *The political economy of international relations*. New Jersey: Princeton University Press.

Goldstein, S., and Goldstein, A. (1984). Population movement, labor force absorption and urbanization in China. *Annals of the American Academy of Political and Social Sciences*, 476, 90-110.

Goldstein, A., and Goldstein, S. (1987-8). Varieties of population mobility in relation to development in China. *Comparative International Development*, Winter, 101-124.

Goldstein, A., and Goldstein, S. (1990a). Town and city: New directions in Chinese urbanization. In R.Y-W. Kwok, W. Parish, A.G. Yeh, and X. Xueqiang (Eds.), *Chinese urban reforms: What models now?* (pp. 17-44). Armonk, NY: M.E. Sharpe.

Goldstein, A., and Goldstein, S. (1990b). China. In C. Nam, W. Serow Jr., and D. Sly (Eds.), *International handbook on internal migration* (pp. 63-83). New York: Greenwood Press.

Goldstein, A., and Goldstein, S. (1996). Migration motivations and outcomes: Permanent and temporary migrants compared. In A. Goldstein and W. Feng (Eds.), *China: The many facets of demographic change* (pp. 187-212). Boulder, CO: Westview Press.

Guangzhou Ribao (Guangzhou Daily) 1992-5.

Guangzhou Shehui (Guangzhou Society) 1992-5.

Guest, P. (1993). The determinants of female migration from a multilevel perspective. In *Internal migration of women in developing countries* (pp. 223-243). Conference Proceedings. New York: United Nations.

Harris, J. and Todaro, M.P. (1970). Migration, unemployment and development: A two-way analysis. *The American Economic Review*, March, 126-142.

He, Q. (1997). *The primary capital accumulation in contemporary China*. Missisauga, ON: Mirror Books.

He, Z, and Xin, C. (1997-8). Women's lament: A perspective on the flagrant violation of the legal rights of women workers. *Chinese Sociology and Anthropology*, 30(2), 76-84.

Hein, M. (1996). Reform of the Hukou System. *Chinese Sociology and Anthropology*, 29(1), 3-14.

Huang, N.C. (1984). The migration of rural women in Taipei. In J.T. Fawcett, S-E. Koo, and P.C. Smith (Eds.), *Women in the cities of Asia: Migration and urban adaptation* (pp. 247-268). Boulder, CO: Westview Press.

Jacka, T. (1997). *Women's work in rural China: Change and continuity in an era of reform*. Cambridge: Cambridge University Press.

Johnson, G.E. (1989). Rural transformation in South China? View from the locality. *Revue Europeene des Sciences Sociales*, 27(84), 191-226.

Jones, G. (1993). The role of female migration in development. In *Internal migration of women in developing countries* (pp. 325-344). Conference Proceedings. New York: United Nations.

Knight, J., and Song, L. (1995). Towards a labor market in China. *Oxford Review of Economic Policy*, 11(4), 97-117.

Kojima, R. (1996). Breakdown of China's policy of restricting population movement. *The Developing Economies*, 34(4), 370-401.

Lan, D. (1996). An investigative report on the migrant population of Caitang Village, Xiamen special economic zone. *Chinese Sociology and Anthropology*, 28(4), 57-74.

Lee, C.K. (1995). Engendering the worlds of labor: Women workers, labor markets, and production politics in the South China economic miracle. *American Sociological Review*, 60(3), 373-397.

Li, R. (1994). Zhujiang Sanjiaozhou laodong shichangzhong de wailai laodong de yanjiu (A study of labor migrants in Pearl River Delta's labor market). *Renkou yu Jingji*, 4, 34-38.

Li, S. (1995). Population mobility and urban and rural development in Mainland China. *Issues and Studies*, 31(9), 37-54.

Li, S., and Yat-Ming, S. (1994). Population mobility. In Y.M. Yeung and David K.Y. Chu (Eds.), *Guangdong: Survey of a province undergoing rapid change* (pp. 373-400). Hong Kong: Chinese University Press.

Lim, L.L. (1993). The structural determinants of female migration. In *Internal migration of women in developing countries* (pp. 207-222). Conference Proceedings. New York: United Nations.

Lin, G.C.S. (1997). *Red capitalism in South China: Growth and development of the Pearl River Delta*. Vancouver, BC: University of British Columbia Press.

Lin, J.Y. (1988). Rural factor markets in China after the household responsibility system. In B.L. Reynolds (Ed.), *Chinese economic policy: Reform at midstream* (pp. 169-204). New York: Paragon House.

Lipton, M. (1980). Migration from rural areas of poor countries: The impact on rural productivity and income distribution. *World Development*, 8, 1-24.

Liu Yuanyuan (1993a). Wailaigong shengsi beige (The sad songs of life and death among labor in-migrants). *Chongyezhe*, 11, 8-12.

Liu Yuanyuan (1993b). Yiwei liulang nuhai de zibai (Confessions of a vagrant young woman). *Chongyezhe*, 12, 29-30.

Lo, C.P. (1989). Recent spatial restructuring in Zhujiang Delta, South China: A study of socialist regional development strategy. *Annals of the Association of American Geographers*, 79(2), 293-308.

Ma, L.J.C., and Xiang, B. (1998). Native place, migration, and the emergence of peasant enclaves in Beijing. *China Quarterly*, 155, 546-581.

Ma, Xia (1994). Changes in the pattern of migration in urban China. In L. Day and M. Xia (Eds.), *Migration and urbanization in China* (pp. 193-216). Armonk, NY: M.E. Sharpe.

Nanfang Nongcun Bao (Southern Village News) 1992-5.

Nanfang Ribao (Southern Daily)1992-95.

Ngai, P. (1999). Becoming dagongmei (working girls): The politics of identity and difference in Reform China. *China Journal*, 42, 1-18.

Oshima, K. (1990). The present condition of inter-regional movements of the labor force in Rural Jiangsu Province, China. *The Developing Economies*, 28(2), 202-20.

Pedraza, S. (1991). Women and migration: The consequences of gender. *Annual Review of Sociology*, 17, 303-325.

Peng, F. (1992). Guangdong liudong renkou xiankuang (The mobile population in Guangdong). *Nanfang Renkou*, 3, 23-27.

Portes, A. (1978). Migration and underdevelopment. *Politics and Society*, 8(1), 1-48.

Potter, S.H., and Potter, J.M. (1990). *China's peasants: The anthropology of a revolution*. Cambridge: Cambridge University Press.

Prybyla, J.S. (1989). China's economic experiment: Back from the market? *Problems of Communism*, 38(1), 1-18.

Riley, N.E., and Gardner, R.W. (1993). Migration decisions: The role of gender. In *Internal migration of women in developing countries* (pp. 195-206). Conference Proceedings. New York: United Nations.

Roberts, K.D. (1997). China's tidal wave of migrant labor. *International Migration Review*, 31(2), 249-293.

Rodenburg, J. (1993). Emancipation or subordination? Consequences of female migration for migrants and their families. In *Internal migration of women in developing countries* (pp. 273-289). Conference Proceedings. New York: United Nations.

Sassen-Koob, S. (1984). Notes on the incorporation of Third World women in wage labor through immigration and off-shore production. *International Migration Review*, 18(4), 1144-1167.

Smart, J., and Smart, A. (1991). Personal relations and divergent economies: A case study of Hong Kong investment in South China. *International Journal of Urban and Regional Research*, 15(2), 216-233.

Solinger, D. (1993). Chinese transients and the State: A case of civil society? *Politics and Society*, 21(1), 91-122.

Solinger, D. (1995). The floating population in the cities: Chances for assimilation? In D. Davis, R. Kraus, B. Naughton, and E. Perry (Eds.), *Urban spaces in contemporary China: The potential for autonomy and community in post-Mao China* (pp. 113-142). Cambridge: Cambridge University Press.

Standing, G. (1985). *Circulation and the labor process*. London: Croom Helm Press.

Stark, O. (1965). Introduction to symposium on advance migration theory. *Journal of Development Economics*, 17, 1-3.

Stark, O., and Levhari, D. (1982). On migration and risk in LCDs. *Economic Development and Cultural Change*, 31(1), 191-6.

Sung, Y. (1991). *The China-Hong Kong connection: The key to China's open door policy*. Cambridge: Cambridge University Press.

Sun, S. (1996). Shichang jingji yu nuxing liudong renkou yanjiu (A study of market economy and female mobile population). *Nanfang Renkou*, 4, 41-44.

Thadani, V.N., and Todaro, M.P. (1984). Female migration: A conceptual framework. In J.T. Fawcett, S-E. Koo, and P.C. Smith (Eds.), *Women in the cities of Asia: Migration and urban adaptation* (pp. 36-59). Boulder, CO: Westview Press.

Todaro, M.P. (1969). A model of labor migration and urban unemployment in less developed countries. *The American Economic Review*, 59, 138-148.

Todaro, M.P. (1976). *International migration in developing countries*. Geneva: International Labor Organization.

Tzeng, F. (1991). The political economy of China's coastal development strategy: A preliminary analysis. *Asian Survey*, 31(3), 270-284.

Vogel, E.F. (1989). *One step ahead in China: Guangdong under reform*. Cambridge, MS: Harvard University Press.

Wan, G.H. (1995). Peasant flood in China: Internal migration and its policy determinants. *Third World Quarterly*, 16(2), 173-196.

Wong, L. (1994). China's urban migrants—The public policy challenge. *Pacific Affairs*, 67(3), 335-356.

Wong, L., and Wai-Po, H. (1998). Reforming the household registration system: A preliminary glimpse of the Blue Chop Household Registration System in Shanghai and Shenzhen. *International Migration Review*, 32(4), 974-994.

Wood, C.H. (1981). Structural changes and household strategies: A conceptual framework for the study of rural migration. *Human Organization*, 40(4), 338-43.

Woon, Y. (1999). Labor migration in the 1990s: Homeward orientation and its implications for Interior China. *Modern China*, 25(4), 475-512.

Xiao, Y. (1995). Shilun shichang jingji yu liudong renkou (Preliminary discussion of market economy and mobile population). *Nanfang Renkou*, 4, 35-37.

Xu, X., and Siming, L. (1990). China's open door policy and urbanization in the Pearl River Delta region. *International Journal of Urban and Regional Research*, 14(1), 49-69.

Xu, X., Qi, L., and Xiangzhang, Z. (1988a). *Zhujiang Sanjiaozhou chengshi huanjing yu chengshi fazhan (The urban environment and urban development of the Pearl River Delta region)*. Guangzhou: Zhongshan University Press.

Xu, X., Qi, L., and Xiangzhang, Z. (1988b). *Zhujiang Sanjiaozhou de fazhan yu chengshihua (The Development and Urbanization of the Pearl River Delta Region)*. Guangzhou: Zhongshan University Press.

Yang, D. (1990). Patterns of China's regional development strategy. *China Quarterly*, 122, 230-257.

Yang, D. (1991). China adjusts to the world economy: The political economy of China's coastal development strategy. *Pacific Affairs*, 64(1), 42-64.

Yang, Q., and Guo, F. (1996). Occupational attainments of rural to urban temporary economic migrants in China, 1985-1990. *International Migration Review*, 30(3), 771-787.

Yang, X., and Goldstein, S. (1990). Population movement in Zhejiang Province, China: The impact of government policies. *International Migration Review*, 24(3), 509-533.

Zhang, H.X. (1999). Female migration and urban labor markets in Tianjin. *Development and Change*, 30(1), 21-41

Zheng, G., and Wenda, H. (1995). Liudong renkouzhong de funu wenti (Women's problems within the mobile population). *Nanfang Renkou*, 3, 37-41.

Zheng, G., and Yuexin, C. (1997). Nongcun liudong funu laodongli de zhiye bianhua (Occupational changes amongst rural female labor migrant). *Nanfang Renkou*, 3, 50-53.

Zhou, D. (1992). Zhujiang Sanjiaozhou wailai laodongli renkou yanjiu (A study of labor migrant population in the Pearl River Delta). *Shehuixue Yanjiu*, 5, 71-79.

Zhou, D. (1996). Investigation and analysis of migrant odd-job workers in Guangzhou. *Chinese Sociology and Anthropology*, 28(4), 75-94.

Zhou, K.X. (1996). *How the farmers changed China: Power of the people*. Boulder, CO: Westview Press.

Chinese Migrations and Implications for Canada: A Human Security Perspective

Robert Bedeski

Professor, Department of Political Science, University of Victoria

> *Give me your tired, your poor,*
> *Your huddled masses yearning to breathe free,*
> *The wretched refuse of your teeming shore,*
> *Send these, the homeless, tempest-tossed to me:*
> *I lift my lamp beside the golden door.*
>
> Emma Lazarus (1883)

A GLOBAL QUESTION

During the summer of 1999, four rusty, barely seaworthy ships were captured by Canadian authorities off Vancouver Island on the west coast of Canada. The ships contained nearly 600 Chinese migrants who had just survived a voyage lasting over 2 months. Well-organized criminal groups, with an extensive network of safe houses and underground transportation links, had orchestrated their voyage, arrival, and plans for subsequent deployment to the US— probably New York City. In Canada, public debate focused on whether these migrants were criminals who should be deported, genuine refugees and victims who should be accepted, or even a windfall of hard workers to Canada's multi-ethnic mosaic. These captured migrants expected to apply for refugee status and to be released into the community, as is the usual practice, but public outcry, especially after a number disappeared following release, resulted in their internment in Prince George, BC.

The arrival of a few hundred illegal migrants hardly represents a major crisis, when compared with the thousands without identification who appear annually at airports claiming to be refugees. However, the sophistication of the smuggling infrastructure and the potential migrant pool of tens of millions in China and elsewhere in the Third World should force Canada to rethink its soft approach to immigration. Is this situation a temporary phenomenon arising out of the opportunity offered by historic American economic expansion, drawing desperate migrants via Canada's unguarded borders, or is it a manifestation of the population explosion predicted by demographers and doomsayers for decades? For Canadians, this challenge will increase in the coming years, and the trajectory of multiculturalism and liberal immigration policy may not be sustainable under these pressures.

THE CHINESE DIASPORA

In Canada, as in other modern industrial societies, immigration policies arouse strong pro and con opinions. The pro-immigration camp argues for humanitarian concerns, citing the World War II Holocaust and recent murderous, genocidal regimes as the universal rationale for welcoming refugees. Pro-immigration pragmatists point to migrants as willing and eager workers, sustainers of family values, and a counter-balance to the Canadian birth dearth. They see young migrants as crucial to the work force—vital if the aging baby boomers are to have their pensions funded.

The anti-immigration sector leans more toward former Prime Minister Mackenzie King's pronouncement:

> *Immigration is a matter of domestic policy and is subject to the control of Parliament. Canada is perfectly within her rights in securing the immigrants she wants. An alien has no 'fundamental human right' to enter Canada. This is a privilege. ... The people of Canada do not wish to make a fundamental alteration in the character of their population through mass immigration. The government is therefore opposed to 'large-scale immigration from the Orient,' which would certainly give rise to social and economic problems, which might lead to serious international difficulties* (1947).[1]

Anti-immigrationists[2] posit a number of negative outcomes for Canada from illegal immigration:

1. Without normal entry checks, illegal immigrants may be carriers of communicable diseases.

2. Large-scale illegal immigration generates losses to local and state/provincial treasuries in the form of expenses for education, welfare, medical, and other costs, as they provide services to non-tax paying residents. Such pressures led to the passage of a referendum in California denying welfare and other services to illegal aliens.

3. Having entered a country illegally, owing large debts to snakeheads, and often living at the fringes of mainstream society, illegal immigrants will be tempted or forced to engage in other unlawful activities, including drugs and prostitution.

4. Large-scale illegal immigration often boomerangs against legal immigrants, who will be regarded with suspicion by the general population on the one hand, and subjected to crime and coercion by illegal countrymen, on the other hand.

5. Easy entry and unlikely deportation of illegal immigrants has also made Canada a haven for terrorists.[3] The US capture of Algerian terrorists at the end of 1999 highlighted the security inadequacies of Canadian monitoring of alien movements domestically, and if unremedied, could negatively affect the open border with the US.

Critics further argue that large-scale immigration—legal or otherwise—creates unfair competition for jobs that become scarce when the economy slows. Also, the favourable treatment of immigrants with relatives in the receiving country (family reunification) presents an open-ended invitation to further inflows over subsequent years. Illegal channels of immigration have grown rapidly to accommodate Chinese pressures, and the high costs of passage on ships through the "underground network" are worthwhile to families who have one of their own members establish a beachhead in a wealthier country.

Reasons for the population outflow from China include:

1. A large and growing population—China's huge population is approaching 1.3 billion people. Beijing has lifted some of the previous restrictions on travel and emigration as labour mobility becomes more important in economic development.

2. Travel into and out of China has become relatively easier since the early 1980s, due to economic liberalization, cheap and frequent air flights, and rapidly expanding maritime traffic. A network of Overseas Chinese (*Huaqiao*) in practically every country provides a network ready to facilitate living and employment for migrants.

3. The softening and liberalization of Western resistance to non-Caucasian immigration, along with domestic and international laws, charters and declarations of human rights, mandates accepting migrants who satisfy the minimal criteria of refugee claims. In Canada, a sector of the legal profession—often government-funded—provides representation for migrants, and public-funded multicultural entrepreneurs advocate open immigration while expanding their clientele. Criticism of open immigration is often branded as racist, resulting in closure of open discussion. These trends are reinforced by the voting patterns of immigrants, who tend to remember which party facilitated their acceptance and spoke in favour of their entry.

4. Rapid economic growth requires labour input in receiving countries, at all levels of skill. During the 1980s, high growth in Japan, Taiwan, South Korea and elsewhere created labour deficits often filled by imported labour. The entry of local women into the workforce mitigated this need, but aliens often filled dirty and dangerous jobs.

5. Higher living standards in China provide capital for travel and foreign investment, and reports of higher wages abroad lead many Chinese to attempt to improve their living standards through immigration. Trying to stem the exodus from countryside to cities, China makes changing legal residence expensive and difficult, so mobility for permanent economic improvement is available only by going abroad.

Contemporary population movements are driven by economics. Over the past decade, tens of thousands of Somalis migrated to eastern Canada to escape chaos in their homeland, and their increased presence has changed the complexion of parts of Ottawa, the national capital. Vancouver and other cities across the country now have a significant Chinese and other Asian ethnic presence. Immigration tends to be an urban phenomenon, and the impact on housing, social services, and schools is readily apparent. Chinese is now a major language in BC.

While race has not been a point of contention in Canadian immigration, nationality could emerge as a problem. Many of the earlier Chinese migrants came from pre-1998 Hong Kong as well as Taiwan—societies more notable as economic dynamos than regional powers. The recent influx of mainland migrants adds a new factor to the equation. The People's Republic of China (PRC) is a major regional and rising global military and economic power, and citizens who leave there do not necessarily reject old allegiances, in contrast to migrants from Hong Kong who worry about how long Beijing will tolerate the former British colony's autonomy. Although Taiwan has been a bastion against Communist Chinese military threats,[4] its future is far from secure, as recurrent saber-rattling from Beijing reminds the world.

Recent espionage cases by China and charges of ethnic Chinese illegal election contributions in the US hint at Beijing's leverage in the most powerful nation in the world. Even without the increasing presence of educated (and probably loyal to the US) ethnic Chinese in academic, scientific, and business sectors, emigration provides a number of benefits to China:

1. Emigrants often remit part of their earnings to their families in their home country, a net gain to local and national income.

2. Valuable networks for trade and business are established between China and foreign countries through ethnic Chinese.

3. Chinese students who study abroad usually specialize in high-technology fields, at the leading edge of a number of fields. While China is unable to provide either the facilities or prospects to entice these scientists and engineers back home, in a decade or two, the country may find itself in a situation similar to Taiwan in the 1960s and 70s—advanced growth with a deficit of sophisticated skills. The Taiwan solution was to greatly expand university and institutional opportunities to attract and recruit overseas Taiwan students and specialists back home, reaping a windfall of highly trained personnel.

4. China is overpopulated, and there are few social and environmental problems that would not be ameliorated by having fewer people. Emigration offers a safety valve to those who might be alienated at home. While people are the greatest resource in development, the large populations of China, India, Indonesia, and other Third World countries are probably an impediment to industrialization due to sheer numbers, and it is in China's interest to encourage—or at least to not impede—any movement out of the country.

It is important to note that there is no evidence that the Chinese government either encourages or overtly facilitates emigration, nor that it has any plans to do so. There is always the danger that suspicions can inflame prejudice, as occurred in Indonesia at the time of demonstrations against Suharto. Chinese transnational migration, however, is a growing phenomenon, and demands objective analysis, not only from the perspective of Chinese national interests, but also from the interests of societies receiving immigrants.

A Human Security Approach

Foreign Minister Lloyd Axworthy has defined human security as "much more than the absence of military threat. It includes security against economic privation, an acceptable quality of life, and a guarantee of fundamental human rights."[5] Human security contrasts with, but does not exclude, national security, which is state-centered, and aims to defend national sovereignty and the collective safety of its citizens. Preserving the nation-state, national security is a prerequisite to human security,[6] which seeks to safeguard individuals from environmental, economic, demographic, criminal, and technological threats. In the area of human rights, human security also seeks to protect individuals from oppressive government.

To include national security within the scope of human security, we formulate an operational definition of human security:

> *Human security is the totality of knowledge, technology, and institutions that protect, defend and preserve the biological existence of human life, and the processes that protect and perfect collective peace and prosperity to enhance civil society and human freedom.*

In this definition, "institutions" include state structures that are absent in Axworthy's definition. "Knowledge" refers to what Michael Oakeshott called technical and practical knowledge, and as the information revolution transforms into a new knowledge revolution, all security concerns may combine these two forms of knowledge, plus a third—"self knowledge." This last form of knowledge, philosophical, sociological, and introspective, enables political and social consensus.

Pro-immigration arguments demonstrate the benefits of immigration, while anti-immigration advocates focus on the costs, leaving most people with a sense of ambivalence. The immigration issue can be divided into two separate but related issues: population growth and migration.

Whether in China or Canada, population growth is primarily a human security issue. More people in a country means more pressure on resources, environment, space, and food. Thomas Malthus claimed that unchecked reproduction will eventually result in scarcity, and his modern disciples argue that humanity cannot continue to expect science and technology to find ways of supporting population growth indefinitely. Even if we remain at a constant world population (around six billion), it is very problematic to support these numbers for the remainder of the 21st century. The population optimists who see a happy hundred million Canadians may believe that our resources will be adequate to maintain present or even improved standards of living, or that multiculturalism will result in a North American version of Swiss tolerance, but the sorry record of mankind is more of the Yugoslav variety in questions of ethnic coexistence; and if predictions of global warming or global cooling prove correct, prospects for Canada will be altered as well.

Higher population density usually creates pressures on all levels of government for intervention: litigation over property and human rights, crime control, welfare and redistribution of wealth, protection of citizens' health, and confiscation of weapons are among the governmental human security activities likely to increase as population size grows. Therefore, as societies become more crowded, libertarian values will be the first casualties, as the state becomes the dominant source of human security and individuals are forced to reduce their latitudes of decision.

Immigration, on the other hand, is primarily an issue of national security, intrinsic to citizenship, loyalty, and sovereignty. Despite being bound to 20th century hot and cold wars, national security summarizes the modern concerns of safety and survival of the nation-state. National security and human security have at times been in opposition. Sending men to war to fight and die for their country, executing spies, suspending civil rights, and infringing freedoms were all normal and largely accepted sacrifices necessary to protect a nation. Since the Cold War, Canadians no longer accept these curtailments on human security by the state. Indeed, in an era of globalization, many doubt the future of the sovereign nation-state as a viable form of political organization; and if the sovereign nation-state has no future, then borders and citizenship become obsolete, and immigration should not be a concern of the state, but a matter of free choice. The European Union, with its trend to dissolving sovereignty, demonstrates a possible future.

More importantly, with cheap transportation and millions of desperate Third World workers and peasants longing to accept Emma Lazarus's invitation, many—probably most—Canadian bourgeoisie do not want unlimited immigration, at least not in their neighborhood. Immigration not only produces inconvenience, but also ethnically reconstitutes society. Recurring violence in BC Sikh communities has not contributed to ethnic tolerance. As host to large-scale, non-Western immigration, Canada may be witnessing the growth of non-assimilable ethnic enclaves, and laying the ground for a future of fragmentation and "Babelization."

National security is seen largely as a concern with military preparedness and protection of official secrets, but it has also been used during the last century as defense against subversion, bringing to mind Senator Joseph McCarthy and the House Un-American Activities Committee of the 1950s, with its loyalty oaths and alleged intimidation of political expression. The outrages to liberty in the Cold War pale to insignificance in the face of the Soviet gulags, genocides and auto-genocides of the Communist world, crimes which were never punished.[7]

Because of the lineage of World War II and the Cold War, national security has become the child nobody claims today, and not without reason—there do not seem to be any state or states aiming to destroy, or erode, or subvert the industrial democracies—including Canada. "National interest" is the more refined term in current usage, and reflects the less-intense temper of our age, but still seems unnecessarily nationalistic to the advocates of world government.

Before we consign "national security" to the dust heap of history, we must ask if another notion preserves its essence—the defense of our nation-state. Critics will reproach my use of the pronoun "our," because it implies a "their." But this is exactly my point—a country is not an abstraction or a territorial convenience, but the accumulation of effort, achievements, experiences, and sacrifices—the Burkean unity of the living, the dead, and the yet unborn. It is not a trifle to be given away or denied. Furthermore, human security is not possible without national security—Lloyd Axworthy's use of human security as an element of Canadian foreign policy implicitly rests on the existence of national security in Canada. A country that dissipates its energies, wealth, and virtues by denying it has any nation to secure will not long be able to have any foreign policy.

Immigration involves moving physically from one country to another with the intention of remaining permanently. It is assumed that the migrant individual will become a citizen of the new country as well. The immigrant has economic dimensions—he/she brings labour, skills, and knowledge, and will be a producer and/or consumer in the new country. The migrant also brings old attachments, culture, and values, some of which may be helpful to adjusting to the new culture, while others may be at odds with it. Generally, the more migrants from the same society, the less incentive there is to adjust to the new country. In Canada, official multiculturalism provides a further disincentive to assimilation.

When immigrants retain old loyalties and values—easily done under the high tolerance and low demands of citizenship in Canada—there is a tendency toward fragmentation, and the country, as a "community of communities" does not materialize. With the launching of the *Nis'gaa* treaty system in BC, for example, this fragmentation may be exacerbated, and any past visions of a Canadian nation may be compromised.

National security also requires, at minimum, territorial and border defense —control of who enters and leaves. Canada remains one of the freest countries in the world, and thus illegal immigration has not aroused excessive reaction. Court decisions have made it more difficult to exclude criminals and undesirables, and a domestic immigration industry (largely government-funded) of lawyers and multicultural entrepreneurs has facilitated passage from abroad into Canada.

In the case of the Chinese Diaspora, Canadian authorities have requested that the Chinese government help with the influx of illegal migrants. Certainly official corruption and collusion between the Triad gangs and military and civilian officials eases the exit of Chinese citizens for overseas destinations. Beijing sees it as a Canadian problem: soft policies invite these headaches.

Canada's failure to treat immigration as a national security problem could, in future, result in a demographic threat to Canadian human security. So far, the Canadian government has used human security as part of a humanitarian foreign policy—that is, we have all the human security we need, so now we should help others to achieve more of it. This position assumes that our problems of human security (and by implication, national security) have been solved, or are at least manageable. The human security dimensions of weakly-controlled or ill-monitored immigration will be manifested in a continued dilution of citizenship, social fragmentation of society along ethnic lines, importation of new and drug-resistant diseases, and Canada as a sanctuary for terrorists.

Guilt and charity have been powerful engines for current Canadian immigration policy—guilt over the pre-1945 Holocaust, perhaps a nagging sense that our comfort is fortuitous and unearned, and charity to alleviate poverty by welcoming the poor to our wealthy society. The irony of this version of charity is that by attracting the risk-takers and adventurous from developing countries to Canada, we deplete their scarce human resources for our own benefit.

Chinese Immigration to Canada

According to the 1991 census, there were about 4.3 million immigrants in Canada, or 16% of the total population.[8] A 1994 breakdown of the bases of these immigrant figures indicates that 49% were business, 42% were social or family class, and 9% humanitarian. Of BC residents, 22% were immigrants.

In 1991, there were 157,410 Chinese living in Canada, comprising 4% of all immigrants.[9] Between 1991 and 1994, Chinese represented 10% of all immigrant arrivals to Canada. In 1991, 43% of Chinese immigrants lived in Ontario, and 34% in BC. If immigration advocates argue for replenishing the youth pool, the Chinese case is not encouraging: in 1991, 22% of all immigrants from China were 65 and over, compared with 18% of all immigrants, and 10% of people born in Canada. Of immigrants from Hong Kong, on the other hand, only 2% were 65 or older.[10] Only 8% of Chinese immigrants were under 25 years of age, compared to 39% of the Canadian-born population. Employment rates for Chinese are slightly less than other groups, including native Canadians, but they are more likely to be self-employed and to have full-time, full-year jobs. The Chinese tend to sponsor parents, who then draw 53% of their incomes from the public purse. A combination of work, welfare, and stability remains a powerful drawing card to Canada.

Unlike many other societies, China has been weak in organized religion, even before the sustained Marxist persecutions that have occurred since 1949.

Daoism, Buddhism, and Confucianism (a quasi-religion) claimed many adherents in traditional society, but with little exclusivism, so individuals might practice rituals and visit temples of more than one faith with hardly any sense of irony or contradiction.

Religion has always been a major social force in the assimilation of immigrants into Western societies, which explains why earlier Canadian policies opposed non-Christian immigration—the difficulty of integration. Among the Chinese, 67% of immigrants claim no religion, compared to 15% of all immigrants, and 12% of Canadian-born. In our increasingly secularist society, these figures may be less relevant, but they point to an indicator of a "cultural firewall" between Chinese immigrants and mainstream Canadian society.

In the brave new secular, globalized, and multicultural Canada, the Chinese segment may be the most ideal, with little of the baggage of allegiance to their previous polity. They may be the most mobile as well. When Lee Kwan Yu was Prime Minister of Singapore—a mostly Chinese city—government officials often admitted that the commitment of citizens was only tentative. Singaporeans usually preferred to invest in expensive autos rather than property and homes (in Chinese, real estate is translated as "non-movable property"—*budongchan*), a symptom of readiness to pick up and leave. Hong Kong prospered after the Chinese Communist revolution because many of the Shanghai business and industrial elite relocated there, and now they and their families are moving again, or at least hedging their bets abroad.

This trend partly fueled the Asian boom in BC in the years preceding the turnover of Hong Kong, and has declined due to increased Canadian federal and provincial taxes and regulations, as well as economic recession in East Asia. The former factors are driving an Asian-Canadian brain drain—commerce, science, and engineering students and graduates recognize more long-term opportunity in the US than in Canada. For many immigrants, Canada is a stopover on the way to the US—even if the sojourn lasts for a generation or two.

These characteristics raise some fundamental questions about citizenship. Does the cultural pragmatism of Chinese immigration dilute their long-term commitment to settling in a country? Is citizenship reduced to the simplest requirements of residence and paying taxes, with open-ended benefits of welfare, health, and education? The trend of the past decades indicates a movement in this direction, combined with the politics of identity based on sex and ethnicity, rather than nation. Here, the question of national security may become moot, as loyalty becomes a formality and the notion of community becomes defined by ethnicity.

A Framework to Study Chinese Immigration to Canada

Immigration becomes a national security question in that it has the potential to alter civil society in significant ways. At the very least, the rapid increase of aliens in a national territory creates demands for accommodation of their values and culture, and modification of dominant institutions to minimize offense to newcomers. Other challenges include funding of indigent immigrants during a transition period, control of imported diseases, terrorist elements who may use the new host country as a base of operations, formation of ghettos where laws of the state may be ignored or neutralized, and pressure on government to change foreign policy to conform to the desires of a new minority. Certainly immigrants also make major contributions to their new homeland as well,[11] and the risks may be worth the rewards. But we must not assume that there will be easy assimilation of immigrants, or that Canadian society will avoid unforeseen transformations, or that massive immigration will not produce a ghettoized or balkanized nation.

AN ANALYTICAL MODEL OF CHINESE MIGRATION TO CANADA

Discussions on immigration tend to focus on the receiving country, and thus provide only half the picture. It is vital to look at the sending country, and the effects emigration has on that society. China is no longer a poor and struggling economy, nor is it a military or radical dictatorship. It is no longer ruled by Maoist true believers, and has shifted to quasi-capitalist pragmatism in economics under an authoritarian party dictatorship. But it is overpopulated, with nearly 1.3 billion people—around 50 times more than Canada. For China, the question is how to transform a redundant 100 million or so persons into a national asset, rather than a source of opposition or a growing claim on existing resources. Emigration is one answer, and it is not necessary for government to lift a finger to encourage it—there are millions of Chinese who want a better life abroad for themselves and their families. Is it Canada's obligation or in Canada's interest to facilitate and welcome these aspirations?

In order to explore and clarify the immigration phenomenon, I propose eight variables of analysis—four Chinese and four Canadian, as indicated in the two following tables. Each variable has its advocates, its beneficiaries, as well as benefits and costs. This analysis is restricted to the first generation of migrants. Its breakdown along lines of the variables is suggestive rather than definitive, and the two tables can provide a point of departure for further refinement of the two sides of China to Canada migratory behaviour, costs, and benefits. This framework also enables the analyst to distinguish among different categories of migrants. To speak of a homogeneous Chinese identity seriously distorts the complex reality of that society, and invites generalizations unjustified by evidence.

In conclusion, the contemporary outmigration from China—the current Diaspora—cannot be explained by a breakdown of state or civil order, and so the illegal immigrants recently pouring into Canada should not be treated as

Table 4.1 Analytical framework on Mainland Chinese migrations to Canada: China as sending society

China: Variables of Emigration	Benefits to China	Beneficiaries in China	Costs to China	Category of Emigrant
National interest = Demographic mercantilism (using emigrants as positive factors in economic development)	Investment; access to technology; foreign earnings through remittances and future returned emigrants	State and economy – less population pressure, income and networks provided by emigrants	Education investment; entrepreneurial and risk-taking spirit (This suggests that Canada is 'mining' Third World for free skills at expense of developing countries)	Students; entrepreneur; professionals
Local interest (county, town, village)	Foreign beachhead for future migrants; remittance of earnings back home	Families remaining in China	Loss of labour and skills	Entrepreneurs; labourers; itinerants
Relief of population pressure	Malcontents and dissidents leave the country; less pressure on unemployment and social services; decrease in land pressure and environmental stress	State and society	Loss of labour and skills	Labourers; farmers; retirees
Criminal networks and gangs	Profits; cheap labour	Snakeheads; corrupt officials; criminal gangs; employers in North America	Voluntary contract servitude; erodes credibility of laws; enriches criminal elements	Rural sector; unskilled

Table 4.2 Analytical framework on Mainland Chinese migrations to Canada: Canada as receiving society

Canada: Variables of Immigration (source of variables)	Benefits to Canada	Beneficiaries in Canada	Unintended Costs to Canada (potential)	Category of Immigrant
National Interest (Canadian government calculations)	Cheap labour; high work ethic; family values; needed skills	Canadian society and economy; immigration industry[12]	Competition for scarce jobs; higher unemployment rates for Canadian-born labour; depression of wage rates	Legal applicants
Humanitarian values (UN declarations)	Reinforcement of social values; often highly educated persons	Genuine and bogus refugees; immigration industry	Welfare; medical care; danger of new disease; public cynicism; high costs of coastal patrols and internment;	Refugee claimants
Libertarian values (individual calculations)	Economic mobility; matching of skills to jobs; enhancement of human freedom	Canadian society and economy; immigration industry	Competition for scarce jobs	Legal applicants; family members of immigrants; fraudulent applicants
Social engineering (multicultural expectations)	Increased diversity; multiculturalism	Immigration and multicultural industry; public sector	Transformation of Canadian society; dominance of groups most skilled in manipulating the immigration system	Generally non-white

refugees in most cases. This wave of migrants, combined with globalization trends in Canada, can pose a challenge to national security in the next few years, and a human security problem over the longer period, if not addressed with more self-interested scrutiny than evident in the past.

ENDNOTES

1 William Lyon Mackenzie King, Statement on Canada's Long-Term Immigration Program of May 1, 1947, quoted in *Canadian Immigration Hotline*, Number 118, November, 1999, p. 1.

2 One example of anti-immigration agitation can be found at *http://ww.canadafirst.net*.

3 See Diane Francis, "Ottawa pursing an incompetent, dangerous policy," *National Post*, January 4, 2000, p. C3.

4 PRC President Jiang Zemin, in his speech at the Macau turnover, insisted that the examples of Hong Kong and Macau 'will give a positive push to the early settlement of the Taiwan question.' Taiwan officials described his speech as 'insulting and provocative.' *Far Eastern Economic Review*, "Target Taiwan," December 30, 1999 and January 6, 2000, p. 10.

5 "Canada and human security: the need for leadership," *International Journal* (Spring 1997), p. 184.

6 As Dean Oliver writes: In many corners of the Third World, the problem of human security lies in collapsed states which have lost legitimacy and the power ot providing for the basic human and political security needs of their citizens. "Pulpit diplomacy: A critical assessment of the Axworthy doctrine." *International Journal* (Summer 1998), p. 386.

7 See *The Black Book of Communism* (Harvard University), and Stephane Courtois, "Red crimes are toted up in a big Black Book," *National Post*, January 8, 2000, B1, B10.

8 Government of Canada, Immigration Research Series, "Total Immigrant Population," p. 1.

9 Government of Canada, Immigration Research Series, "Profiles People's Republic of China," p. 1.

10 Government of Canada, Immigration Research Series, "Profiles Hong Kong," p. 5.

11 A new report by the Center for Immigration Studies (Washington, DC), "Reconsidering Immigrant Entrepreneurship: An Examination of Self-Employment Among Natives and the Foreign-Born," finds that while immigrants do seem to have been significantly more entrepreneurial than natives in the past, since 1980 self-employment patterns among natives and immigrants have been very similar.

12 This refers to lawyers, multicultural entrepreneurs, charities, advocacy groups, and others who receive direct or indirect remuneration for involvement in immigration affairs.

The Determinants of Elderly Immigrants' Social Support

Zheng Wu

Professor, Department of Sociology, University of Victoria

Randy Hart

Department of Sociology, University of Victoria

INTRODUCTION

The number of older Canadians is increasing. In 1996, about 3.3 million Canadians (9% of the population) were aged 65 years or older; and by 2021 this number is expected to double (Statistics Canada, 1999; Statistics Canada, 2000a). Moreover, the most recent data indicate that 27% of the elderly are foreign-born (Statistics Canada, 1999). This high proportion of elderly immigrants raises a number of important issues.

As people reach old age, and subsequently experience declining health, they often are in greater need of social support. Indeed, the availability of social support has been shown to greatly improve physical and mental health, as well as stabilize poor health (Kiefer et al., 1985; Lai and McDonald, 1995; Lee, Crittenden, and Yu, 1996; Noh and Avison, 1996; Noh, Wu, and Avison, 1994; also see Thoits, 1995, for a review). It may be thought that immigrants to Canada experience an inadequacy of social support due to the uprooting process. However, research indicates that immigrants tend to "chain migrate" with their immediate families, and thus the main components of their support structures remain intact (Kuo and Tsai, 1986). Furthermore, immigrants to Canada establish support networks within their ethnic-cultural communities, and may well receive support from the broader communities of the host society (Kuo and Tsai, 1986; Noh and Avison, 1996). Kuo and Tsai (1986) also have suggested that the identification of support resources may begin prior to emigration.

Overall, very little research has been conducted on social support among elderly immigrants, and most of the existing literature focuses on the effects of social support on physical or mental health (Kiefer et al., 1985; Lai and McDonald, 1995; Lee, Crittenden, and Yu, 1996; Noh and Avison, 1996; Noh, Wu, and Avison, 1994). The research that does exist on the determinants of immigrants' social support generally involves areas studies based on small, non-probability samples, and centres on immigrants of specific ethnic-cultural origins (Tsai and Lopez, 1997). In this study, we analyse data from Canada's National Population Health Survey (NPHS)—a large, nationally representative sample—and concentrate on the determinants of social support among Canada's foreign-born elderly.

Research Hypotheses

Social support, commonly viewed as multifaceted, is usually separated into three components: support resources; support behaviours; and perceived support (Vaux, 1985; Barrera, 1986). Support resources simply describe the extent of one's social support network, and can be considered the source of one's social capital, or the advantages one receives through social interaction (Coleman, 1988; Portes, 1998; Sampson, Morenoff, and Earls, 1999). Frequency of social contact and social involvement are its usual measures (Krause and Borawski-Clark, 1995). Supportive behaviours describe the actual emotional and/or instrumental support one receives. This support is not always welcome, as it can be uninvited and negatively perceived (Krause and Borawski-Clark, 1995). Perceived support refers to one's subjective assessment of both the availability and adequacy of social support. Research suggests that perceived support has as much an effect on one's well being as does received support (Wethington and Kessler, 1986). In this study, we focus on two dimensions of social support: perceived availability of support, and support resources (i.e., social involvement and social contact). Received support is not examined, as the survey does not provide the necessary information.

Although much research has focused on the effects of social support on physical and mental health, health may also affect social support. More specifically, the experience of poor health and stress may activate a support system (Pearlin, Lieberman, Menaghan, and Mullan, 1981), as people search for aid. Conversely, poor physical or mental health may result in a reduction of support because some people may disengage rather than search for, or accept, help (Krause, 1991). This study will determine the impact of health and stress on elderly immigrant's social support. We expect social contact to increase if health is poor because ill health may activate a support network. However, we expect less social involvement and contact for those with mobility and dexterity problems, as these disabilities likely reduce social interaction.

Age, gender, marital status, children, and siblings are all known to influence social support, but research findings have been somewhat equivocal. For example, while a positive association between age and perceived support has been found (Barrett, 1999), there is some evidence of an inverse relationship (Thoits, 1984; Turner and Marino, 1994). This study determines the relationship between age and perceived support among elderly immigrants, but also explores the relationship between age and support resources, that is, social involvement and social contact.

Most research suggests that gender influences the provision and receipt of informal support among the elderly, with women generally experiencing more social support than men (Antonucci and Akiyama, 1987; Campbell, Connidis, and Davies, 1999; Connidis, Rosenthal, and McMullin, 1996; Shye, Mullooly, Freeborn, and Pope, 1995; Wu and Pollard, 1998). In their study, however, Krause and Keith (1989: 623) found that elderly women and men were equally likely to activate a support network in the face of "global stressful life events," whereas gender differences occurred only when dealing with financial strains. We have included gender in our models in order to determine whether there are gender differences among Canada's foreign-born elderly.

There is also some dispute about the relationship between marital status and social support. In a recent study, Barrett (1999) found that among the elderly, the never-married have lower levels of involvement and perceived support, as well as a lower probability of having a confidant, than the married. In younger populations, however, the never-married and the married have more similar social support, with the never-married having more contact with friends and family than the currently or previously married. Furthermore, Connidis and McMullin (1994) found that the divorced and the single are more likely than the married to rely on formal support and paid assistance. Neither Choi (1996) nor Wu and Pollard (1998), however, find a significant relationship between marital status and social support.

Both availability and receipt of support for older persons increases greatly when grown children are available (Connidis and McMullin, 1994; Litwak, 1985; Lynch, 1998), so we include a measure of whether the respondent has children. Similarly, research shows siblings to be an important source of support (Campbell, Connidis, and Davies, 1999), and so we include siblings in our models as well.

We have incorporated a measure of whether or not the respondent lives in a house, because living in a detached dwelling can increase the need for assistance—for example, help with yard work or housekeeping. So, there may be a positive relationship between social support and living in a house. On the other hand, living in a house may reduce the chances of interaction with others because, unlike apartments or nursing homes, the sources of support may not be nearby.

Previous research suggests that social support in later life may vary by socioeconomic status (SES). For example, Krause and Borawski-Clark (1995) found that those with higher SES tend to have more contact with family and friends, and are generally more satisfied with the support they receive. The authors also found that contact with friends and support satisfaction increase with educational attainment and income. In the current study, we presume that employment will increase the availability of social support because of the increased likelihood of social involvement. As a result, those working outside the home also may have a greater perception of available support because their social network may be greater than that of the unemployed. Our measures of socioeconomic status include working outside the home, educational attainment, and income adequacy.

Finally, we include in our models a number of immigrant-specific variables. We assume that the number of years residing in Canada will relate positively to social support: a longer time of residence allows the formation of a larger support network, and a greater likelihood of assimilation into the host society. We also include a quadratic term because the relationship between length of residence and social support may be non-linear. More specifically, the effect of length of residence may stabilize over time. We also provide a measure of whether the respondent speaks either of Canada's two official languages, English or French. Speaking either language indicates acculturation, and should extend the availability of social support beyond the respondent's own cultural/ethnic community.

Increasingly, new Canadian immigrants come from Asia (see Statistics Canada, 1999), but there is little research on their availability of social support, or their social resources in this country (see Noh, Wu, and Avison [1994] and Noh and Avison [1996] on Koreans in Canada; see Lai and MacDonald [1995] on elderly Chinese immigrants in Calgary). We therefore include a measure of whether the respondent originated from China or Southeast Asia, to discover whether social support among these immigrants differs from that of other foreign-born Canadian residents.

Data and Methods

Our empirical analysis draws cross-sectional data from the second cycle of the National Population Health Survey (NPHS), conducted by Statistics Canada in 1996-97. The NPHS was designed to collect in-depth information on the physical and mental health of Canadians and on population health determinants. In addition to cross-sectional information, the NPHS collects longitudinal data from a panel of individuals at 2-year intervals for up to two decades. The first cycle of data collection, in 1994-95, was comprised of a nationally representative sample of 17,626 Canadians aged 12 and older in all provinces and territories except First Nations reserves and Canadian Forces bases. Using the same target population, the second cycle, in 1996-97, included 15,670 respondents from the longitudinal panel (those who provided complete information in both cycles). In cycle 2, additional respondents were surveyed for cross-sectional purposes only. A total of 81,804 respondents, including those on the longitudinal panel,[1] completed the in-depth interview in cycle 2, with an overall response rate of 79%.[2]

Although it would be desirable to use the longitudinal data from the NPHS in this study, the small number of elderly immigrants from the panel (N = 359) was inadequate for proper analysis. For this reason, we use instead the cross-sectional data from cycle 2 of the NPHS, restricting the sample to respondents born outside Canada (immigrants), who were aged 65 years or older at the time of the interview. With these restrictions, our study sample includes a total of 3,009 elderly immigrants (1,737 women and 1,272 men). The primary statistical tools used in this analysis are ordinary least squares (OLS) models.

Measures

As noted above, social support is often assessed in three categories, of which we concentrate on two, perceived support and social resources. To assess perceived support, we use the social support index (4 items), which reflects whether the respondents feel they have someone they can confide in, count on, who can give them advice, and makes them feel loved. As Thoits (1995: 64) has stated, this index is the "simplest and most powerful measure of social support."

We consider two measures of social resources available in the NPHS: a social involvement index and social contact. The social involvement index (two items) indicates the frequency of participation in associations or voluntary organizations, and frequency of attendance at religious services in the last year. Social contact reflects the average number of contacts in the past 12 months with family members and friends who are not part of the household, and with neighbors. Table 5.1 presents descriptive statistics for these measures.

Table 5.1 also provides both definitions and descriptive statistics for our independent variables. Because health status and activity of daily living (ADL) impairments are known to be the strongest strain predictors (Arling, 1987; Revicki and Mitchell, 1990), we include six health indicators to measure the physical and mental health of the respondent. Chronic conditions are a continuous variable, indicating the number of chronic conditions (e.g., arthritis/rheumatism, high blood pressure, diabetes, heart disease, Alzheimer's disease or other dementia). Self-reported health status is an ordinal variable, ranging from "poor" to "excellent." Cognitive function is a composite index (two items) used as part of the Comprehensive Health Status Measurement System (CHSMS) implemented in the NPHS (see Statistics Canada, 1998). Measuring the respondent's ability to remember, think, and solve problems, the index is coded as an ordinal scale, ranging from "no cognitive problems" to "unable to remember and/or think."

The last three health indicators also form part of the CHSMS used in the NPHS. Like cognitive function, dexterity function is a composite index (four items), measuring the level of dexterity. However, because of its skewed distribution (less than 2% of the respondents reporting any dexterity problems), we decided to measure dexterity as a dummy variable indicating whether the respondent has any dexterity problems at all. We measure mobility function (a 7-item index) in the same manner, for the same reason. Finally, emotional function is measured by a single-item ordinal scale on five levels, which range from "happy and interested in life" to "so unhappy that life is not worthwhile."

As noted, we consider a number of demographic variables pertaining to social support for the elderly. Age is measured at four levels: 65-69, 70-74,

Table 5.1 Definitions and descriptive statistics for variables used in the analysis of social support of elderly immigrants: Canada, 1996-97

Variable	Variable Coding	Mean or %	S. D.
Dependent Variables			
Social Support	Perceived social support in 5 levels (4 = most,..., 0 =least)a	3.65 2161.65	0.87 1674.82
Social Involvement	Social involvement in 9 levels (8 = most, ..., 0 = least)a	3.17	2.67
Social contact	Average frequency of social contact in 7 levels (6 = most,..., 0 = least)a	4.14	0.98
Health Indicators			
Chronic condition	Number of chronic conditions (10 = 10 or more, ..., 0 = none)	2.14	1.81
Health	Self-reported health status in 5 levels (5 = excellent, ..., 1 = poor)	3.19	1.09
Cognitive function	Cognitive function in 6 levels (6 = no cognitive problems, ..., 1 = unable to remember/ to think)	5.19	1.24
Dexterity problem	Dummy indicator (1 = yes, 0 = no)	1.90	--
Mobility problem	Dummy indicator (1 = yes, 0 = no)	10.70	--
Emotional problem	Emotional problem in 5 levels (5 = very unhappy,..., 1 = very happy)	1.31	0.64
Demographic Indicators			
Age			
65-69	Dummy indicator (1 = yes, 0 = no)	33.4	--
70-74	Dummy indicator (1 = yes, 0 = no)	29.6	--
75-79	Dummy indicator (1 = yes, 0 = no)	15.9	--
80+	Reference group	21.1	--

Table 5.1   continued

Variable	Variable Coding	Mean or %	S. D.
Demographic Indicators (continued)			
Marital status			
Married/Cohabiting	Dummy indicator (1 = yes, 0 = no)	60.2	--
Never married	Dummy indicator (1 = yes, 0 = no)	4.1	--
Widowed/ Separated/Divorced	Reference group	35.3	--
Presence of children	Dummy indicator (1 = yes, 0 = no)	85.3	--
Presence of siblings	Dummy indicator (1 = yes, 0 = no)	63.8	--
Live in a house	Dummy indicator (1 = yes, 0 = no)	44.3	--
SES Indicators			
Work outside the home	Dummy indicator (1 = yes, 0 = no)	6.1	--
Educational status	Educational attainment in 12 levels (1 = no schooling, ..., 12 = masters or above)	5.04	3.22
Income adequacy	Income adequacy in 5 levels (5 = adequate, ..., 1 = inadequate)	3.09	0.83
Immigrant-Specific Variables			
Years in Canada	Years in Canada (since landing)	42.46	18.88
Years in Canada squared	Quadratic term of years in Canada	2161.65	1674.82
Speak English or French	Dummy indicator (1 = yes, 0 = no)	90.4%	--
Chinese/Southeast Asian	Dummy indicator (1 = yes, 0 = no)	9.1%	--
N		3,009	

Note: Weighted means or percentages, unweighted N.

[a] See text for detailed description.

75-79, and 80 or older. Marital status is a 3-level categorical variable: married or cohabiting, previously married, or never married. Table 5.1 indicates that about 60% of elderly immigrants are currently in a marital or a nonmarital union, 35% are separated, divorced or widowed, and about 4% have never married. We use two dummy indicators measuring the presence of living children and siblings.

As housing status may also affect an individual's desire and opportunity for social contact, we include a dummy variable indicating whether the respondent lives in a house. At the time of the interview, 44% of elderly immigrants were living in a single detached or undetached house (see Table 5.1). The comparable figure for overall Canadian households was 66.3% in 1997 when the survey was completed (Statistics Canada, 2000b).

We include three SES indicators. We use a dummy variable indicating whether the respondent works outside the home. As would be expected, only 6% of elderly immigrants were employed outside the home at the time of the interview. For educational status we use an ordinal variable, ranging from no formal schooling to a masters degree or above. To measure income, we use the NPHS income adequacy scale, which is based on household income relative to the size of the household (see Statistics Canada, 1998).

Finally, three variables are used for immigrant-specific characteristics. Duration of residence in the host country (in years) provides an indicator of assimilation. However, we add a quadratic term to the multivariate models to capture any possible non-linear effect of length of residence. As ability to speak the host language is often used as a measure of acculturation, we use a dummy variable indicating whether the respondent is able to conduct a conversation in either official language (English or French). Table 5.1 shows that most elderly immigrants (90%) are able to speak either language. Finally, to capture the recent increase in the number of Asian immigrants, we include a dummy variable indicating whether the respondent's ethnic origin is Southeast Asian or Chinese.

RESULTS

Recent Trends in Canadian Immigration

Immigration to Canada has been somewhat uneven, and has fluctuated over the past 40 years or so. However, a consistent and prolonged increase occurred between 1985 and 1996 (Figure 5.1). To a large degree, this trend is probably attributable to the greater number of immigrants arriving from Asia. Throughout much of the nation's history, the majority of immigrants arrived from "traditional" source countries in the UK, Europe, as well as from the US. The 1960s saw Canada's immigration policy come under attack as discriminatory on the basis of national origin. Officially, the Canadian federal government lifted the source country restriction in 1962, and introduced the point system in 1967; the 1976 Immigration Act reinforced the nondiscriminatory policy towards independent immigrants, family reunification, and refugee issues (Beaujot, 1991). Since the 1960s, Canada has been admitting increasing numbers of immigrants from "non-traditional" source countries in Asia and the Pacific Islands, South and Central America, and Africa and the Middle East. Indeed, Figure 5.2 shows clearly that the proportion of immigrants arriving from Asia has increased steadily, with a slight decline after about 1996.

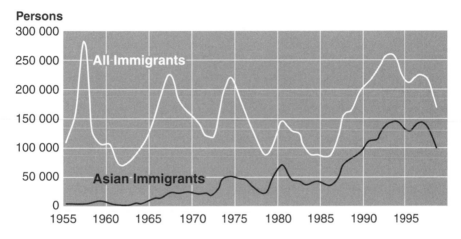

Figure 5.1　Number of immigrants to Canada, 1955-1998 (Source: Employment and Immigration Canada, SDDS 3601. Update: 29 June, 1999)

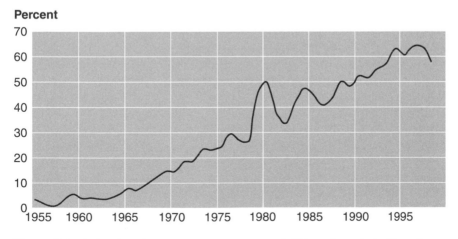

Figure 5.2　Asian immigrants as a percentage of all immigrants to Canada, 1955-1998 (Source: Employment and Immigration Canada, SDDS 3601. Update: 29 June, 1999)

Although immigration to Canada increasingly stems from Asia and the Middle East, the majority of elderly immigrants in our sample came to Canada some time ago—the average length of residence is 43 years (see Table 5.1), which indicates that most of these people probably came from Europe and the UK, the primary sources of Canadian immigration at the time. Table 5.2 shows that about 41% of immigrants from the UK, 56% of immigrants from Northern/Western Europe, 39% of immigrants from Eastern Europe, and 32% of immigrants from Southern Europe, all arrived in Canada prior to 1961. By comparison, 39% of immigrants from West-central Asia/Middle East, 43% of immigrants from Eastern Asia, 29% of immigrants from Southeast Asia, and 40% of immigrants from southern Asia arrived between 1991 and 1996.

Table 5.2 also shows that prior to 1961 about 25% of immigrants to Canada were from the United Kingdom, and about 65% from various European regions. During this period only 3% of Canadian immigrants originated in Asia. Between 1991 and 1996, however, only about 2% of new immigrants were from the United Kingdom; about 17% were from Europe, and about 57% of immigrants were from Asia. About 9% of the elderly in our sample are of either Chinese or Southeast Asian origin (Table 5.1). In the coming years, these numbers are expected to rise as the population of recent Asian immigrants age, and it is crucial that we begin to gain an understanding of social support among this population, as well as other populations of elderly immigrants.[3]

Determinants of Elderly Immigrants' Social Support

Table 5.3 provides our OLS regressions of social support on selected independent variables among elderly immigrants. The first model is concerned with perceived support. While most of the health indicators in this model are statistically insignificant, there is a significant negative relationship between emotional problems and the dependent variable, which indicates that elderly immigrants who experience emotional problems are less likely to believe that they have adequate support when needed. The model also shows that female immigrants are more likely than their male counterparts to perceive support.

Perceived support is further shown to vary by age. More specifically, those who are between 65-69, or between 70-74, perceive less support compared to immigrants who are 80 years of age or over. This probably indicates that the oldest immigrants are already receiving social support, perhaps due to age-related health problems, and are thus more likely to perceive the availability of support. The married/cohabiting are seen to experience higher perceived support than the widowed/separated/divorced. Finally, the model shows a positive relationship between the presence of children and perceived support.

Social involvement is the dependent variable in the second model in Table 5.3. As would be expected, good health is generally associated with increased involvement, while poor physical or mental health results in a decrease. For

Table 5.2 Immigration population by place of birth and period of immigration: Canada, 1996[a]

| Place of Birth | Period of Immigration | | | | | | |
	<1961	1961-70	1971-80	1981-90	1991-96	Total[b]	%
United States	45,050	50,200	74,015	46,405	29,025	244,695	4.9
	18.4%	20.5%	30.2%	19.0%	11.9%	100.0%	
Central and South America	6,370	17,410	67,470	106,230	76,335	273,815	5.5
	2.3%	6.4%	24.6%	38.8%	27.9%	100.0%	
Caribbean and Bermuda	8,390	45,270	96,025	72,405	57,315	279,405	5.6
	3.0%	16.2%	34.4%	25.9%	20.5%	100.0%	
United Kingdom	265,580	168,140	132,950	63,445	25,420	655,535	13.2
	40.5%	25.6%	20.3%	9.7%	3.9%	100.0%	
Other Northern/ Western Europe	284,205	90,465	59,850	48,095	31,705	514,320	10.3
	55.3%	17.6%	11.6%	9.4%	6.2%	100.0%	
Eastern Europe	175,430	40,855	32,280	111,370	87,900	447,835	9.0
	39.2%	9.1%	7.2%	24.9%	19.6%	100.0%	
Southern Europe	228,145	244,380	131,620	57,785	52,455	714,385	14.4
	31.9%	34.2%	18.4%	8.1%	7.3%	100.0%	
Africa	4,945	25,685	58,150	64,265	76,260	229,305	4.6
	2.2%	11.2%	25.4%	28.0%	33.3%	100.0%	
West-central Asia/ Middle East	4,975	15,165	30,980	77,685	82,050	210,855	4.2
	2.4%	7.2%	14.7%	36.8%	38.9%	100.0%	
Eastern Asia	20,555	38,865	104,940	172,715	252,340	589,415	11.9
	3.5%	6.6%	17.8%	29.3%	42.8%	100.0%	
Southeast Asia	2,485	14,040	111,700	162,490	118,265	408,980	8.2
	0.6%	3.4%	27.3%	39.7%	28.9%	100.0%	
Southern Asia	4,565	28,875	80,755	99,270	140,055	353,520	7.1
	1.3%	8.2%	22.8%	28.1%	39.6%	100.0%	
Oceania and Other[c]	4,250	9,240	15,420	10,240	9,875	49,025	1.0
	8.7%	18.8%	31.5%	20.9%	20.1%	100.0%	
Total	1,054,947	788,592	996,158	1,092,403	1,039,003	4,971,090	100.0

[a] Includes only the first four months of 1996.

[b] Total may not add up to 100% due to rounding errors.

[c] "Other" includes Greenland, St. Pierre and Miquelon, the category *other country*, as well as immigrants born in Canada.

Source: Statistics Canada. *1996 Census* (Online).
          http://www.statcan.ca/english/Pgdb/People/Population/demo25a.htm.

Table 5.3   OLS regressions of social support on selected independent
variables among elderly immigrants: Canada, 1996-1997

| | | Dependent Variable | |
Independent Variable	Support	Involvement	Contact
Health Indicators			
Chronic condition	-0.001	0.038	0.017
Health	0.015	0.139**	0.007
Cognitive function	0.013	-0.040	0.075***
Dexterity problem (1 = yes)	0.066	-0.684*	-0.034
Mobility problem (1 = yes)	-0.026	-0.423**	0.072
Emotional problem	-0.212***	-0.354***	-0.103***
Demographic Indicators			
Female (1 = yes)	0.258***	0.374***	0.225***
Age			
65-69	-0.107*	0.066	-0.097
70-74	-0.134**	0.180	-0.136**
75-79	-0.056	0.146	-0.062
80+[a]			
Marital status			
Married/Cohabiting	0.248***	0.250**	0.038
Never married	0.051	0.477*	0.045
Widowed/Separated/ Divorced[a]			
Presence of children (1 = yes)	0.381***	0.183	0.093
Presence of siblings (1 = yes)	-0.040	0.385***	-0.402***
Live in a house (1 = yes)	-0.008	-0.246**	-0.101**
SES Indicators			
Work outside the home (1 = yes)	0.004	0.377*	-0.006
Educational status	-0.008	0.025	-0.005
Income adequacy	0.003	-0.171**	-0.041

Table 5.3   continued

Independent Variable	Dependent Variable		
	Support	Involvement	Contact
Immigrant-Specific Variables			
Years in Canada	-0.002	0.022	0.002
Years in Canada squared	0.000	0.000	0.000
Speak English or French *(1 = yes)*	0.108	-0.724*	0.134
Chinese/Southeast Asian *(1 = yes)*	-0.083	0.487	-0.203
Intercept	3.231***	2.865***	3.992***
R^2	0.073***	0.036***	0.073***

[a] Reference group.

* $p < .05$ ** $p < .01$ *** $p < .001$ (two-tailed test)

example, self-reported health status is positively related to the dependent variable, while dexterity, mobility, and emotional problems all significantly reduce involvement. The model also shows that female immigrants are more socially involved than their male counterparts. The married/cohabiting, as well as the never married, have higher levels of social involvement than the widowed/separated/divorced, while the presence of siblings tends to increase involvement.

As expected, living in a detached dwelling reduces social involvement, which may mean that these immigrants are somewhat isolated. Employment outside the home is seen to increase involvement probably because the opportunities for social contact are increased through the availability of workplace interactions and friendships. The model further shows that both income adequacy and being able to speak either of Canada's official language are negatively related to social involvement.

The third model regresses social contact on our independent variables. Cognitive functioning is positively associated with the dependent variable, while the relationship between emotion problems and contact is significantly negative. As with perceived support and social involvement, female immigrants experience more social contact than males. Compared to immigrants who are 80 years of age or older, those who are between the ages of 70 and 74 have significantly less contact. Surprisingly, immigrants with siblings have lower levels of social contact than those who do not. Finally, the model reveals that living in a house reduces immigrants' social contacts.

DISCUSSION AND CONCLUSION

This study has focused on the determinants of social support among the for-eign-born elderly in Canada. We have assessed two dimensions of support: perceived support and social resources. We regard social resources as the struc-tural determinants of social capital, or the advantages one gains through social interaction. The more one is involved in his/her community and/or with fam-ily and friends, the more advantages accrue from these interactions.

Our OLS models reveal that in general good physical and mental health increase both the availability as well as the perception of support. In this re-gard, the most consistent finding is the negative relationships found between emotional problems and all three dependent variables: elderly immigrants with emotional problems tend to perceive less support, have less social involve-ment, and have fewer social contacts. This suggests support for the hypothesis that emotional stress results in a disengagement from, rather than an activa-tion of, a support network. Of course, we cannot be certain of the direction of the effect, as ours is a cross-sectional analysis. It is possible that a lack of social support and low social capital have led to emotional problems (Turner, 1999). Longitudinal analysis is needed in order to establish causality. It would also be useful to determine if emotional stress is due to the immigration process itself, especially among more recent immigrants, or some other structural and/ or individual factors.

For the most part, the effects of our demographic indicators are consistent with much of the literature. We find that foreign-born elderly women are more likely to perceive the availability of social support, are more socially involved, and experience greater social contact than their male counterparts. Similar gender differences are found among the native-born (Antonucci and Akiyama, 1987; Barrett, 1999; Lynch, 1998; Thoits, 1995). Our results further indicate that the married/cohabiting are more likely than the widowed/separated/ divorced to perceive available support. This may mean that spouses/partners expect each other to provide principal support, but with the loss of this rela-tionship there may be little chance of finding an alternative source. This posi-tion provides some support for the task-specific model, which posits that when a support relationship is unavailable or disrupted, an alternative support rela-tionship is not always found and substituted (Litwak, 1985). Perceived social support is also positively affected by the presence of children, which indicates that elderly immigrants, like native-born residents (Connidis and McMullin, 1994), probably expect their offspring to support them when needed.

Compared to the widowed/separated/divorced, the married/cohabiting and the never married have more social involvement, which may mean that the dissolution of a union disrupts one's activities outside the home. We also find that elderly immigrants' financial security is seen to reduce social in-volvement. This suggests that those who are experiencing financial strains may actively seek support through increased social involvement. Krause and

Keith (1989) have argued that this type of strategy is more common among elderly women, as elderly men have a tendency to seek post-retirement employment when a financial crisis occurs.

The unexpected negative relationship between the presence of siblings and social contact deserves comment. This relationship suggests that those who do not have siblings experience more social contact, which may indicate that these elderly immigrants are more gregarious in nature. Throughout their lives, only children may develop close friendships upon which they can draw for social support. The functional-specificity of relationships model of social support buttresses this view, proposing that people negotiate and rearrange their social support network according to situational contingencies (Campbell, Connidis, and Davies, 1999; Simons, 1983-84). Immigrants without siblings do not suffer an inadequacy of support, but simply have different sources of support than those with siblings.

As expected, living in a house has a negative impact on social involvement and social contact. Detached dwellings may well insulate the elderly from community involvement as well as limit interaction with family and friends. For example, those living in apartments may have more proximate access to activities outside the home, that is, social activities within an apartment complex.

Finally, most of our immigrant-specific variables do not reach statistical significance. However, the ability to speak either of Canada's official languages is seen to reduce social involvement compared to immigrants who do not. It may be that elderly immigrants who do not speak English or French actively seek support from their cultural/ethnic community. This view is consistent with Noh, Wu, and Avison's (1994) and Kuo and Tsai's (1986) research, which suggests that support from within an immigrant's cultural/ethnic community is more extensive and more important than support from the host society. Further research is needed in order to determine the specific effects English/French proficiency have on elderly immigrants' social support networks.

Canada has long been established as an immigrant-based society. As the number of immigrants increases, we must recognize the diverse sources of social support among different ethnic/cultural groups. The well-established, positive relationship between the availability of social support and positive health outcomes tells us little, if we are unaware of the determinants of support in the first place. Knowing these determinants, we are better able to assess possible vulnerabilities and areas of need among Canada's foreign-born residents. For example, we have seen that poor health both diminishes the availability of social resources upon which elderly immigrants can draw for social support, and reduces their perceived availability of support. Although longitudinal research is needed in order to establish causality among these relationships, and more research is needed generally to better understand social support among this population, the present study has made an initial attempt to understand the unique circumstances of elderly immigrants in Canada.

ENDNOTES

1 The questionnaire for each cycle of the NPHS has two separate components. The general component of the questionnaire was completed for all household members. The (in-depth) health component of the questionnaire was completed for one person aged 12 or older who was randomly selected from the household. Cycle 2 of the NPHS collected cross-sectional data from 210,377 respondents for the general component (173,216 aged 12 or older), and 81,804 for the in-depth health component, including those who are on the longitudinal panel. There is also an institutional component of the survey, which covers long-term residents of hospitals and residential care facilities.

2 See Statistics Canada (1998) and Swain, Catlin, and Beaudet (1999) for detailed information about the survey design and data collection of the NPHS.

3 Unfortunately, the number of elderly Asian immigrants in the NPHS is too small to do an adequate analysis solely based on this population.

REFERENCES

Antonucci, T.C., and Akiyama, H. (1987). An examination of sex differences in social support among older men and women. *Sex Roles, 17*, 737-749.

Arling, G. (1987). Strain, social support, and distress in old age. *Journal of Gerontology, 42*, 107-113.

Barrera, M. (1986). Distinctions between social support concepts, measures, and models. *American Journal of Community Psychology, 14*, 413-445.

Barrett, A.E. (1999). Social support and life satisfaction among the never married: Examining the effects of age. *Research on Aging, 21*, 46-72.

Beaujot, R. (1991). *Population change in Canada: The challenges of policy adaptation.* Toronto: McClelland & Stewart.

Campbell, L.D., Connidis, I.A., and Davies, L. (1999). Sibling ties in later life: A social network analysis. *Journal of Family Issues, 20*, 114-148.

Choi, N.G. (1996). The never married and divorced elderly: Comparison of economic and health status, social support, and living arrangement. *Journal of Gerontological Social Work, 26*, 3-25.

Coleman, J.S. (1988). Social capital in the creation of human capital. *American Journal of Sociology, 94*, S95-121.

Connidis, I.A., and McMullin, J.A. (1994). Social support in older age: Assessing the impact of marital and parent status. *Canadian Journal on Aging, 13*, 510-527.

Connidis, I.A., Rosenthal, C.J., and McMullin, J.A. (1996). The impact of family composition on providing help to older persons: A study of employed adults. *Research on Aging, 18*, 402-429.

Kiefer, C.W., Kim, S., Choi, K., Kim, L., Kim, B.L., Shon, S., and Kim, T. (1985). Adjustment problems of Korean American elderly. *The Gerontologist, 25*, 477-482.

Krause, N. (1991). Stress and isolation from close ties in later life. *Journal of Gerontology: Social Sciences, 46*, 183-194.

Krause, N., and Borawski-Clark, E. (1995). Social class differences in social support among older adults. *The Gerontologist, 35*, 498-508.

Krause, N., and Keith, V. (1989). Gender differences in social support among older adults. *Sex Roles, 9/10*, 609-628.

Kuo, W.H., and Tsai, Y. (1986). Social networking, hardiness and immigrant's mental health. *Journal of Health and Social Behavior*, 27, 133-149.

Lai, D.W., and McDonald, J.R. (1995). Life satisfaction of Chinese elderly immigrants in Canada. *Canadian Journal on Aging*, 14, 536-552.

Lee, M.S., Crittenden, K.S., and Yu, E. (1996). Social support and depression among elderly Korean immigrants in the United States. *International Journal of Aging and Human Development*, 42, 313-327.

Litwak, E. (1985). *Helping the elderly: The complementary roles of informal networks and formal systems.* New York: The Guilford Press.

Lynch, S.A. (1998). Who supports whom? How age and gender affect the perceived quality of support from family and friends. *The Gerontologist*, 38, 231-238.

Noh, S., and Avison, W.R. (1996). Asian immigrants and the stress process: A study of Koreans in Canada. *Journal of Health and Social Behavior*, 37, 192-206.

Noh, S., Wu, Z., and Avison, W.R. (1994). Social support and quality of life: Sociocultural similarity and effective social support among Korean immigrants. *Advances in Medical Sociology*, 5, 115-137.

Pearlin, L.I., Lieberman, M.A., Menaghan, E.G., and Mullan, J.T. (1981). The stress process. *Journal of Health and Social Behavior*, 22, 337-356.

Portes, A. (1998). Social capital: Its origins and applications in modern sociology. *Annual Review of Sociology*, 24, 1-24.

Revicki, D.A., and Mitchell, J.P. (1990). Strain, social support, and mental health in rural elderly individuals. *Journal of Gerontology: Social Sciences*, 27, 108-113.

Sampson, R.J., Morenoff, J.D., and Earls, F. (1999). Beyond social capital: Spatial dynamics of collective efficacy for children. *American Sociological Review*, 64, 633-660.

Shye, D., Mullooly, J.P., Freeborn, D.K., and Pope, C.R. (1995). Gender differences in the relationship between social network support and mortality: A longitudinal study of an elderly cohort. *Social Science and Medicine*, 41, 935-947.

Simons, R.L. (1983-84). Specificity and substitution in the social networks of the elderly. *International Journal of Aging and Human Development*, 18, 121-139.

Statistics Canada. (1998). *National Population Health Survey: Public Use Microdata Files.* CD-ROM version. (Product no. 82M0009XCB.) Ottawa: Statistics Canada.

Statistics Canada. (1999). *Statistical Report on the Health of Canadians.* (Catalogue no. 82-570-X1E). Ottawa: Statistics Canada.

Statistics Canada. (2000a). Online. Population projections for 2001, 2006, 2011, 2016, 2021 and 2026, July1, *http://www.statcan.ca/english/Pgdb/People/Population/demo23c.htm.*

Statistics Canada. (2000b). Online. Selected dwelling characteristics and household equipment, *http://www.statcan.ca/english/Pgdb/People/Families/famil09a.htm.*

Swain, L., Catlin, G., and Beaudet, M.P. (1999). The national population health survey: Its longitudinal nature. *Health Reports*, 10, 69-82.

Thoits, P. (1984). Explaining distributions of psychological vulnerability: Lack of support in the face of life stress. *Social Forces*, 63, 453-481.

Thoits, P. (1995). Stress, coping, and social support processes: Where are we? What next? *Journal of Health and Social Behavior*, extra issue, 53-79.

Tsai, D.T., and Lopez, R.A. (1997). The use of social supports by elderly Chinese immigrants. *Journal of Gerontological Social Work*, 29, 77-94.

Turner, R.J. (1999). Social support and coping. In A.V. Horwitz and T.L. Scheid (Eds.), *A handbook for the study of mental health: Social contexts, theories, and systems* (pp. 198-210). New York: Cambridge University Press.

Turner, R.J., and Marino, F. (1994). Social support and social structure: A descriptive epidemiology. *Journal of Health and Social Behavior*, 35, 193-212.

Vaux, A. (1985). Variations in social support associated with gender, ethnicity, and age. *Journal of Social Issues*, 41, 89-110.

Wethington, E., and Kessler, R.C. (1986). Perceived support, received support, and adjustment to stressful life events. *Journal of Health and Social Behavior*, 27, 79-89.

Wu, Z., and Pollard, M.S. (1998). Social support among unmarried childless elderly persons. *Journal of Gerontology*, 53B, 324-335.

Public Choices on Modes of Caregiving for the Elderly with Disabilities

Tru-gin Liu

Associate Professor, Graduate Institute of Economics,
National Sun Yet-sen University

INTRODUCTION

In advanced societies, aging of the population has been prevalent for decades because of improved life expectancy and even more because of a decline in fertility. Care for the elderly has been characterized by a decline in the role of family and of kinship, and increased demand for participation by government. In developed countries, caregiving, public pensions, and medical services are generally very critical in providing these services: there is a strong demand for care of the elderly, especially for those with disabilities. Government services are usually insufficient to meet the demands; therefore, families must assume a large portion of the work involved in caring for their aged parents. In countries experiencing enormous demographic and social changes, such as Taiwan, however, the provision of care for the elderly becomes more difficult for families.

In Chinese societies, the care of the elderly is usually the responsibility of adult females, such as daughters or daughters-in-law. This has been a tradition in family ethics in the Chinese culture for centuries. Until very recently, care of the elderly was not institutionalized in Taiwan. As the issue has intensified in recent years, however, the government has recognized the necessity of establishing organized care for the elderly. Experts and scholars of social welfare have disputed such issues as an incentive scheme for rewarding caregivers, including housewives caring for the elderly at home, and whether the major mode of caregiving should be directed towards institutionalized agencies or community networks. The main issue under dispute is the efficiency of different modes of caregiving, and whether it is appropriate that the housewife continue to assume the role of sole caregiver of an old person at home as her duty and hers alone. Among the potential solutions proposed, the locally integrated support network, based on long-term residence and active community involvement, has gained wide support from professionals.

This chapter examines whether the proposal put forth by professionals in the field of social welfare will be the winner under a simple majority rule of voting. Public choice issues of this type inevitably involve multi-dimensional aspects. For instance, according to traditional Chinese family ethics, taking care of her parents-in-law is considered a virtue in a housewife. However, this point of view has met with enormous challenges as women's participation in the job market and their educational achievements have increased in recent decades. Thus, the propensity for co-residence with the elderly may differ between husbands and wives.

Let us look at the problem this way first. Suppose voters can be divided by sex. Male voters would likely vote for the traditional method of caregiving, because, as men, they do not need to "commit" themselves to the task, which is generally considered very time-consuming. But female voters may prefer not to co-reside with the elderly, if co-residence implies the responsibility of caregiving. Female voters may prefer institutionalized caregiving to other modes. Therefore, from the perspective of sexual discrimination against females in caring for the elderly, the attitudes of males and females may be opposed.

In addition to the different gender preferences to be considered, voters must also consider this issue from the dimension of efficiency. As is argued by Coase (1937), transaction costs play an important role in the determination of an institution or the configuration of economic organizations. Following his argument, the choice among the three potential modes would certainly involve comparing the transaction costs these modes may incur. The infra-marginal analysis developed by Yang and Ng (1993) is appropriate for this work. I will apply their approach to the present issue to examine the relationships between the modes of caregiving and family welfare, as well as the effects of alternative government supports on resource allocation and family welfare.

This chapter is organized as follows: the second section discusses why females may be more averse toward the mode of a family dependent support network for caring for the elderly, who are normally their parents-in-law. The third section deals with the efficiency problem. Three models will be built, each corresponding to a mode of caregiving for the elderly, with a specific type of family composition implied. Here, it is assumed that the young couple is not biased against any type of family composition. The criterion adopted is efficiency, i.e. the mode of caregiving that realizes the highest family welfare and is neutral to government's supporting program will be considered as an efficient mode. The fourth section concludes the chapter.

PREFERENCES OF HUSBANDS AND WIVES REGARDING SUPPORT NETWORKS FOR THE ELDERLY

According to the 1996 survey on the living conditions of the elderly (defined as those aged over 65) conducted by the Bureau of Statistics, Ministry of Internal Affairs, among the 1.7 million elderly people in Taiwan, 1.3 million revealed a strong desire for the government to provide services for long-term care. This figure is nearly double the figure of those who revealed a desire for medical care or elderly pensions from the public sector. It is interesting to note that the same report also reveals that the percentage of the elderly and their children living in co-residence decreased from 70.24% to 64.28% over the last decade. Such a transition in household composition certainly reflects demographic and social changes. However, psychologically, or perhaps ideologically, some elderly have difficulty adjusting to these changes. For example, Zheng and Wang (1998) reported that many of the elderly prefer the in-home care to other modes, and demonstrate a high propensity for co-residence with their adult children.

The same report also covers the statistics on the opinions of people aged 25 to 60 on issues considered most urgent for the government in providing services for the elderly. It states that over 70% of people in each age group indicate their priorities in long-term caregiving. The result accords with the findings of Zheng and Wang, which shows that young adults or people in middle age seem to favour community-based caregiving services, such as daytime or part-time caregiving assistance provided by community service agencies. Ironically, this mode only accounts for 0.4% of the elderly who are given long-term care, much less than the 28.2% of the elderly cared for by institutionalized caregiving agencies. Such a sharp contrast may reflect the fact that either the transaction costs involved in the locally integrated support network are much higher than other formal support networks, or the government's support for community integration is rather limited relative to the desires of young adults, and couples.

Perhaps partly in response to this finding, many scholars in the field of social welfare have proposed greater government involvement in community-based caregiving services in the future. Certainly, there are some practical reasons deserving attention, since this proposal is rather eclectic. Among these reasons, the one most frequently enumerated is the rise of feminism in recent years. Therefore, we need to consider the preference orderings of males and females in possible modes of caring for the elderly.

To simplify the discussion, let us focus on the following three modes of support networks for caring the elderly:

Mode A   the family-dependent support network, i.e., most commonly the old person relies primarily on daughters-in-law and children;

Mode B   the locally integrated support network, which is usually based on long-term residence and active community involvement;

Mode C   the institutionalized agency support system.

It has been recognized that gains from family division of labour can be realized if a husband specializes in market activities and a wife in home-related activities, or vice versa. However, this case is seldom observed in most advanced countries, nor is it in present-day Taiwan. Undoubtedly, the increasing job opportunities available to females offer a strong explanation for this phenomenon. Among others, the following are considered as critical as well: freedom and rights (Sen, 1987), bargaining power inside the family, and the positive correlation between marriage instability and risk of investing in the accumulation of domestic human capital (Cigno, 1991). For example, Cigno has argued that women with children suffer financially from divorce, and suggests that family law and public marriage contracts might not adequately protect the interests of a marriage partner specializing in home-related activities (typically the woman) (Cigno, 1991). All these factors will affect women's decision to deviate from some traditional family ethics, especially caregiving of the elderly, which requires "sacrifices." As has been well-argued by Sen:

> ...*traditional family relations in many societies have called for asymmetric sacrifices by some members of the family, e.g. women. The survival of these traditions have often been helped by the acceptance of a particular type of "ethic" in which gross inequalities in living standards may not appear unacceptable and sometimes may not in fact be consciously recognised and presented for assessment and acceptance. The issue of perception is a central one in understanding sex bias in traditional societies, and an ethical challenge to the traditional moralities call for some cognitive arguments* (Sen, 1987, p. 20).

As far as preference ordering in the three modes of caring for the elderly is concerned, the above discussion seems sufficient to indicate that, as a society is more open to the marketplace, the ideal point of a wife will be closer to mode C than mode A. By contrast, if we assume altruism between generations, then the ideal point of a husband will be closer to A or B, and away from C since the old person is normally his father or mother. Therefore, mode B will likely be the median point of all voters, along with the dimension of feminism. According to the median voter theorem of Enelow and Hinich (1984), if an issue is single-dimensional, and all voters have single peaked preferences defined in it, then the median position cannot lose under majority rule. This may explain why professionals propose mode B. However, the issue has the other dimension—the efficiency criterion—to be examined.

Efficiency Criterion

Assume that each young couple is neutral towards whether to co-reside with the elderly or not. Their only concern is efficiency, that is, the couple wishes to maximize family welfare. Assume further that there is an old person with disabilities in each family who needs caregiving. To simplify the analysis, the model does not take into account caring for children.

Mode A

The Configuration

This support network is composed of independent families. In each family, an old person lives with the son and daughter-in-law. Each person can either engage in the production of a composite good, say x, for daily consumption, or care for the elderly person at home, say y, or both. The family is guided by the principle of family welfare maximization. Members redistribute x within the family and share y together. Suppose that both x and y are necessary goods, and the law of diminishing marginal rate of substitution between them prevails, the family welfare function can be expressed as U_A:

$$U_A = x\,y \qquad\qquad (1)$$

Denote l_{xi} and l_{yi} as the shares of labour input in the production activities of x and y of the ith person. Assuming that there exist economies of specialization, the production functions of x and y can then be given by (2), where a and b are production parameters of values greater than 1. Equation (3) gives the labour constraint for each person.

$$x = l^a_{x1} + l^a_{x2},\, y = l^b_{y1} + l^b_{y2},\ a,b > 1 \qquad (2)$$

$$l_{xi} + l_{yi} = 1,\text{ for } i = 1,2 \qquad\qquad (3)$$

The optimal solution of the family's objective function can be easily solved from the first order conditions given by the above system:

$$x^* = y^* = 1,\, U^*_A = 1,\, l^*_{xi} = l^*_{yj} = 1,\text{ for } i \neq j \qquad (4)$$

It is suggested from (4) that the optimal combination of the family's collective labour supply is complete division of labour to realize the economies of specialization.

Government Intervention and Policy Effect

Suppose society is composed of this type of family. If the government levies a lump-sum tax, say t, from the person engaging in the production of x, and transfers t to the other person specializing in caregiving at home, would this policy cause distortion? Denote the resultant consumption of x and y inside the family as x^c and y^c, then the following relationship must hold true:

$$x^c = (x-t) + t = x,\, y^c = y \qquad\qquad (5)$$

The resultant family welfare function will be:

$$U_A = x^c\, y^c \qquad\qquad (6)$$

Since this policy does not cause any changes in the disposable resources of the family, the optimal solution as (4) remains undisturbed. In other words, this policy has the merit of neutrality.[1]

Mode B

The Configuration

The characteristics of this support network are the existence of a caregiving centre for the elderly in the community, and the co-residence of the old person, his son, and daughter-in-law. There is a market in the community for caregiving, either during daytime or part-time; the young couple has the choice to specialize in the production activity of x. If this configuration emerges naturally without the government's intervention, then there exist two markets. Some people sell x in exchange for y, while others sell y for x. Denote x/y as the family whose working labourers specialize in the production of x in the daytime, and take care of the elderly after work. Denote y/x as the family whose working labourers not only give care to their own old person, but also provide caregiving services to the elderly of other families. Denoting the transaction efficiency coefficients of x and y markets as k and r, it can be reasonably assumed that the former is larger than the latter, i.e. $1 > k > r > 0$.

The x/y Family

The optimization problem of the x/y family is as follows:

$$\text{Maximize}_{x, y^d} \; U_{x/y} = x\, r\, y^d \qquad (7)$$

$$\text{subject to} \; x + x^s = 2$$
$$P_x\, x^s = P_y\, y^d$$

where x^s is the amount of x commodity sold to the market, x is self-consumed, and y^d is the amount of y services purchased from the market.

Solving (7), we have:

$$x^* = 1, \; y^{d*} = p_x/p_y, \; U^*_{x/y} = r\, p_x/p_y \qquad (8)$$

From (8), it is evident that the welfare of the x/y family, measured by $U^*_{x/y}$, is determined by the transaction efficiency of the caregiving market, r, and the relative price of p_x/p_y.

The y/x Family

The optimization problem of the y/x family is as follows:

$$\text{Maximize}_{x^d, y} \; U_{y/x} = k\, x^d\, y \qquad (9)$$

$$\text{subject to} \; y + y^s = 2$$
$$P_x\, x^d = P_y\, y^s$$

The solution to (9) is:

$$x^{d*} = p_y/p_x, \; y^* = 1, \; U^*_{y/x} = k\, p_y/p_x \qquad (10)$$

In parallel to (8), (10) says that the welfare of the y/x family is conditioned by the transaction efficiency of the commodity market, k, and the relative price of p_y/p_x.

Equilibrium of the x/y and y/x Configuration

Through the negative feedback adjustment mechanism, above all free mobility of individuals between job markets, the following relationship will hold true in equilibrium:

$$U^*_B = U^*_{x/y} = U^*_{y/x} = (kr)^{1/2} \qquad (11)$$

Comparing U^*_A in (4) with U^*_B in (11), we have:

$$U^*_B < U^*_A \qquad (12)$$

The result implies that the locally integrated support network will be inferior to the family dependent support network, because of the loss incurred from the transaction for caregiving, even if we assume that k is approaching 1. Therefore, it can be argued that if the opinion survey shows that young couples' preference is in favour of the former, it would suggest that economic concern might not be the chief reason.

Determination of Employment in x and y Markets

Denote Y^d and Y^s as the aggregate demand for and supply of y of the community, and M_x and M_y as the numbers of x/y and y/x families respectively. By definition, we have:

$$Y^d = M_x \, y^d = M_x \, p_x/p_y \qquad (13)$$
$$Y^s = M_y \, y^s = M_y \qquad (14)$$

The market-clearing condition is:

$$Y^d = Y^s \qquad (15)$$

By the use of (11), it can be easily shown that the relative professionals in equilibrium is:

$$M_x \, / \, M_y = (k/r)^{1/2} \qquad (16)$$

Since $k > r$, (16) implies that the larger (k/r) is, the more community working labourers will be required for caregiving in this configuration. This may help explain the significant difference between the strong subjective desires of young couples for the locally integrated support network and the low occurrence in reality.

Policy Effects

Suppose the government levies a T amount of lump-sum tax against each x/y family, and makes a lump-sum transfer of G to each y/x family, while maintaining public budget balance, i.e., $G = T \, M_x \, / \, M_y$. Under this circumstance, the optimization problem facing a family will be:

For the x/y family:

$$\text{Maximize } UT_{x/y} = x \, r \, y^d \qquad (17)$$
$$x, y^d$$
$$\text{s.t. } x + x^s = 2$$
$$p_x \, x^s = p_y \, y^d + T$$

where the superscript of T denotes government intervention in this case.

Solving for (17), we have:

$$x^* = 1 - T/(2p_x), \quad y^{d*} = p_x/p_y - T/(2p_y) \qquad (18)$$

By comparing (8) and (18), it is clear that the government's intervention will reduce the x/y family's consumption level of x, and may also reduce that of y if the relative price holds constant. In the case where p_x/p_y is held constant, then the welfare level of the x/y family will decrease, as shown below:

$$UT_{x/y} = r\,[p_x/p_y - T/p_y + T^2/(4p_xp_y)] < U^*_{x/y} = r\,p_x/p_y \qquad (19)$$

For the y/x family, the optimization problem is:

$$\text{Maximize } UT_{y/x} = k\,x^d\,y \qquad (20)$$
$$x^d, y$$
$$\text{s.t. } y + y^s = 2$$
$$p_x\,x^d = p_y\,y^s + G$$

The optimal solution is given by:

$$x^{d*} = p_y/p_x + G/(2p_x), \quad y^* = 1 + G/(2p_y) \qquad (21)$$

By comparing (10) and (21), it is clear that the government's intervention will increase the y/x family's consumption level of y, and may also increase that of x if the relative price holds constant. In the case where p_x/p_y is held constant, then the welfare level of the y/x family will increase, as shown below:

$$UT_{y/x} = k\,[p_y/p_x + G/p_x + G^2/(4p_xp_y)] > U_{y/x} = k\,p_y/p_x \qquad (22)$$

New Equilibrium After the Government's Intervention

Since given the original relative price, the y/x family will be better off, while the x/y family will be worse off, the mobility of labour will be guided toward y/x and away from x/y, which will certainly cause the relative price to change. The latter implies that this intervention will not be neutral. As the new equilibrium is reached, i.e., $UT_{x/y} = UT_{y/x}$, the following condition must hold:

$$(p_x - \tfrac{1}{2}T)/(p_y + \tfrac{1}{2}G) = (k/r)^{\tfrac{1}{2}} \qquad (23)$$

Because T and G are both positive, it also implies:

$$(p_x/p_y)^T > (k/r)^{\tfrac{1}{2}} \qquad (24)$$

where the superscript of T again denotes the case of government intervention.

Meanwhile, the relative number of professionals will also change, as shown below:

$$M_y/M_x = (p_x/p_y)^T > (k/r)^{\tfrac{1}{2}} \qquad (25)$$

The non-neutrality property of government's intervention into the local caregiving market is evident from either (24) or (25). Both inequalities reflect misallocation of labour resources.

Mode C

The Configuration

In this configuration, there are professional caregiving centres, denoted by $y/l_y,x$, which supply full-time care and residence to the elderly. The employers hire labourers who supply labour l_y, which is required for the production of y, and receive wages, w. Thus, the labour market of l_y emerges. Assume that the employers themselves manage the centres. The management services, termed as Z, are considered as an intermediate factor. In this configuration, there are three markets: x, y, and l_y. The corresponding transaction efficiency coefficients are k, r_1, and s, with $0 < k, r_1, s < 1$.

The families are all nuclear families since the elderly live in the caregiving centres. Young couples either specialize in x activity, or work in the centres. The latter is denoted as $l_y/x,y$.

The x/y Family

The problems facing the x/y family in this configuration are similar to those of the x/y family under the locally integrated support network. The only difference is in the transaction efficiency of caregiving. Since the caregiving centre is more specialized in caring for the elderly, it can be assumed that $r_1 > r$. The optimal solutions are:

$$x^* =1, y^{d*} = p_x/p_y, U^*_{x/y} = r_1 p_x/p_y \qquad (26)$$

The $l_y/x,y$ Family

Its target is:

$$\text{Maximize}_{x^d,y^d} \ U_{l_y} = k\, x^d\, r_1\, y^d \qquad (27)$$

$$\text{s.t. } p_x\, x^d + p_y\, y^d = 2w$$

Solving (27), we have:

$$x^{d*} = w/p_x, y^{d*} = w/p_y, U^*_{l_y} = k\, r_1 w^2/(p_x\, p_y) \qquad (28)$$

The $y/l_y,x$ Family (the owner of the caregiving centre)

Its production and income flows are to produce y by combining l_y and Z, then it sells y^s to the market. On the other hand, a part of its receipt is paid to l_y, and the other part is to buy x^d.

Let each centre hire N labourers to provide for l_y, and each labourer produces y^s on average. The production of y^s requires the input of Z. Let the average amount of Z over labourers be Z^d. Besides, the actual labour hired by the employer is $s\, l_y$ since l_y is hired from the market, which causes some transaction costs. The production of y^s is expressed as:

$$y^s = (Z^d\, s\, l_y)^c = (Z^d\, s)^c, \ c \ Î \ (½ ,1) \qquad (29)$$

In (29), the value of the parameter c lies between ½ and 1 reflecting the fact that total factor productivity (TFP) in the production of y exhibits economies of specialization. Next, let $Y + Y^s$ represent the total output of each centre, we will have:

$$Y + Y^s \equiv N\, y^s \qquad (30)$$

With regard to the supply of management, we assume that a couple which specializes in managing their centre owns each one. Consequently, the total supply of management services of each centre is the sum of the maximum labour shares of the couple, i.e., $Z^s = 2$, and the average amount of Z over labourers is:

$$Z^d = 2\,/\,N \qquad (31)$$

Substitute (31) into (29), bearing in mind that $l_y = 1$, we shall have:

$$Y^s = (2s/N)^c \qquad (32)$$

Together with (30), (31), and (32), the optimization problem facing the owner of a caregiving centre will become:

$$\text{Maximize } U_y = k\, x^d\, Y \qquad (33)$$
$$X^d, Y, N$$

$$\text{s.t. } Y + Y^s = N\,(2s/N)^c$$
$$p_y\, Y^s = w\, N + p_x\, x^d$$

Solving for (33), we will have the optimal choices for the owner of a caregiving centre, x^{d*}, N^*, and Y^*, which determine the welfare attainable, i.e., U^*_y, as shown in (34).

$$x^{d*} = c\,(1\text{-}c)^{(1\text{-}c)/c}\, s\, p_y^{1/c}\, p_x^{-1}\, w^{(c\text{-}1)/c}, \quad N^* = (1\text{-}c)^{1/c}\, 2\, s\, (p_y/w)^{1/c}$$
$$Y^* = s\, c\,(1\text{-}c)^{(1\text{-}c)/c}\,(p_y/w)^{(1\text{-}c)/c}, \quad U^*_y = k\,(p_y/p_x)\, c^2\, s^2\, [(1\text{-}c)\,(p_y/w)]^{(1\text{-}c)/c} \quad (34)$$

Equilibrium of the Institutionalized Agency Support System

Equating $U^*_{x/y}$, $U^*_{ly/x,y}$, and $U^*_{y/ly,x}$ by using (26), (28), and (34), the welfare level of each family in equilibrium can be solved as below:

$$U^* = r_1^{(2\text{-}c)/2}\, k^{\frac{1}{2}}\, c^c s^c\, (1\text{-}c)^{1\text{-}c} \qquad (35)$$

Policy Effect

The calculation of policy effect in this case is much more complicated than in the former two cases. However, this will not affect the judgement on whether government intervention is neutral or not. Due to the fact that government intervention will affect relative prices, which appear asymmetrically in the in-direct welfare functions of families of different specialties, the policy effect will not be neutral.

Discussion

The findings of this section can be summarized as follows. Firstly, if the government does not intervene in the caregiving business, it is clear that Mode A, the family dependent support network, will realize the highest welfare level. However, the ordering of the locally integrated support network, Mode B, and the institutionalized agency support system, Mode C, is ambiguous. As I noted earlier, in reality, Mode B only accounts for 0.4% of the elderly who are given long-term care, much less than the 28.2% of the elderly who are cared for by Mode C. Since there is little evidence that the government supported Mode C strongly in the past, this sharp contrast may reflect the fact that the transaction costs involved in the locally integrated support network are much higher than other formal support networks. Therefore, the ordering of the three modes in terms of efficiency might be A, C, and B. Secondly, the family dependent support network is also independent of government interventions, while the other two systems are not. Due to the fact that Mode A is most efficient and also independent of government intervention, the family dependent support network, that is, Mode A, will be supported by voters even under a unanimity rule, if efficiency and policy effects on distortions are voters' chief concerns.

CONCLUSION

The discussion in the second section indicates that Mode B will be the winning issue under majority rule, if female voters are concerned with feminism only, and male voters demonstrate altruism toward their former generation. Since mode B is a median issue, the preference ordering of the three modes may be either B > C > A, or B > A > C. The discussion in the third section indicates consistently that the ordering is very likely to be A > C > B, if only efficiency is concerned, bearing in mind that Mode A is also the most preferred issue of males. Together with the finding in the second section, it becomes clear that the preference ordering of male voters may be either A > B > C or A > C > B when the two dimensions are considered simultaneously. Suppose males weight filial piety towards their own parents more than economic considerations, as is normally observed in Taiwan, then the ordering of A > B > C is more likely. However, for female voters, their preference orderings are less transparent. On the first issue, it is C > B > A. On the other issue, it shows that A > C > B. Hence, C > A > B may be the possible ordering of females when the two dimensions are considered altogether.

Now, how are we going to predict the likely outcome of the social ordering among the three issues under majority rule? The aggregate preference ordering of males may be A > B > C, while that of females may be C > A > B. Will the outcome be A, C or B. In this battle of the sexes, I will not make a prediction.

However, in reality, what has been proposed turns out to be the locally integrated support network. This may suggest that professionals of social welfare are more concerned with feminism than efficiency.

REFERENCES

Bureau of Statistics, Ministry of Internal Affairs, Taiwan (1997). 1996 Survey on the living conditions of the elderly, Taipei.

Bureau of Statistics, Ministry of Internal Affairs, Taiwan (2000). 1999 Survey on the living conditions of the elderly, Taipei.

Baggett, S.A. (1989). *Residential care for the elderly: Critical issues in public policy*. New York: Greenwood Press.

Brearley, C.P. (1990). *Working in residential homes for elderly people*. London and New York: Tavistock/Routledge.

Cigno, A. (1991). *Economics of the family*. Oxford: Clarendon Press.

Coase, R. (1937). The nature of the firm. *Economica*, November, 386-405.

Coase, R. (1960). The problem of social costs. *Journal of Law and Economics*, October, 1-44.

Enelow, J.M., and Hinich, M.J. (1984). *The spatial theory of voting*. Cambridge: Cambridge University Press.

Mogey, J. (Ed.) (1990). *Aiding and aging: The coming crisis in support for the elderly by kin and state*. New York: Greenwood Press.

Roberto, K.A. (Ed.) (1993). *The elderly caregiver: Caring for adults with developmental disabilities*. Newbury Park, CA: Sage.

Sen, A. (1987). *On ethics and economics*. Oxford: Blackwell.

Suong, D.S., Chi, L., and Lee, M.L. (1997). *Population aging and caring for the elderly, Taipei* (in Chinese).

Veall, M.R. (1986). Public pensions as optimal social contracts, *Journal of Public Economics*, 31, 237-251.

Wen, M. (1996). *Division of labor in economic development*, Ph.D. Dissertation, Department of Economics, Monash University.

Yang C. (1999). Living arrangement of the elderly in Taiwan. *Journal of Population Studies*, 20, 167-183, Population and Gender Studies Center, National Taiwan University.

Yang, X., and Ng, Y.K. (1993). *Specialization and economic organization*. Amsterdam, Netherlands: North-Holland.

Zheng, C.N., and Wang, C. (1998). *The elderly, caregiving, family ethics: A study on the long-term allocation of caregiving resources*. Conference on the Elderly Issue and Policy, Taipei: Academic Sinica.

ENDNOTES

[1] Certainly, the bargaining power between family members may change. However, given the assumption of family welfare maximization, the policy effect remains neutral because of the redistribution mechanism inside the family. This is not to say that the policy is meaningless since it could be used to reflect the opportunity costs of labour, which is directed towards the caregiving of the elderly.

Immigrants to British Columbia: Distinctiveness of the Taiwanese Elderly Compared With Those From Hong Kong and Mainland China

Neena L. Chappell

Canada Research Chair in Health and Aging, and
Professor, Department of Sociology, University of Victoria

INTRODUCTION

Often North American research assumes a static and localized view of Chinese culture, despite the fact that it, like North American culture, is evolving. Furthermore, Chinese culture encompasses many different societies and nations, including but not restricted to Taiwan, Hong Kong, and Mainland China. In addition, as the world becomes a global village via advanced communication technology, increasing urbanization and industrialization affect traditional values, both within and outside of Asia. Like other countries, Taiwan is affected by global change.

In traditional Chinese societies, kinship relations governed almost all aspects of life, from mate selection and marriage to old age support. The filial piety of Confucianism was not only the building block of family relations but also a key criterion for appointing government officials (Garnet, 1982). To be associated with the old was an important way to earn respect. Family elders controlled considerable assets, often had the final say, and enjoyed relatively high social and economic status. Even today, with urbanization, mass industrialization, increased geographic mobility, and increased numbers of nuclear families, traditional filial practices, such as holding family reunions around major holidays or elders' birthdays, providing financial and instrumental support to older parents, and worshipping ancestors, remains to a certain extent (Zhu et al., 1994). Respect and deference from the young to the old remains strong.

By contrast, in Canada and North America in general, aging tends to be associated with an image of poverty and feebleness. Even the elderly themselves hold more pessimistic beliefs about the physical and mental health of older adults and their associated functional capacity than objective data warrant (Kite and Johnson, 1988). Although Canadian culture promotes healthy and active aging, independent living, and free choice, people tend to view health-related declines associated with aging as inevitable and even normal (Clark, 1969). It is unknown how traditional Chinese culture and how North American culture affect Chinese immigrants in their adaptation to Canadian society.

Taiwan maintains the Chinese tradition, which, despite 50 years of Japanese rule, was not heavily influenced by Japanese culture. Much of the literature on Taiwanese elders suggests that although the traditional culture is changing, they nevertheless remain somewhat distinct from Western society, notably in the area of social support. Yet much of the empirical research that examines predictors suggests that the old age Taiwanese experience is very similar to that reported in Western societies. For example, Ofstedal, Zimmer, and Lin (1999) report that predictors of cognitive functioning decline are similar in Taiwan and in the US, including increasing age, female gender, lower education, depression, and selected health conditions. In addition, cognitive functioning, although a significant predictor of both Activities of Daily Living (ADL) and Instrumental Activities of Daily Living (IADL), is more powerful with respect to IADL. Chong, Li, and Chang (1997) report that in Taiwan, elders who have been provided with more informal support before they were disabled are less likely to be institutionalized. Li (1994) notes that the likelihood of receiving intergenerational monetary support is positively associated with age and the availability of children. Krause and Liang (1992) note that there do not appear to be major cross-cultural differences in the way depressive symptoms are manifested in the US, Japan, and Taiwan.

However, Taiwanese culture does appear to be distinct, with a clearly Asian emphasis that differs from Western society, but also a specifically Taiwanese aspect. For example, Raymo and Cornman (1999) notice that older women are more engaged in economic activity, especially in Singapore and Taiwan, compared with the Philippines and Thailand, a situation which also starkly contrasts with North America. Ingersoll and Saengtienchai (1999) argue that although expressions of respect for older adults are changing in Singapore, Thailand, the Philippines, and Taiwan, respect for the elderly remains a central value nevertheless. Elderly co-residing with children appears to still be a norm (Asis, Domingo, Knodel, and Mehta, 1995; Lee, Lin, and Chang, 1995). Despite the heavy reliance of elders on the younger generation (Tu, Freedman, and Wolf, 1993), some community services exist, such as the Evergreen Cultural and Recreational Centre (Sheppard, 1988) and the Taxi Nurses Program (Cowart and Streib, 1987).

As there are both similarities and differences between Taiwanese and Western culture, no doubt there are also similarities and differences between Taiwan and other Asian countries. This chapter takes a preliminary look at similarities and differences among elderly Chinese from Taiwan in British Columbia, Canada, compared with those from Mainland China, and those from Hong Kong. Hong Kong, a British colony for 100 years before it was turned over to the Chinese government, is unique in that it is very commercialized: its production in service industries is very developed even by western standards, but in terms of culture Hong Kong identifies with the Chinese mainstream value system, albeit one influenced by western culture. With no social security or pension system, and a social welfare system much lower than in Canada or Mainland China, most Hong Kong elderly must rely on their children for old age support unless they plan well ahead of retirement. Mainland China, influenced by 50 years of Communist rule, represents Chinese tradition affected by Communism which de-emphasized family values. It has a less developed economy than either Hong Kong or Taiwan.

METHODS

A unique strategy was used to obtain a representative sample of Chinese elders aged 65 and over in the Greater Victoria and Greater Vancouver areas of British Columbia. As many Chinese surnames as possible were listed; vital statistics of the provincial government then drew a random sample of all persons with these surnames aged 65 and over living in Greater Victoria and Greater Vancouver. While this strategy may underestimate Chinese women married to non-Chinese, it is likely that among this population of elders, few would fall into such a category. Furthermore, the strategy is superior to the use of local telephone directories, typical in studies of minority group elders. The sample was purposely overdrawn and telephone screening ensured that individuals self-identified as Chinese and aged 65 or over.

Data were collected in face-to-face interviews, averaging an hour and fifteen minutes, during the summer and fall of 1995. Of the original 2,158 names, 35.9% were ineligible for various reasons: not being Chinese, having died, being away for an extended period, or being ill or too frail. Another 13.7% could not be contacted after 10 attempts. Several callbacks, however, obtained an overall refusal rate of 22.5% of those eligible. This refusal rate is very similar to those in other community surveys of this type with the general population of seniors in Canada.

Interviews were conducted in the elder's language, the vast majority (77.2%) in Cantonese. An additional 11.1% were conducted in Taishan, 5.8% in Putonghua, 5.2% in English and less than 1% in each of the Shantou, Hakka, Fujian and Chaozhou dialects. In total, 830 interviews were completed, 580 (69.6%) in Greater Vancouver and 250 (30.1%) in Greater Victoria. Victoria was over-sampled to allow sufficient numbers for separate analyses of that sample for comparisons with Suzhou, its political twin retirement city in China, located just outside of Shanghai (not the focus of this chapter).

To the extent possible, the questions asked had been validated with general populations of seniors in North America to allow comparison. However, in some instances, this was not possible—where no validated questions existed on the topics to be included, or when questions used frequently in North America were not culturally appropriate. An expert steering committee consisting of individuals from the Chinese communities assisted with wording the questions; then they were piloted (with several Chinese elders individually), revised, piloted again, and revised again. The questions were translated into Chinese, back-translated to English, revised, pilot tested in Chinese, revised, piloted again in Chinese and revised again.

For this chapter, all who were born in Taiwan (N=11) were identified, then a random sample of the same number was drawn from those born in mainland China (N=11) and those born in Hong Kong (N=11). Total N=33. All those who emigrated from Taiwan were also identified (N=31) and a random sample of the same number was drawn from those who emigrated from mainland China (N=31) and Hong Kong (N=31). Total N=93. The two groups were analysed separately. Table 7.1 shows birth place and place of immigration for both samples. The vast majority (72.7%) of those born in Taiwan also immigrated to Canada from Taiwan. Similarly, the vast majority (95.5%) of those born in either Hong Kong or mainland China immigrated to Canada from those places. However, the vast majority emigrated from Hong Kong (77.3%). Looking at Table 7.1B, the larger sample focusing on place of immigration rather than place of birth, it is evident that all eight who were born in Taiwan also emigrated from there. However, those born in mainland China emigrated from Taiwan, Hong Kong, or mainland China, and the three born in Hong Kong also emigrated from there.

VARIABLES

A variety of data was collected including demographic, health-related, social support, immigration, and other information. Demographic variables included: age (continuous), gender (male, female), personal monthly income categories, perceived adequacy of finances, country of birth (Canada, Hong Kong, mainland China, Taiwan, Macao, other), ability to speak English (well), English-speaking (yes, no), and employment status.

Service utilization was measured by asking the number of times respondents used the services of general practitioners, specialist MDs, and dentists in the past year. Health was measured in terms of perceived health, illness, and disability. Perceived health was measured using the standard question found in gerontological research: "How would you describe your state of health? Compared to other persons of your own age, would you say it was excellent, very good, good, fair, poor?"

Table 7.1 Birth place by place of emigration

A) Birth Place by Place of Emigration (N=33)

	Born In:	
Immigrated From:	Hong Kong/ Mainland China	Taiwan
Taiwan	1 (4.5%)	8 (72.7%)
Hong Kong	17 (77.3%)	1 (9.1%)
Mainland China	4 (18.2%)	0 (0%)
United States	0 (0%)	1 (9.1%)
Brazil	0 (0%)	1 (9.1%)
TOTALS	**22**	**11**

B) Birth Place by Place of Emigration (N=93)

	Born In:				
Immigrated From:	Hong Kong	Mainland China	Taiwan	Macau	Other
Taiwan	0 (0%)	22 (27.5%)	8 (100%)	1 (100%)	0 (0%)
Hong Kong	3 (100%)	27 (33.8%)	0 (0%)	0 (0%)	1 (100%)
Mainland China	0 (0%)	31 (38.8%)	0 (0%)	0 (0%)	0 (0%)
TOTALS	3	80	8	1	1

Participants were asked the standard question about chronic conditions: "For *each* condition I will now list, please indicate whether or not you currently have it, and whether or not you are being treated for it." The list included: allergy; problems with joints, back, etc.; heart disease/troubles; anaemia or other blood diseases; high blood pressure (hardening of the arteries); problems due to stroke; cancer; mental health problems (including Alzheimer's/dementia, nerves/emotional problems); recurrent stomach ache or other gastrointestinal problems excluding incontinence; problems with the urinary tract including kidney and bladder troubles, not incontinence; dental problems (teeth need care, dentures don't fit); diabetes; chronic obstructive/lung diseases including chronic bronchitis, asthma, emphysema; Parkinson's disease; foot trouble; skin problems; other (specify). These items were summed to give an indication of the number of chronic conditions individuals have.

Functional ability was measured in terms of the individual's ability to do both basic (ADL) and instrumental activities of daily living (IADL). The ADL and IADL included: washing, bathing, grooming; eating, feeding; personal mobility; using the toilet; light housework chores; heavy household chores; house maintenance and yard-work; transportation; shopping; food preparation; personal business affairs such as paying bills; using the phone. Response categories included no help needed, minimal help required, much help required, completely dependent. These items were summed, Cronbach's alpha=.87, for the total sample.

The interviewees were also asked about a number of symptoms: falls, fainting, breathing difficulties, tiredness, headaches, rashes, bladder problems, bowel problems, hearing difficulties. The number of symptoms experienced was summed. Cronbach's alpha=.73, for the total sample.

Social support variables consisted of household size (continuous), marital status (married, widowed, other), frequency of interaction with family (less than or equal to once a year, at least once a month, at least once a week), who their main helper is generally when there is a minor illness, when there is a serious illness, and about support when upset and when ill.

Immigration variables included: age at immigration (continuous), period of immigration (prior to 1947, 1948-1966, 1967-1977, 1978-1982, 1983, and later), who they immigrated with, whether family sponsored them, and years in BC.

Other variables of interest included visits to Chinatown (yes, no), life satisfaction (the Andrew's and Withey Terrible/Delightful Scale) and loneliness (the revised UCLA Scale) (see Table 2).

Table 7.2   Variables of interest

Demographic:	Social Support:	Other:
Age	Marital status	Visits to Chinatown
Gender	Number in household	Life satisfaction
Language (ability in English)	Contact with family	Loneliness
Employment status	Main helper	
Personal monthly income	Helper for minor illness	
Perceived finance	Helper for serious illness	
	Support when upset	
Health Related:	Support when ill	
Perceived health		
Chronic conditions	**Immigration:**	
Symptomatology	Immigrated alone	
Disability	Immigrated with children	
Visits to GP	Immigrated with spouse	
Visits to specialist MD	Sponsored by family	
Visits to dentist	Period of immigration	
Main helper	Years in BC	

Because of the small sample sizes, analyses are restricted to bivariate correlation coefficients for non-parametric data.

Findings

Significance levels of .10 are indicated because of the small sample size of only 33. However, the discussion focuses on those that are significant at the .05 and .01 levels. Table 7.3 shows significant differences at the bivariate level for elderly immigrants living in British Columbia, from Taiwan, Hong Kong, and the mainland. The first two columns compare those born in Taiwan with those born in mainland China and those born in Taiwan with those born in Hong Kong. The third column compares those born in Taiwan with those born in mainland China and Hong Kong grouped together. The data reveal that, compared with those born in mainland China, the elderly born in Taiwan are more likely to be able to read English, to suffer from less functional disability, and to be less lonely. Compared with the elderly from Hong Kong, those from Taiwan live in smaller households, are more likely to turn to their spouse as the main helper when seriously ill, and are less likely to suffer from functional disability. Those born in Taiwan compared with those from either Hong Kong or mainland China live in smaller households and suffer less from functional disability.

Table 7.3   Taiwan born Chinese elders in BC: Bivariate comparisons

Born in Taiwan   11
Born in Hong Kong   11 (randomly drawn)
Born in Mainland China 11 (randomly drawn)

	Taiwan & Mainland China	Taiwan & Hong Kong	Taiwan & Other
Age (T+ - younger)	-0.3	-0.39*	-0.31*
Can read English (T - yes)	-0.63***	-0.06	-0.26
Marital status (T - married)	0.29	0.38*	0.31*
Number in household (T - fewer)	-0.41*	-0.56***	-0.42**
Immigrated alone (T - no)	-0.40*	-0.40*	-0.33*
Immigrated with children (T - no)	-0.09	-0.18	-0.13
Sponsored by family (T - no)	-0.41*	-0.19	-0.29*
Main helper when seriously ill (T - spouse)	-0.16	0.44**	-0.28
Disability (T - less)	-0.54***	-0.43**	-0.44***
Satisfaction with life as a whole (T - more satisfied)	0.32	0.27	0.30*
Lonely (T - less lonely)	-0.46**	-0.19	-0.30*

Not significant: employment status, personal monthly income, perceived health, symptomatology, chronic conditions, gender, visits to GP, visits to specialist MD, visits to dentist, contact with family, perceived finances, period of immigration, immigrated with spouse, immigrated with children, years in BC, support when upset, support when ill, main helper generally, main helper for minor illness, visits to Chinatown.

+ T = Taiwan   * p < .10; ** p < .05; *** p < .01

In each instance, those from Taiwan tend to be in better health and indicate a higher quality of life. Importantly, economic status as measured in terms of personal income, perceived adequacy, and employment status, does not differ significantly between these groups. Furthermore, period of immigration is not significantly related either.

Table 7.4 presents data on significant differences in the domains of life satisfaction. Compared with those born in mainland China, those born in Taiwan are happier in the recreational sphere of their lives and in terms of their overall life satisfaction. Compared with those born in Hong Kong, those born in Taiwan are happier with their friendships, with the recreational sphere, and with transportation. Compared with the other two groups collapsed together, those born in Taiwan are happier with their recreational sphere and with transportation. In all cases where significant differences emerge, those elderly born in Taiwan express higher levels of life satisfaction than those born in either Hong Kong or mainland China. In other words, from this small sample with bivariate analyses the Taiwanese emerge as distinctive. Where differences are evident, they are healthier, have more social support, and are happier. That is, they have a better quality of life.

Table 7.4   Born in Taiwan: domains of life satisfaction

Domains of Life Satisfaction	Taiwan & Mainland China	Taiwan & Hong Kong	Taiwan & Other
Health	ns	ns	ns
Finances	ns	ns	ns
Contact with family	ns	ns	ns
Family responsibilities	ns	ns	ns
Contact with friends	0.26	0.47**	0.33*
Housing	ns	ns	ns
Spouse	ns	ns	ns
Recreation	0.46**	0.59***	0.47***
Spirituality	ns	ns	ns
Yourself	ns	ns	ns
Transportation	0.29	0.46**	0.34**
Food	ns	ns	ns
Children/grandchildren	ns	ns	ns
Overall life satisfaction	0.32*	0.27	0.30*

ns = not significant   N = 33
Note: In all instances, T = happier
* p<.10; **p<.05; ***p<.01

We turn now to a comparison of those who emigrated (irrespective of birthplace) from Taiwan compared with those who emigrated from Hong Kong or mainland China. The initial bivariate correlations are shown in Table 7.5. Due to the larger sample size, significance levels are shown at the .05, .01, and .001 levels. Only the stronger correlations (.01 and .001) are discussed within the text. Unlike the comparisons within the smaller sample, there appears to be a clear difference between those born in mainland China and Hong Kong, and there are many more differences between the Taiwanese compared with those from mainland China and many fewer differences between those from Taiwan and Hong Kong. Compared to those who emigrated from mainland China, those who emigrated from Taiwan are more likely to be able to read English, to have spent fewer years in Canada, to be married, to have immigrated with someone and that someone is likely a spouse, their main helper is likely a spouse, generally with a minor illness, and with serious illness. Compared to those from Hong Kong, those from Taiwan are more likely to have immigrated with a spouse and are more likely to not be lonely.

Table 7.5   Emigrated from Taiwan to Canada: Bivariate comparisons

Immigrated from Taiwan N=31
Immigrated from Hong Kong N=31 (randomly chosen)
Immigrated from Mainland China N=31 (randomly chosen)

	Taiwan & Mainland China	Taiwan & Hong Kong	Taiwan & Other
Can read English (T-yes)	-0.37**	-0.17	-0.26**
Years in Canada (T-fewer years)	-0.47***	-0.26*	-0.31**
Marital Status (T-married)	0.33**	0.17	0.23*
Immigrated alone (T-not alone)	-0.34**	-0.31*	-0.29**
Immigrated with spouse (T-spouse)	0.43***	0.32**	0.34***
Live alone (T-no)	-0.26*	-0.19	-0.20*
Main helper (T-spouse)	-0.40**	-0.20	-0.29**
Care when minor illness (T-spouse)	-0.45***	-0.25*	-0.31**
Care when serious illness (T-spouse)	-0.45***	-0.24*	-0.32**
Disability (T-less)	-0.29*	-0.08	-0.17
MD specialists (T-more visits)	0.27*	0.25*	0.29**
Lonely (T-not lonely)	-0.23	-0.35**	-0.27**

Note: The following were not significant: age, employment status, personal monthly income, size of household, perceived health, symptomatology, chronic conditions, gender, use of general practitioner services, dentist services, perceived finances, contact with family, life satisfaction, main support when upset, place of emigration, immigrated with children, sponsored by family, visits to Chinatown.

* p< .05; ** p< .01; *** p<.001

When grouping those from mainland China and Hong Kong together most of the same differences emerge, although in this instance visits to specialist MDs increases in significance with those from Taiwan making more visits. Once again, there are no significant differences between the groups in terms of economic status as measured by personal monthly income, perceived adequacy of finances, and employment status. Similarly, immigration history in terms of age of immigration, period of immigration, or years living in British Columbia reveal no significant differences between the groups. Once again, the Taiwanese elderly emerge as distinctive, particularly from those coming from mainland China in terms of social support and quality of life.

Table 7.6 shows differences in the domains of life satisfaction. Fewer differences emerge in this sample, although those from Taiwan differ significantly from those from mainland China and from Hong Kong in expressing greater satisfaction with the spiritual domains of life. They also express greater life satisfaction from those from mainland China in terms of transportation.

Table 7.6   Immigrated from Taiwan to Canada:
Domains of life satisfaction

Domains of Life Satisfaction	Taiwan & Mainland China	Taiwan & Hong Kong	Taiwan & Other
Health	ns	ns	ns
Finances	ns	ns	ns
Contact with family	ns	ns	ns
Family responsibilities	ns	ns	ns
Contact with friends	0.27*	0.1	0.17
Housing	ns	ns	ns
Spouse	ns	ns	ns
Recreation	ns	ns	ns
Spirituality	0.34**	0.31**	0.31**
Yourself	ns	ns	ns
Transportation	0.31**	0.05	0.18
Food	ns	ns	ns
Children/grandchildren	ns	ns	ns
Overall life satisfaction	ns	ns	ns

ns = not significant   N = 93
Note: In all instances, T = happier
* p<.05; **p<.01; ***p<.001

CONCLUSION

This preliminary examination into the distinctiveness of elderly Taiwanese immigrants living in British Columbia, Canada, suggests those both born in and emigrating from Taiwan (of which there is a large overlap) are indeed distinctive in some ways. Importantly, they emerge as healthier, happier, and with more social support than those from Hong Kong, and especially in comparison with those from mainland China. They seem to exhibit a significantly better quality of life than do the other two groups. Interestingly, there is less distinction between those born in and those emigrating from Taiwan than perhaps might be expected.

The reasons for this distinctiveness call for more research and particularly, in-depth research into their culture, both the culture they have left and the one that they have adopted in terms of beliefs, attitudes, and behaviours. That type of information was not available in this data set. Nevertheless, the data suggest that the Taiwanese, who among the three groups examined, arguably maintain the strongest or truest Chinese tradition, including more traditional family values, have increased feelings of satisfaction with life. They were more likely to emigrate with a spouse and to be able to speak English, perhaps leading to their feeling less isolated and lonely within their new land.

It is interesting that the Taiwanese discussed were no more likely to exhibit higher economic status than the other two groups. Equally interesting, there were no differences by how long the individual had lived in BC, length of time since they had emigrated, nor the period of immigration in which they had moved. The lack of differences in socioeconomic status among the groups suggest that the distinctiveness of the Taiwanese is not due to a selectivity of, for example, the more affluent. Of course there could be a selectivity in terms of attitudes and beliefs that were not measured in this data set from which the secondary analyses were drawn. The data do suggest rather strongly, though, a distinctiveness by birth place and place of emigration, and that the Taiwanese in British Columbia are somewhat different. The reasons are purely speculative but indicate that further research is warranted, particularly into the culture of immigrants from different Asian countries.

REFERENCES

Asis, M.M.B., Domingo, L., Knodel, J., and Mehta, K. (1995). Living arrangements in four Asian countries: A comparative perspective. *Journal of Cross Cultural Gerontology*, 10, 145-162.

Chong, W.S., Li, C.Y., and Chang, A.L. (1997). Influence of intergenerational exchange on nursing home admission in Taiwan. *Journal of Cross Cultural Gerontology*, 12, 163-174.

Clark, M. (1969). Cultural values and dependency in later life. In R.A. Kalish (Ed.), *The dependencies of old people*. Ann Arbor, MI: Institute of Gerontology, University of Michigan.

Cowart, M.E., and Streib, G.F. (1987). Taiwan and its elderly: Taxi nurses and home care. *Journal of Applied Gerontology*, 6, 156-162.

Garnet, J. (1982). *A history of Chinese civilization*. Translated from French by J.R. Foster. Cambridge: Cambridge University Press.

Ingersoll, D.B., and Saengtienchai, C. (1999). Respect for the elderly in Asia: Stability and change. *International Journal of Aging and Human Development*, 48, 113-130.

Kite, M.E., and Johnson, B.T. (1988). Attitudes toward older and younger adults: A meta-analysis. *Psychology and Aging*, 3, 233-244.

Krause, N., and Liang, J. (1992). Cross-cultural variations in depressive symptoms in later life. *International Psychogeriatrics*, 4, 185-202.

Lee, M.L., Lin, H.S., and Chang, M.C. (1995). Living arrangements of the elderly in Taiwan: Qualitative evidence. *Journal of Cross Cultural Gerontology*, 10, 53-78.

Li, R.M. (1994). Aging trends - Taiwan. *Journal of Cross Cultural Gerontology*, 9, 389-402.

Ofstedal, M.B., Zimmer, Z., and Lin, H.S. (1999). Comparison of correlates of cognitive functioning in older persons in Taiwan and the United States. *Journals of Gerontology: Series B: Psychological and Social Sciences*, 54B, S291-S301.

Raymo, J.M., and Cornman, J.C. (1999). Labor force status transitions at older ages in the Philipines, Singapore, Taiwan, and Thailand, 1970-1990. *Journal of Cross Cultural Gerontology*, 14, 221-244.

Sheppard, H.L. (Ed.) (1988). Social service and aging policies: Taiwan, Hong Kong, and the United States. Report from the International Exchange Center on Gerontology, University of South Florida, Tampa, FL.

Tu, E.J.C., Freedman, V.A., and Wolf, D.A. (1993). Kinship and family support in Taiwan: A microsimulation approach. *Research Aging*, 15, 465-486.

Zhu, X-Y, Kitano, H., Chi, I., Lubben, J., Berkanovic, E., and Zhang, C.C. (1994). Living arrangements and family support of the elderly in Beijing. In G.H. Stopp Jr. (Ed.), *International perspectives on healthcare for the elderly* (pp. 69-83). New York: Peter Lang.

Effects of Demographic Transformations Upon Social and Political Changes[1]

Dan Koenig

Professor, Department of Sociology, University of Victoria

An Overview

It is common knowledge that demographic outcomes are influenced by social and structural variables. It may be less understood that demographic changes also influence social or structural changes. As has been pointed out by others, for example Easterlin (1978, 1987), the relationship between social or structural changes and demographic changes is not unidirectional. One-sided extrapolation of the causal effects of social or structural changes upon demographic changes, as well as of demographic changes upon social or structural changes, is insufficient. There is a dynamic interplay between social and structural factors on the one hand and of demographic factors on the other.

The following, an admittedly oversimplified historical analysis, outlines how social and structural changes contributed to an imminent population implosion, an aging population, and a significant change in the sex ratio of many Western societies. Cultural differences constrain generalizing these experiences to other societies. It is suggested, nonetheless, that the constraining influence of cultural differences is being eroded by economic and cultural globalization, which, in turn, is being fuelled by the globalization of the mass media and ongoing quantum advances in telecommunications and computing technologies.

This chapter considers some of the advantages of demographic analysis for anticipating the future. It offers three examples of how demographic changes have influenced popular culture and political behaviours in Canada and other developed western societies: the outbreak of social activism in the 1960s, the political empowerment of the elderly, and the movement towards gender equality. The conclusion raises some questions about the possible relevance of the above analysis for China. Given China's large shadow, the ramifications for Taiwan may have some parallels.

DEMOGRAPHIC ANALYSIS

Demographic analysis is a bit like owning a crystal ball. Based upon trends in the number of births, a review of trends in migration, and age-specific death rates, one can reliably predict whether we will need more or fewer schools in the near future, and where such schools should be built—or closed, as the case may be. One can also make rather good prognostications about other longer term phenomena, such as the demand for university spaces, future supply-demand curves involving the labour force, the supply-demand curve for mating partners as it is affected by increasing or decreasing age specific fertility rates,[2] the volume and nature of housing stock that will be in demand, planning needs or investment opportunities in the provision of specific types of leisure pursuits, future demands for upgraded infrastructure such as roadways, water supply, and waste disposal, as well as future demand curves for various types of health services, including care of that portion of the elderly whose physical or mental functioning becomes limited.[3]

However, for such demographic analysis to be fruitful, simple unidirectional extrapolation is insufficient: the analyst must bring to the analysis what C. Wright Mills (1959) described as "the sociological imagination." As Easterlin (1978, 1987) has argued, the analyst must be mindful that social and structural changes feed back to influence demographic changes, and vice versa. Thus, the analyst must examine not only how demographic change will be *affected* by social change, but also how demographic trends will *create* social changes. Depending on the state of a country's development, one may, as it were, anticipate the future with the benefit of hindsight by examining what has already happened elsewhere. The following section provides an example.

SOCIAL AND STRUCTURAL INFLUENCES UPON DEMOGRAPHIC CHANGES

Increasing industrialization intensified the pull of people to large cities. The advent of the internal combustion engine and its widespread availability enabled these urban populations to disperse their dwellings over large geographical areas surrounding the central cities. By studying the experiences of other countries that have already undergone transformations of this nature, one can seek to avoid the myriad problems associated with these trends. Thus, the analyst can both anticipate problems like the alienation of productive agricultural land, as discussed by Brown (1999), and pro-actively embrace advanced alternatives to minimize such problems.[4]

In agricultural societies, children are productive assets, while provision of food, shelter, and so forth entails only nominal incremental costs; in developed urban societies, however, the productive contribution of children all but disappears, while provision for their subsistence entails significant incremental costs. It is not surprising that urban living was accompanied by smaller family size and a concomitant increased emphasis upon individual happiness. The reduced number of children had important implications for women's roles, as did the differing productive relations which characterized urban-industrial (compared to agricultural) economies. The variety of economic functions performed within the home declined, both for women and for the family units. Reduced family functionality, coupled with fewer children to be born and parented, freed women from what had become their "traditional" role. This freedom, in turn, expedited their availability for accelerating entrance into the paid labour force when, at least initially, labour markets became tight. As Ogburn and Nimkoff (1955) have documented in detail, urban living also produced an increase in anonymity (impersonality), as well as a weakening of both household stability and extended family ties.

The falling fertility rates associated with the reduction in family size dramatically transformed the age and sex structure of Western societies. This transformation, in turn, directly influenced three major developments within highly industrialized societies: a population implosion rather than explosion, an aging population, and a changed sex ratio causing the emergence of women as population majorities, particularly among those of voting age. It is likely that these changes also prefigure the future for currently developing countries —possibly for none more so than China.

Rapid declines in both births and deaths have significantly transformed what, in the absence of plague, famine, and war, were the more traditional age and sex distributions of populations.[5]   Figure 8.1 illustrates how this transformation unfolded within Canada during the twentieth century. As can be seen, at the beginning of the century there was a broad base at the young ages reflecting the already falling, but still substantial fertility and mortality rates. By the end of the century, there were increased proportions of the older age's population, caused by significant declines in age-specific death rates, particularly early in life. There was also a serious contraction of the proportions of the population at young ages caused by lower birth rates. As can also be noted, the cohorts in the childbearing ages were not reproducing sufficiently to replace themselves. Over the longer term, the total Canadian population will begin a precipitous decline in the absence of massive net immigration.

The effects of this transformation can be seen in Figure 8.2, which shows Canada's age structure in 1986 and its age structure projected for 2031. It is expected that in 2031 there will be fewer and fewer people within each succeeding age cohort from age 40 down to birth. In fact, the decline would begin at an even older age range except for very high levels of net immigration and a small birth echo from the large cohorts born during the so called "baby boom", which was particularly strong from 1946 until the mid 1960s. Immigrants also age, however, and the transitory baby boom has long since resumed its downward trajectory to become a "baby bust."

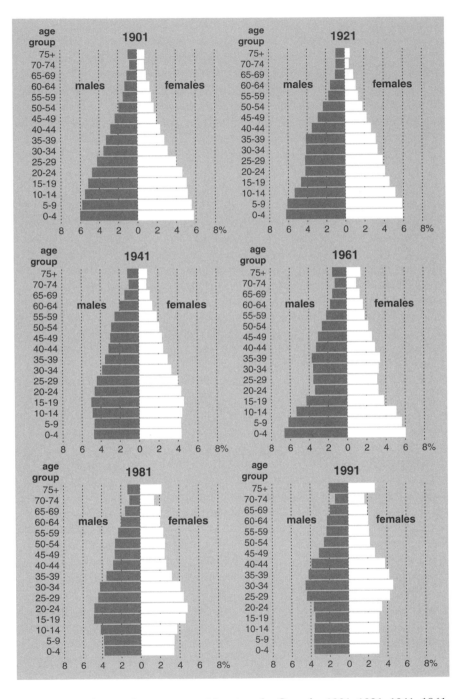

Figure 8.1   Age and sex composition trends, Canada: 1901, 1921, 1941, 1961, 1981, 1991 (McVey and Kahlbach, 1995)

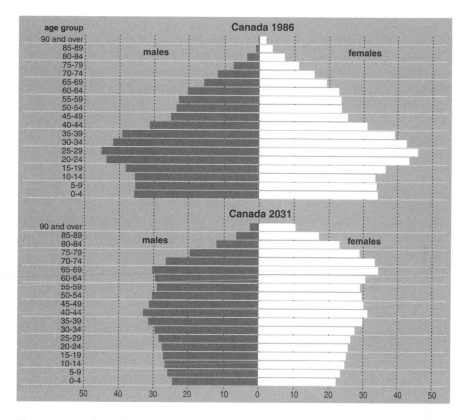

Figure 8.2   Canada's age structure: 1986 and projected for 2031 (Canada, 1989)

A careful inspection of Figure 8.2 demonstrates three important demographic phenomena. First, substantially more people will be dying than will be being born to replace them. Statistics Canada (1996) projects that this process will begin to occur about the year 2030. The result will be a rapidly declining population without unprecedented levels of net immigration. Computer modelling reveals that if age-specific fertility and mortality rates remained constant and emigration and immigration flows equalled one another, Canada's population would decline by about one half during this century.

Secondly, because fewer people are being born and those that are born have higher survival rates at all ages, the overall population is aging (from a median age of 25.6 in 1966 to a projection of around 40 by 2011). Populations with falling fertility rates will age. The process is exacerbated when falling age-specific mortality rates accompany falling fertility rates, as has been the case in developed Western countries. For example, Statistics Canada (1996) reports that those over the age of 65 accounted for 8% of Canada's population in 1961 but are expected to have increased to 23% of the Canadian population by 2041. The global nature of aging populations was recognized by the United

Nations' designation of 1999 as the International Year of Older Persons (Canada Co-ordinating Committee, 1998). Additional indications of its widespread occurrence and its importance can be inferred by the attention given to it by the United Nations (1994) in the case of Asian populations, and the detailed attention being given to its implications for Euroland countries, for example in Schroots, Fernandez-Ballesteros, and Rudinger (1999).

In the absence of cultural interference, nature appears to favour males over females in the probability of conception and birth. That is, in virtually all societies more male than female babies are born. However, males also have higher probabilities than females of dying at virtually every age following birth (and probably also higher probabilities of being spontaneously aborted or stillborn). This causes a third significant change: the initial numerical advantage of males over females in birth cohorts tends to reverse later in life. As can be seen in Figure 8.3, the initial numerical advantage of males over females at birth reverses past age 55, and becomes more pronounced with each succeeding older cohort. Thus as populations age, women become the numerical majority. Their numerical majority becomes even more pronounced if one focuses only on the population of voting age.

CULTURAL DIFFERENCES

Before suggesting a few ways in which these demographic changes have influenced popular culture and political behaviours, brief attention should be given to the issue of cultural differences. There is no denying that East Asian cultures are less oriented toward the individual than North American cultures. Are cultural differences likely to intervene between any demographic transformations and corresponding changes among different societies? Will cultural differences cause the effects of demographic structural changes to differ for East Asian societies from what has occurred in Western societies?

This question cannot conclusively be answered either affirmatively or negatively. Moreover, the question likely has different answers depending upon whether one takes a short or long-range perspective. Cultural differences *will* likely temporize changes over the short term; however, it is doubtful that any differences will be able to withstand the strong tide of economic and cultural globalization over the longer term. In this connection it is pertinent to observe that those Asian societies which were earliest to echo the demographic structural changes that had been underway in the West for centuries were those which were arguably most economically integrated with the developed West: Japan, Hong Kong, and Singapore and, to a lesser extent, South Korea and Taiwan.

Cultural globalization is occurring increasingly alongside of economic globalization. There is increasing convergence in the multinational branding one sees from one city to another throughout the world, as well as in dress and in

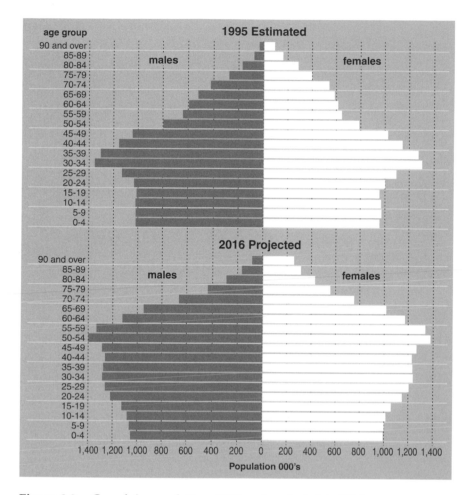

Figure 8.3   Canada's population: 1995 and projected to 2016
(Statistics Canada, 1996)

other materialist aspects of life. There also has been an ongoing exponential global penetration by gigantic multimedia media corporations: AOL-Time Warner, (CBS-) Viacom, Disney (-ABC), NewsCorp, Sony, and Bertlesmann. It is probably no coincidence that a goddess of liberty was erected in Tiananmen Square during the 1989 Chinese anti-corruption uprisings or that there has been a proliferation of cybercafes around the world (whose Internet content comes overwhelmingly from the developed countries, particularly from the United States). Western, primarily "American" films, television programs, recordings, and other cultural exports are in high demand around the world. Media specialists also contend that users absorb the embedded cultural values within these products, though the process is as subtle as it is profound.[6]

One media analyst has gone so far as to say that, through his vast media empire, Rupert Murdoch has more influence over Western media and popular culture than any other person (Silkos, 1992). Moreover, Lippman has observed how newer technologies, such as satellite channels, permit media instantly to penetrate national borders, with or without the consent of governments, and to affect the cultural values of those whom they reach. As Lippman wrote:

> *Asked once what had caused the stunning collapse of communism in Eastern Europe, Polish leader Lech Walesa pointed to a nearby TV set. 'It all came from there.' If it has helped topple totalitarian governments and promote global democracy, television has also, for better or for worse, led a modern Crusade, spreading pop culture over the Earth as medieval knights once spread Christendom. The rapid inroads of satellite-based borderless television are changing the way the world works, the way it plays, even the way it goes to war and makes peace.*

> *Countries that have long limited what their countries can watch on nationalized TV are slowly being forced to relax their grip.... Truly global 'super channels' such as MTV reach hundreds of millions of households, while CNN is seen in 137 countries.... The cultural, political, and economic effects of this global television revolution are enormous.... Television is how most people now experience history, as happened when viewers watched live satellite pictures of Scud missiles whistling down on Israel during the Gulf War. Conversely, history is now symbolized by television, a reality eloquently symbolized by East German youths when they hoisted MTV flags over the Berlin Wall as it was torn down.... With satellites beaming down literally hundreds of TV channels over whole continents and oceans, countries lose control over the information crossing their borders—an unstoppable migration of ideas, images, and culture that raises basic questions about the meaning of national sovereignty in the modern world. The nation-state is less and less able to control what goes in and out of it.*

> *Even more than on politics, however, the greatest influence of satellite television is on culture. Whereas it used to take decades or centuries for one culture to seep into another, television today can spread lasting images in a matter of seconds* (1992: A5).

It is likely that the far-reaching changes in telecommunications and computing technologies will facilitate and accelerate cultural globalization.[7] As the automobile earlier transformed societies, today the telecommunications revolution is transforming society. Telecommunications and computer technology are advancing exponentially, as new technologies make wireless connectivity possible anywhere. They are also doing so with ever increasing bandwidth for the transmission not only of voice but also of enormous encrypted data files and video. Whether it is distance education, recreation, long distance health care provided by expert systems, cyber-tourism, or cyber-friendships (and more), these newer technologies have not only changed the way that we do things but also what it is that we do.[8]

ILLUSTRATIVE CANADIAN TREND DATA

A persuasive case can be made that many changes in popular culture and political behaviours in modern Western democratic market economy societies have been demographically driven. For present purposes, three will be discussed and illustrated with Canadian trend data. The first of these is the rise of the "hippie" movement alongside of the social activism among youth of the 1960s, the second is the empowerment of the elderly, and the third is the empowerment of women and the movement towards gender equality.

The so-called "Quiet Generation" of the 1950s in the US (and Canada) evolved into the visible presence of hippies and social activists in the 1960s. This phenomenon was not confined to North America, but was also in evidence in Western Europe and, indeed, even behind the "Iron Curtain," as witnessed by the Prague uprising of 1968 in what was then Czechoslovakia. An argument can be advanced that there was a common demographic transformation occurring on both sides of the Atlantic Ocean, and that this transformation was strongly influenced by the fertility trough that occurred during the Great Depression of the 1930s.

The 1950s generation of youth was relatively small as a consequence of the baby bust of the 1930s, which did not recover more than nominally until the so-called baby boom from 1946 until the mid 1960s. Their small size made 1950s youth relatively invisible, which, compounded by three (US) recessions during the 1950s, kept this generation relatively quiet. This phenomenon is illustrated graphically in Figure 8.4, which shows bar graphs of the percentage of the total Canadian population under the age of 15 on the left and the percentage 65 or over on the right. As can be seen, the proportion of the population 0-14 reached a then all time low in 1941. These would have been the youth and young adults of the 1950s. As a share of the population, the youth population recovered over the next two decades before resuming a secular decline.

Meanwhile the proportion of the population age 65 and over was beginning what would turn into a rapid, long-term expansion. Figure 8.5 demonstrates this same transformation in the Canadian population age structure, though over a shorter time period and for somewhat different age ranges (the relative shares of the population age 15 through 24 and 55 or over, respectively).[9]

As can be seen, the 1960s saw a rapid increase in the youth population both relative to the total population and in absolute numbers. In addition, there was a major economic stimulus provided by consumer spending for both durable and non-durable goods because of the continuing large numbers of household formations attributable to the increased number of children and youth in the

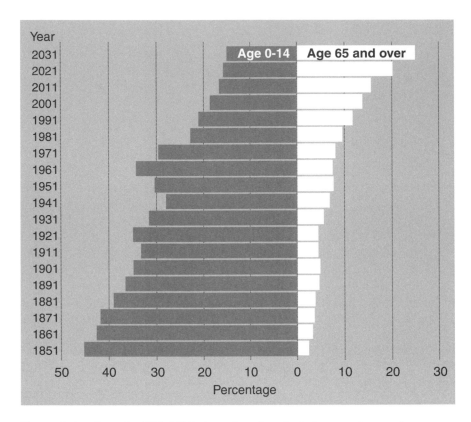

Figure 8.4   Canada 1851-2031: Actual and projected percentages of population under 15 and 65 or over (Canada, 1989)

population.[10] The vastly increased war expenditures following the 1965 American military intervention in Southeast Asia created further economic stimulus; it also took hundreds of thousands of youth out of the civilian labour market.

Cumulatively, these factors had several consequences. First, the increasing number of youth became more visible both to others and to themselves. They also had a tendency to see themselves as different ("Don't trust anyone over 30" was a popular slogan) and to become more assertive. Jobs were easy to obtain and one could quit a job one didn't like, for good reasons or bad, and not have trouble obtaining another when and where one chose. This freed the young from social control in the form of economic pressure that their forebears had experienced. Some, such as the hippies, had an opportunity to drop out of mainstream society in favour of a lifestyle of self indulgence (including dress, demeanor, behaviour, sex, music, drugs, hair length, etc.), while others of a reform bent also became free to vigorously pursue social activism without risking the dire consequences that would result had alternative options been closed.

Rate per 100,000 population

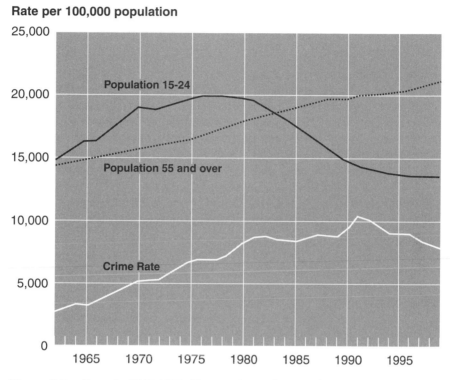

Figure 8.5   Canada 1962-1999: Shares of population of those
aged 15-24 inclusive and 55 or over (Tremblay, 2000)

Later, as the baby boom gave way to a renewed baby bust in the 1960s
(continuing until today despite a muffled echo), youth once again became relatively invisible, less politically important, and more constrained by a harsher
economic reality. Simultaneously, the continually declining death rates across
virtually the entire age spectrum resulted in an explosion of the older population, and particularly the older population of voting age. This transformation is retrospectively illustrated by Figure 8.6 and prospectively illustrated by
Figure 8.7.

The elderly have become such a potent political force that their pressure
tactics persuaded former Prime Minister Mulroney to reverse a previously an-
nounced policy change affecting their pensions. They continue to increase both
in size and power, particularly since an increasing number of them are affluent
as a result of having been childless or having been in relationships in which
both partners were remuneratively employed.

These circumstances have contributed to a third change. It has been noted
already that women have become the numerical majority, rather significantly
so among those who have reached voting age, as populations have aged. This

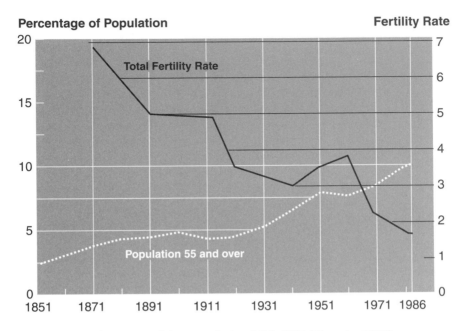

Figure 8.6   The aging of the population 1851-1986 (Canada, 1989)

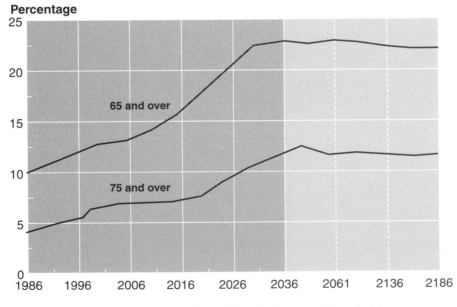

Figure 8.7   Percentage of population 65 and older and 75 and older: 1986-2186 (Canada, 1989)

situation gives them potential power to pressure for further improvement in their situations.[11] When spurred to action, Canadian women today constitute a potent political force: any elected or appointed official who responds to women dismissively or derisively is likely to rue his or her action.

As women have become a majority of the electorate, the movements for women's rights have been making more substantial and sustained progress. For instance, Figure 8.8 indicates that approximate parity in labour force participation rates between men and women has become an enduring feature of the labour force rather than a transitory response to tight labour markets. The process of empowerment for women has fed upon itself. *Newsweek* (2000: 34), for example, noted that by 1984 college enrollment of women had surpassed that of men in the US, and the gap has become steadily wider; at present about a million more women than men attend college in the US. A similar situation exists in Canada.

Participation rate (%)

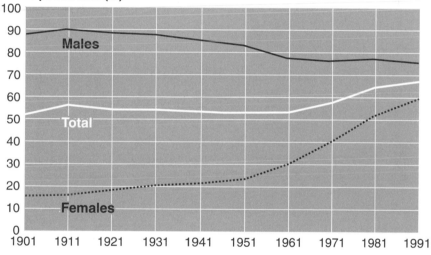

Figure 8.8   Labour force participation rates by sex: Canada 1901-1991
             (McVey and Kahlbach, 1995)

There are other factors that could be discussed in addition to those that have been noted. As the population has aged, electoral patterns have become more conservative, recreational patterns have changed (televised golf and curling reflect such change), and consumption and savings patterns have changed, as they will again when the "baby boomers" increasingly depart from the paid labor force and become heavy consumers of their accumulated capital. As well, there has been a long range trend for growth in the labor force of advanced economies to be disproportionately in the service sector rather than in traditional sectors such as manufacturing and extractive industries.

Conclusion

Can one predict demographically driven social, cultural, or structural changes for China? In the absence of a cataclysmic disaster, demographic changes can be predicted with considerable accuracy because of the long lead times involved. It takes a generation for a baby boom or bust to hit the work force, and another generation to hit middle age, etc. As a simple sketch, consider the implications of the one-child policy for the following questions.

- How will the very dramatic aging of China's population over the coming decades create a large dependency problem of older people, compounded by the fact that there may be only one potential child to assist the elderly in their old age.

- How will health care resources be affected as a large proportion of the population moves into advanced age?

- What will be the implications for the labour force as large numbers of people age and leave the labour force, while a decreasing pool of new labour force entrants is available to replace them? Will this situation create conditions for significant and destabilizing wage-driven inflation? With what consequences?

- If cultural norms are influencing intervention in the relative proportion of females being born, will their status increase and cultural norms be reversed as women become in short supply at mating and marriageable ages?

- Will a whole generation of "only children" have been so spoiled by being the centre of attention all of their lives that they will contribute to an erosion of aspects of traditional Chinese culture?

However these implications unfold on the mainland will undoubtedly cast a long shadow over Taiwan. But perhaps even that influence will be less than the influence of the media-driven globalization of culture.

Endnotes

[1] I thank Drs. Yuen-Fong Woon and Zack Zimmer for their helpful comments when this paper was originally presented at National Sun Yat-sen University in Kaohsiung.

[2] For example, see Veevers (1988).

[3] Many examples of the above can be found in Merrick and Tordella (1988), or, more recently, in Foot and Stoffman (2000).

[4] A discussion of such proactive alternatives can be found in Roodman (1999).

[5] Van de Kaa (1987), provides a good illustration of this phenomenon.

[6] See, for example, Parenti (1986, 1992) for extensive elaboration on this point.

[7] Parallel advances in biotechnology, including identification of the genome, are equally important, but of less relevance to this paper.

[8] For elaboration of these points, see STRATFOR (1999).

⁹ The crime rate trends, while consistent with the argument presented because street crime is committed predominantly by young males, is beyond the scope of the present discussion.

¹⁰ Parenthetically, it is interesting to note that the unprecedented expansion of the 1990s has also been driven largely by consumer spending, though it is financed by private debt rather than public debt.

¹¹ For examples of this process, see Baud and Smyth (1997).

REFERENCES

Baud, I., and Smith, I. (Eds.) (1997). *Searching for security: Women's responses to economic transformations.* London: Routledge.

Brown, L.R. (1999). *Feeding nine billion.* In L. Starke (Ed.), *State of the world, 1999: A Worldwatch Institute report on progress toward a sustainable society* (pp. 115-132). New York: W.W. Norton and Company.

Canada Coordinating Committee for the International Year of Older Persons (1998). *Canada, a society for all ages* (Cat. H39-449/1998E). Ottawa, ON: Minister of Supply and Services Canada.

Canada, Health and Welfare (1989). *Charting Canada's future: A report of the demographic review.* Ottawa, ON: Minister of Supply and Services Canada, 1989.

Easterlin, R.A. (1987). *Birth and fortune: The impact of numbers on personal welfare* (2nd ed.) Chicago, IL: University of Chicago Press, 1987.

Easterlin, R.A. (1978). What will 1984 be like? Socioeconomic implications of recent twists in age structure. *Demography*, 15(4), 397-432.

Foot, D.K., and Stoffman, D. (2000). *Boom, bust and echo 2000: Profiting from the demographic shift in the new millennium.* Toronto, ON: Stoddart, 2000.

Lippmann, J. (1992). Global village tightens its grip, *Times-Colonist*, November 1, p. A5 (reproduced from the *Los Angeles Times*).

McVey, W.W. Jr., and Kahlbach, W.E. (1995). *Canadian population.* Scarborough, ON: Nelson Canada.

Merrick, T.W., and Tordella, S.J. (1988). Demographics: People and markets. *Population Bulletin*, 43(1). Washington, DC Population Reference Bureau, Inc., February, 1988.

Mills, C.W. (1959). *The sociological imagination.* New York: Oxford University Press.

Newsweek (2000). *The 21ˢᵗ Century: America and the world.* January 1, 2000.

Ogburn, W.F., and Nimkoff, M.F. (1955). *Technology and the changing family.* Boston, MS: Houghton Mifflin Company.

O'Meara, M. (1999). Exploring a new vision for cities. In L. Starke (Ed.), *State of the world, 1999: A Worldwatch Institute report on progress toward a sustainable society* (pp. 133-150). New York: W.W. Norton and Company.

Parenti, M. (1986). *Inventing reality: The politics of the mass media.* New York: St. Martin's Press.

Parenti, M. (1992). *Make-believe media: The politics of entertainment.* New York: St. Martin's Press.

Roodman, D.M. (1999). Building a sustainable society. In L. Starke (Ed.), *State of the world, 1999: A Worldwatch Institute report on progress toward a sustainable society* (pp. 169-188). New York: W.W. Norton and Company.

Schroots, J.J.F., Fernandez-Ballesteros, R., and Rudinger, G. (Eds.) (1999). *Aging in Europe* (Volume 17 of *Biomedical and Health Research*). Amsterdam: IOS Press.

Silkos, R. (1992). Murdoch: His empire strikes back. *Financial Post*, September 7, p. S12.

Statistics Canada (Tina Chui) (1996). Canada's population: Charting into the 21st century. *Canadian Social Trends*, 42 (Autumn), 3-7.

Stratfor Inc. (1999). *Stratfor's decade forecast—2000-2010: Can America's new golden age be sustained?* Austin, TX: Stratfor.Com (*http://www.stratfor.com*), December 21, 1999.

Tremblay, S. (2000). Crime statistics in Canada. *Juristat (Statistics Canada Catalogue no. 85-002)*, 20(5).

United Nations Department for Economic and Social Information and Policy Analysis (1994). *The ageing of Asian populations*. New York: United Nations.

Van de Kaa, D.J. (1987). Europe's second demographic revolution. *Population Bulletin*, 42(1). Washington, DC Population Reference Bureau, Inc., March, 1987.

Veevers, J. (1988). The real marriage squeeze: Marriage, mate selection and the mating gradient. *Sociological Perspectives*, 31, 142-167.

SECTION 11

Democracy and Development

Development Strategies Feasible for Developing Economies, with Special Reference to Unconventional Policies

Peter C. Lin

Professor of Economics, National Sun Yat-sen University and Director, Institute of Operations and Management, Ka Yuan Institute of Technology

INTRODUCTION

Countries throughout the world have long made efforts toward the pursuit of development. Economic development involves more than just economic growth, as measured by an increase in real income per head. Development may be defined as the attainment of a number of "ideals of modernization," such as a rise in productivity, social and economic equalization, modern knowledge, improved institutions and attitudes, and a rationally coordinated system of policy measures that can remove the host of undesirable conditions in the social system that have perpetuated a state of underdevelopment (Black, 1966). Development signifies growth plus change.

Modern development economics began in the late 1940s along with the political independence of the emerging regions of Asia, Africa, and the Caribbean. The theory of economic development evolved after World War II as a separate branch of economics, with its own academic institutions, concepts, and prescriptions. The new development economists went beyond their classical and neoclassical predecessors to consider the kind of policies that an active state or a developing economy could adopt to accelerate a country's rate of development.

The successful economic and social development of East Asian countries has been the subject of considerable interest among economists. The World Bank (1993) report entitled *The East Asian Miracle: Economic Growth and Public Policy*, a widely recognized piece of empirical research, contributes significantly to the understanding of development processes. Understanding the forces of development is essential to designing appropriate policies to accelerate development. The World Bank study stresses the roles played by sound macroeconomic policies, by liberal trade policies, and by the state. It has been established that there is no unique recipe for successful economic development and the conventional or neoclassical recommendations are neither a necessary nor sufficient condition for achieving development.

The East Asian development experience contrasts vividly with that of Latin America. As early as the 1950s, some of the larger Latin American countries such as Brazil, Mexico, Argentina, and Venezuela were considered by many observers to be ready for rapid long-term growth. In fact, the Latin American countries started with higher per capita incomes than were found in Asia. However, Latin America did not realize its potential for growth and, instead, the economy stagnated. During and after the 1980s, most Latin American countries radically revised their development strategies. Policy changes included liberalizing trade and other international economic relations, drastically reducing the role of the state in economic decision-making, opening up their markets and industries to international competition, and privatizing state-owned enterprises.

Examining development strategies and comparing development experience between the two regions would be of great relevance in identifying strategies feasible to development. We understand that there are great divergences between countries in their institutions, and their social and political conditions, which bear significantly on the economic development of individual countries. However, a comparative analysis of the two regions' economic development should help to reach a full understanding of divergent trends in growth in East Asia and Latin America.

Section II outlines classical and neoclassical growth theory; Section III compares development strategies between East Asia and Latin America; Section IV examines some issues that are relevant to the developing economies; and the chapter concludes with some remarks in Section V.

CLASSICAL AND NEOCLASSICAL GROWTH THEORY

Classical economists were very much interested in economic growth. According to Adam Smith, the level of output per head, together with its growth, "must be regulated by two different circumstances: first, by the skill, dexterity, and judgement with which labor is generally applied; and, secondly, by the proportion between the number of those who are employed in useful labor, and that of those who are not employed" (Smith, 1776, p. 10).

Among classical economists, development views emphasized capital accumulation as a driving force in the growth process, concentrated on increasing productivity, and pointed to the possibility of development based on foreign trade. Thus, the major sources of growth are: (1) growth in the labour force and stock of capital (capital accumulation); (2) improvement in the efficiency with which capital is applied to labour through greater division of labour and technological progress; and (3) foreign trade that widens the market and reinforces the other two sources of growth.

Once growth begins, the process becomes self-reinforcing in a progressive state. Growth leads to increases in wealth, which in turn favours profits. As a result, savings and additional capital accumulation are forthcoming, which further propel growth. Growing capital accumulation leads to increased demand for labour, and an additional labour force is absorbed in productive employment.

Smith emphasized the importance of the division of labour: it brings about improved labour efficiency, and increased productivity due to specialization leads to rising per capita income. By promoting the division of labour, improved productivity reduces the cost of production per unit of output, raising competitiveness in the market place. The division of labour increases wealth, which, in turn, widens the market, enabling the division of labour to be carried forward further.

Based on classical growth theory, capital accumulation, division of labour, and foreign trade are sources of a nation's economic growth; and growth can be promoted through the extension of market institutions and the activity of competition.

The neoclassical growth theory is built around the concept of the aggregate production function, involving factors other than physical capital and labour. Increments to any factor of production should ultimately cause output to increase. In measuring the contribution of productive factors to economic growth, factor earnings explained only part of the growth: a substantial amount of growth remained unexplained, which came to be known as the residual. Although the concept of the residual was initially considered to be a coefficient of technical progress (Solow, 1957), it was soon recognized as a composite of the effects of many forces contributing to growth. These forces include: (1) improvement in the quality of labour through education, experience, and on-the-job training; (2) reallocation of resources from low-productivity to higher-productivity uses; (3) exploitation of economies of scale; and (4) improved ways of combining resources to produce goods and services.

The neoclassical growth theory can take into account all sorts of distortions and market imperfections. It defines most of the unexplained amount of growth as stuck in the residual. It identifies sources of growth from capital accumulation, increases in labour quantity and quality, increases in intermediate inputs, and total factor productivity growth within sectors.

DEVELOPMENT STRATEGIES BETWEEN
EAST ASIA AND LATIN AMERICA

A stable macroeconomic foundation is essential to economic growth. When government spending expands too far, the result is often large deficits, excessive borrowing or monetary expansion, and problems in the financial sector.

These conditions in turn lead to inflation, losses of export competitiveness, domestic and external debt problems, and the crowding out of private investment. Most East Asian countries have enjoyed macroeconomic stability in terms of low inflation, competitive and stable real foreign exchange rates, and manageable external debt. Their success stresses the role that is played by sound macroeconomic policies.

East Asian countries have developed their economies through export-oriented strategies designed to take advantage of a dynamic world economy. A market-oriented strategy has led to superior development performance in a number of these countries. By undertaking policies that remove barriers to exports and make it as profitable to produce for export as for the domestic market, these countries achieved significant gains from trade. Since they no longer produce only for their domestic markets, they overcame the diseconomies of being small countries and raised efficiency in the mobilization and allocation of resources in the production process.

East Asia has had more outward-looking trade and exchange rate policies than Latin America. Notwithstanding occasional government intervention, trade regimes in East Asian countries have generally been left to market forces. Unlike the resource-rich larger countries in Latin America, East Asian countries have had few options but to develop outward-looking policies: because of their small markets and lack of natural resources, import-substitution policies are untenable.

One of the striking features of development in East Asian countries has been that it has occurred under fairly equitable conditions, linking growth with equity. The early development experience of Latin America supported the conventional view that, initially, rapid growth would worsen income inequalities. Greater equity and balanced economic and social development contribute to social stability: inequalities commonly generate social and political reactions at various levels. The greater the inequalities, the less stable the socioeconomic system, and in turn the lower the rate of investment and economic growth.

East Asian countries have effectively invested in human capital, emphasizing primary and secondary education and vocational training. The World Bank's Staff Working Paper (July 1980) concludes that economic returns on investment in education seem, in most instances, to exceed returns on alternative kinds of investment, and that developing countries gain higher returns than developed ones. The East Asian success stories have been based, not on abundance of natural resources, but on human resources. All these countries have invested heavily in education.

East Asian countries have also provided incentives encouraging entrepreneurship and private initiative. These countries are well known for their policies emphasizing market and private sector development (World Bank, 1993). Except for Hong Kong, East Asian countries go beyond the fundamentals, and intervene with varying degrees of intensity to alter market incentives.

These intervention policies are intended to correct market distortions or achieve certain social goals that will facilitate the market system. The main areas of incentives include: export push, maintaining interest rates below market-clearing levels, directed credit, and selective intervention.

As previously noted, it seemed to many observers in the 1950s that some Latin American countries were poised for rapid long-term growth. Most of these countries started with higher per capita incomes than those of Asian countries. However, by the 1960s the presumption was already breaking down as several East Asian countries surged ahead in their economies as potentially new industrializing countries. In the late 1970s and through the 1980s, Asia experienced rapid growth, while Latin America stagnated. An examination of development strategies adopted by Latin American countries during the 1960s and 1970s may provide some explanations for the economic divergence between the two regions.

During the 1960s and 1970s, Latin America looked inward in pursuit of import substitution industrialization (ISI). Import substitution held considerable appeal because of the common belief that it would help the balance-of-payment problems of most developing countries. In the course of import substitution, these developing countries protected their incipient manufacturing industries producing for domestic markets. They applied high tariffs or quantitative restrictions that limited, or even excluded, competition from imports. These protectionist policies have resulted in higher prices, domestic products of inferior quality, and inefficient resource use. ISI policies have subsidized import replacement and, at the same time, have inhibited expansion of exports. Realizing the limitations of their inward-looking development strategy of industrialization, many Latin American countries have changed their emphasis and are now seeking measures to promote industrialization through export push.

Lack of sound macroeconomic policies was detrimental to growth in Latin America, and macroeconomic instability became widespread in the region. Extensive borrowing financed the nominal growth of these economies in the 1960s and 1970s, with the borrowed funds too often used not for investment, but for public consumption. Mismanagement of financial sectors and lack of sound macroeconomic policies resulted in excessive external debts and high inflation. Because of the serious distortions caused by inflation and hyperinflation, macroeconomic crises occurred frequently and economic growth was greatly retarded.

Economic inequality and social tensions prevailed in Latin America because social policy neglected to narrow inequalities. Further, a lack of political and macroeconomic stability provided unfavourable preconditions for growth. In the Asian countries, there have been few changes in government leadership in the past two to three decades, and Asia has had more political stability than Latin America. In addition, the economic policies followed by governments in Asia have generally reflected pragmatism rather than a political ideology.

OTHER ISSUES

Private Sector Development

Private sector development plays a very important role in the growth process of emerging economies. Mechanisms should be provided to promote small and medium enterprises (SME). SMEs play an important role in economic development for many East Asian countries: in fact, many of today's major companies started as SMEs. They offer the best opportunity to generate employment with modest investment. The World Bank study describes the role of SMEs in Japan and other East Asian countries: they have significant effects on employment, real wage increases for workers, and, hence, contribute to equitable growth. The part played by SMEs in stimulating the market, in providing vital support to industry, and in initiating innovation makes them crucial for competition in the market and for development.

SMEs fill the role of stable and reliable suppliers of parts and components for the manufacturing industry, enhancing its proficiency in the production process. Thus, they complement the smooth function of the manufacturing industry and form an essential part of the entire industrial structure.

The increasing role and sustained development of the SME sector can be seen most clearly in Taiwan. In 1998, SMEs accounted for 97.8% of the total enterprises in Taiwan; they provided 78.2% of total employment, and their share of sales was 30.4%. The SME sector has become an important cornerstone of Taiwan's economy, a powerful engine of growth. Due to its operating agility and flexibility in dealing with changing environments, it possesses a great capacity to react to adverse situations and is able to meet the challenges of external shocks.

To promote SMEs, resources must be channelled more effectively to the local level for employment-generating small and medium enterprises. A greater share of support is needed to help promote the domestic private sector, especially through the provision of credit to SMEs. In addition, a channel should be provided for direct dialogue with foreign and private sector representatives to discuss ways of improving business and investment environments. Streamlining and simplifying processes for securing government approvals and permits are necessary to reduce bureaucracy and to facilitate business operations for SMEs.

Good Governance

Improved public administration, transparency, and enhanced accountability in the use of public funds are important to improve the efficiency and effectiveness of economic management and the allocation of resources. A commitment to fighting corruption, and a well-trained and properly remunerated civil service are all very important to the proper function of any society and system.

Transparency and open competitive bidding as well as systems of payments and monitoring are necessary to insure sound business practices and operations which contribute to efficiency and cost effectiveness. Lack of transparency, excessive bureaucratic power and a poorly developed judicial system hinder both the running of existing businesses and attracting new ones.

Both domestic and foreign businesses find that the complex and detailed nature of permit requirements, the opaque nature of decision-making, and the prevalence of corruption are barriers to doing business. Removing hindrances, and thus providing a friendlier business environment, would attract more business investment. As things are now, red tape and corruption hamper business operations, leading many firms to postpone expansion plans. In the business world, time is money, and effective competition requires swift responses to changing environments.

Foreign Direct Investment

Investment has traditionally been viewed as one of the driving forces of economic growth. In a closed economy, savings are the only source of investment. However, in an open economy, in addition to domestic sources, borrowing from abroad can finance investment, or it can be achieved through foreign direct investment (FDI).

In less-developed countries, FDI provides a major source of saving and investment for host countries with low domestic saving capacities and weak domestic investment efforts. Attracting foreign investment requires an agreeable environment: extra efforts to promote FDI inflows are clearly needed. In dealing with foreign investors, attitudes need to change at the middle levels of bureaucracy, where government policy is often only implemented with delays or side payments. Removal of out-dated regulations and the liberalization of trade will undoubtedly lead to increases in FDI.

Capital accumulation signifies an increase in the stock of the means of production, which occurs through investment. It is important because it leads to increased productive capacity, creates employment, and permits the absorption of technical improvement. Capital and technology are joint inputs in the production process: the use of one necessarily involves the use of the other.

A shortage of savings presents one of the important economic constraints in developing countries. In the early stages of development, this problem can be alleviated, to some extent, through foreign direct investment. FDI is normally undertaken through transnational corporations (TNC). One of the great sources of power in TNCs lies in their expertise, which includes technological knowledge, understanding of markets and finance, as well as of managerial skills. TNCs are one of the major conduits of the inflow of foreign technology for less-developed countries. TNCs may bring in new technology unavailable domestically, and spillovers to the host country may lead to the domestic adoption and development of the technology.

A Reputable Civil Service

To sustain growth, a bureaucracy must have the competence to formulate effective policies and the integrity to implement them fairly. The more policymakers attempt to fine tune the economy, the greater the need for competence and honesty. The principles of competent and honest bureaucracies are essential and applicable to any developing economy: (1) recruitment and promotion must be merit-based and highly competitive; (2) total compensation, including pay, perks, and prestige, must be competitive with the private sector; and (3) those who make it to the top should be amply rewarded to minimize corruption.

Promotion within a bureaucracy should be based on a combination of seniority and a host of performance indicators. Incentive-based compensation should be encouraged to promote creativity and efficiency. In bureaucracies, as in nearly everything else, you get what you pay for. In general, the more favourably the total public sector compensation package compares to compensation in the private sector, the better the quality of the bureaucracy.

Competence generates integrity, which reduces the temptation for wrongdoing or corruption. Mechanisms that induce competency can also enhance honesty.

The Banking System

Without a sound and efficient banking system, a nation can neither mobilize savings nor channel those savings to their most productive uses. Reforming a banking system is technically and politically difficult, and requires careful sequencing, protection of depositors, isolation of bad loan portfolios, and reduction of potential risks. The reform of the banking system has to focus on the financial vulnerability to crisis, and its weak capacity to mobilize savings and invest efficiently.

A weak banking system, with many bad loans and numerous bureaucratic controls precludes the flow of foreign investment to the host country. The liquidity problems of the domestic banks and their aversion to lending will persist, as more misallocated loans turn bad, the deposit base remains narrow and foreign commercial lenders became more circumspect.

Real rates of interest should be kept reasonably high to provide incentives for savings and curb consumption for the purpose of greater future consumption. Real interest rates are often negative and unpredictable during periods of high inflation and, as a consequence, domestic financial savings are greatly discouraged. There is a positive association between real interest rates and the growth of saving deposits and broad money aggregates. Economic theory and empirical evidence agree that if a government holds real interest rates on deposits too low for too long people will have little or no incentive to accumulate financial assets, financial savings will fall, and economic growth will be adversely affected. A sound financial system and healthy financial intermediaries are essential to win the confidence of people to put their money in the banks. People will only deposit funds with a bank or other financial institution if they are reasonably confident that the institution will return the funds as promised.

CONCLUDING REMARKS

There is no unique solution to successful economic development. The development experiences of East Asia and Latin America provide a good comparison of development strategies and their resultant economic performances. The divergent trends in development in East Asia and Latin America over the past two to three decades were due to economic as well as non-economic factors. While acknowledging that it is impossible to replicate specific experiences under different historical, cultural, and structural conditions, Latin American countries undertook a radical revision of their past development strategies. The two main elements of this revision were the liberalization of trade and other international economic relations, and a drastic reduction in the role of the state in economic development policy-making. Latin American governments swiftly opened their markets and industries to international competition, and privatized state-owned enterprises. The process of structural adjustment without incorporating proper social policies to alleviate the impact on the poor has worsened the plight of the poor, generated wide economic inequalities, and raised several tensions generally.

This study raises some unconventional policies that are relevant to development strategy. They are: private sector development, good governance, foreign direct investment, building a reputable civil service, and creation of a sound and efficient banking system. These measures, though not considered to be on the top of the list of development strategies, are essential and complementary to development.

REFERENCES

Aoki, M, Kim, H-K., and Okuno-Fujiwara, M. (1996). The role of government in East Asian economic development: Comparative institutional analysis. Washington, DC: Economic Development Institute, World Bank.

Black, C.E. (1966). *The dynamics of modernization*. New York: Harper and Row.

Chen, J. (Ed.) (1998). *Economic effects of globalization*. Brookfield, VT: Ashgate.

Eigen, P. (1996). Combatting corruption around the world. *The Journal of Democracy*, 7(1), 158-168.

Hosono, A., and Saavedra-Rivano, N. (Eds.) (1998). *Development strategies in East Asia and Latin America*. London: MacMillan Press Ltd.

King, T. (Ed.) (1980). *Education and income.* World Bank Staff Working Paper, No. 402 (July).

Smith, A. (1776). *An inquiry into the nature and causes of the wealth of nations* (originally published in 1776; Glasgow edition, R.H. Campbell and A.S. Skimer, eds., 1979).

Solow, R. (1957). Technical change and the production function. *Review of Economics and Statistic,* 39(3), 312-320.

World Bank (1993). *The East Asian miracle: Economic growth and public policy.* New York: Oxford University Press.

The Effects of Information and Communications Technology on Development: A Cross-National Study of Non-Governmental Organizations

R. Alan Hedley

Professor, Department of Sociology, University of Victoria

RESEARCH OBJECTIVES

The proposed research involves a retrospective "before and after" questionnaire survey of non-governmental organizations (NGOs) in India, Malaysia, and Japan to determine the impact of information and communications technology (i.e., the Internet) on the achievement of their development objectives. In addition, an analysis of this impact will permit me to postulate which of four development scenarios is emerging on a global scale.

RESEARCH BACKGROUND

The industrial revolution that originated in England just over two centuries ago constituted a pivotal event in human history. The most profound result of this technological revolution was a huge gain in productivity, which in turn significantly raised income in those countries that became industrialized (Hedley, 1992). This event marked the capstone of what was later described as a *Global Rift* (Stavrianos, 1981), which is starkly apparent today in terms of the total value of goods and services produced throughout the world. In 1998, the industrially developed countries, comprising just 15% of the world's population, produced 78% of world GNP. Average per capita GNP in these countries was US $25,510 compared to only US $1,250 in the developing nations (World Bank, 231). In turn, the technological watershed between developed and developing countries also produced differences in rates of natural increase, human capital accumulation, labour force participation, dependency ratios, infrastructural development, and quality of life that serve to compound and magnify this global rift (World Bank, 2000).

Today, we stand on the threshold of what promises to be another momentous technological revolution—an information and communications technology (ICT) revolution that could virtually abolish time and space constraints in the same way that the earlier revolution liberated human beings from many of their physical constraints. Despite claims to the contrary, the ICT revolution is still very much in its beginning stages and is limited primarily to the developed countries. For example, in 1994 the G-7 nations accounted for 80% of the information technology market, as measured by the revenues of primary vendors, and American and Japanese corporations dominated the industry (OECD, 1997). In 1997, developed countries had 269 personal computers per 1,000 people compared to only 12 per 1,000 in the rest of the world (World Bank, 2000). Analysis of the Internet, the worldwide network of personal computers connected to host computers, indicates that it is overwhelmingly American based, English speaking, and Western focused. In January 1999, approximately 71% of the estimated 43.23 million host computers connected to the Internet were in the US, 79% in English-speaking nations, and fully 91% operated out of Western countries (Network Wizards 1999).

Given these facts, an obvious conclusion to draw is that the emerging ICT revolution will exacerbate the existing fault line between rich and poor, and widen the already huge global rift. However, some scholars suggest that due to features unique to this ICT revolution, such an outcome is not necessary (Hedley, 1999; Howkins and Valantin, 1997). Given that the Internet (and its likely successor) is a configuration of two-way, horizontally connected computers, accessed mainly by individuals via personal computers, its technology represents a significant break with previous one-way, top-down communications media, and consequently the potential for mass indoctrination. Although the Internet still permits the exercise of widespread power, its multiple interactive, real-time capability combined with its potential for universal access are novel features never before experienced on a world scale. According to Brown and Brown (1994), the ICT revolution "will provide a virtually seamless world communications network capable of reaching every inhabitant on earth." For the first time ever, a true global village in which all people have the chance to interact and voice their individual concerns is possible, if not yet realized. For the hitherto disenfranchised of the world, the ICT revolution could provide the means to organize and articulate their needs, such that they could eventually participate in a more just and humane and, thus, sustainable world society.

POTENTIAL EFFECTS OF INFORMATION AND COMMUNICATIONS TECHNOLOGY ON DEVELOPMENT

A number of potential scenarios are possible as to the projected outcome of this new technological revolution. Howkins and Valantin (1997) report on the results of a high-level international workshop sponsored by the UN

Commission on Science and Technology for Development, in which participants were directed to develop scenarios on the effects of ICT on development, employing a 15 to 20 year horizon. The key axes upon which participants constructed their model are the global community and individual countries. With respect to the diffusion of ICT, to the extent that it is inclusive, open, and enabling, rather than exclusive, closed, and restrictive, prospects for more equitable and sustainable development are enhanced. Similarly, if national responses to ICT are proactive and engaged rather than reactive and disengaged, individual countries can employ these technologies to further their development objectives.

Figure 10.1 presents four possible development scenarios that could emerge, depending on where the global community and individual countries position themselves on these two crosscutting continua. Since these scenarios are ideal types, there are actually not four, but myriad potential outcomes that could ensue depending upon the relative inclusiveness of the global environment and the degree of receptivity that various countries have to these new technologies. The four scenarios are as follows.

The March of Follies

By 2010 the 'development debate' is virtually dead. Few notice that the UN is moribund. ... every day the stories are the same: some people somewhere with not enough to eat, some cases of mass migration, poor people trying to invade rich areas, scenes of violence. But these problems are no longer in the public sphere and subject to regulation, and they are no longer part of public anxiety.

Cargo Cult

By 2005, all countries have access to an effective global network. However, although the access provider might have a local name, its language, user interface, menu, guide, smart agent, and search agents are usually devised, owned, and managed by foreign companies. The result is widespread frustration. By adopting an uncritical approach, most countries gain access at the expense of substance. They can buy other countries' information; but cannot generate their own. They fail to make the connection between information and development.

Netblocs

As a result of the spread of ICTs, many people become wired into the new global information society. Groups [blocs] emerge, based on shared cultures and languages, initially in the towns and then spreading further afield. At the end of the scenario period, the blocs have achieved much. They have created information societies and economies that reflect their own histories, traditions, cultures, and ways of doing business. But their insistence on their own regional laws, regulations, and trading principles creates centripetal forces that lead to a highly unstable situation.

Networld

By 2000, many corporations realize that the successful sale of a few international brands (such as televisions, food, and clothes) to young urban elites has not produced a broad consumer base, or generated much domestic wealth. Markets for other goods and services are also very small. These companies begin to realize the extent of their failure. Facing saturated markets at home, they want to reach new consumers. There is strong evidence of enlightened self-interest as they seek ways of working with companies and institutions in the developing world. Their awareness is matched by a realization in developing countries that they should work with global corporations to create their own national information society and economy. They cannot go it alone (Howkins and Valantin, 1997).

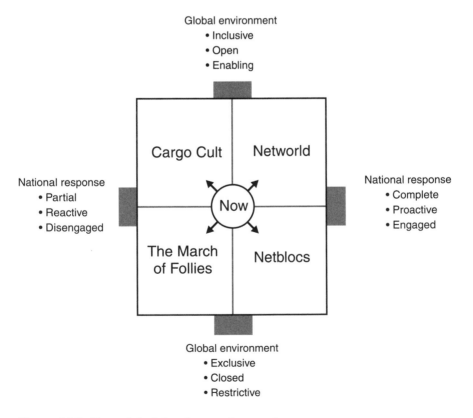

Figure 10.1 Four global development scenarios

Which of these development scenarios is most likely? This research proposes to provide a partial and preliminary indication. Because we are still in the beginning stages of the ICT revolution, the results from this research could be used to inform policy initiatives, should it be discovered that we are not moving toward the *Networld* development scenario.

RESEARCH DESIGN

This study uses a retrospective 'before and after' design intended to measure the impacts of domestic and global access to the Internet on the relative success of indigenous Asian non-governmental organizations (NGOs) in achieving their development objectives. As a result, the units of analysis are national NGOs; the measure of the independent variable (ICT) is relative use of and exposure to the Internet, and the empirical indicator of the dependent variable (development) is the 'after' minus 'before' ability of these NGOs to attain their development goals. Table 10.1 presents the dimensions of development employed by Howkins and Valantin (1997), which will be used as the basis for selecting NGOs.

Table 10.1   Dimensions of development

- **Literacy, education, and skills** (literacy, education, training and skills, and opportunities for all members of society to increase their capacities)

- **Health** (life expectancy, maternal and infant mortality, quality of life, and the levels of health care available in situations of morbidity)

- **Income and economic welfare** (high levels of employment, high incomes per capita, and increased gross national product, with appropriate corrections for environmental protection and for income equity)

- **Choice, democracy, and participation** (participation in social and economic affairs, with fair economic rewards, the availability of reasonable choice, and participation in the democratic process)

- **Technology** (the capacity to develop technological innovations and to make technological choices)

Source: Howkins and Valantin, 1997.

In that it has been previously found that initial levels of national development affect countries' subsequent ability to achieve development objectives (see Figure 10.2), I survey NGOs in India, Malaysia, and Japan to determine whether the relationship between exposure to the Internet and ability to accomplish development goals differs in countries with low, medium, and high levels of

GDP per capita *(1995 U.S. dollars)*

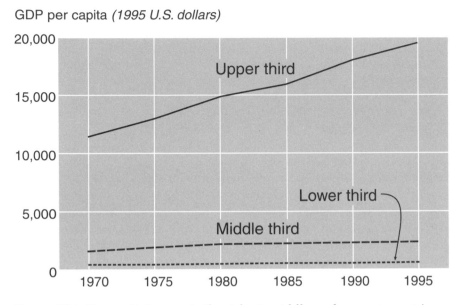

Figure 10.2 Per capita income in the richest, middle, and poorest countries, 1970 to 1995

socioeconomic development. Table 10.2 provides data on the relative development of these three countries according to the criteria specified in Table 10.1.

It should be mentioned that to the extent that differences in the 'before' and 'after' measurements of NGO performance are found, explanations other than the impact of the Internet are possible (Babbie, 1998). For example, higher "after" results could be due to an easing of the financial crisis in Asia (i.e., history) rather than from the effect of the independent variable. Alternatively, higher "after" results could be from NGOs gaining greater experience over time (i.e., maturation), rather than from their exposure to the Internet. Quite simply, this type of research design does not permit unequivocal causal assertions. Great care must be taken in attributing differences in 'before' and 'after' measurements to the independent variable.

To measure the relative inclusiveness and openness of the global environment, I ask these NGOs to assess their "before" and "after" relationships with international development agencies, and to measure the degree of national proactivity and engagement, I request NGOs to describe their reactions to increased access to the international development community, and to assess how accommodating their governments are in establishing infrastructural support and access to the Internet.

To assess the impact of the Internet on NGOs in these three countries in accomplishing their objectives (in the context of the global environment and national responses to ICT), it is necessary to survey NGOs in the official languages of their respective countries. Otherwise a potentially serious sampling

Table 10.2   Human Development in India, Malaysia, and Japan (c. 1997)

Development Indicators		India	Malaysia	Japan
Human Development Index				
Rank		132	56	4
Education				
% Literate	Male	67	90	99
	Female	39	81	99
% enrolled in secondary education		60	64	100
% GNP spent on education		3.4	5.2	3.6
Health				
Years life expectancy at birth		63	72	80
Infant mortality per 1,000 live births		71	10	4
Maternal mortality per 100,000 live births		570	80	18
Doctors per 100,000 population		48	43	641
% GDP spent on health		0.7	1.3	5.6
Economy				
Real GDP per capita (PPP$)		1,670	8,140	24,070
GNP % annual growth rate (1975-95)		5.0	7.1	3.5
% of GDP	Agriculture	25	12	2
	Industry	30	47	38
	Services	45	41	60
Dependency ratio (%)		65	65	45
Carbon dioxide emissions per capita (metric tons)		1.1	5.8	9.3
Polity				
% voting in last election		62	72	59
Year women received right to vote		1950	1957	1947
% seats in parliament held by women		8.3	10.3	8.9
Science and Technology				
Commercial energy use per capita (kilos oil equiv.)		380	1,950	4,058
R&D scientists and technicians per 1,000 population		0.3	0.2	7.1
Personal computers per 1,000 population		2	46	202
Internet hosts per 10,000 population (Jan/99)		0.13	21.36	133.53

Sources: United Nations Development Programme 1999; World Bank 2000.

bias could result, in that only Western-oriented, English speaking, indigenous NGOs would be surveyed. Consequently, a co-investigator in each country has agreed to supervise questionnaire translation and to provide local endorsement and support.

Minimal criteria for the inclusion of development-oriented, indigenous NGOs in the study are as follows:

1. NGOs must be "member-serving grassroots organizations (GROs) based in local communities, ... [or] nationally ... based development assistance organizations called grassroots support organizations (GRSOs)" (Fisher, 1998).

2. NGOs must be concerned with development as specified in Table 10.1.

3. NGOs must have used the Internet (e-mail at a minimum) for at least one year prior to being surveyed.

There are no comprehensive listings of NGOs, which precludes a random sample. Instead, a purposive availability sample of indigenous NGOs based on the five dimensions of development identified in Table 10.1 will be selected from Internet sites concerned with development (e.g., Action Without Borders, Canadian International Development Agency, NGO Net, Pan Asia Network, Society for International Development, Sustainable Development Gateway, Third World Network, and Virtual Library on International Development) and Internet search engines. Co-investigators will also aid in compilation of indigenous NGO directories. Only NGOs with e-mail addresses will be eligible for inclusion: the actual survey will be conducted either by e-mail or fax machine.

HYPOTHETICAL DEVELOPMENT OUTCOMES

This research design permits speculation as to which of the above four development scenarios is most applicable to each of the countries surveyed.

March of Follies

The evidence for this outcome would consist of similar 'before' and 'after' treatment and benign neglect of local NGOs by international agencies, manifest reluctance on the part of national governments to establish viable information and communications infrastructures, and as a consequence, few 'before' and 'after' differences in the achievement of development objectives by indigenous NGOs. In addition, relatively few NGOs, especially in rural areas, would have access to the Internet to pursue their organizational mission.

Cargo Cult

Demonstration of this scenario would be provided by greater affiliation of indigenous NGOs with their international counterparts (and, correspondingly, less local autonomy) and more one-way international-national interaction (much of it in English). Access to the Internet would be provided largely by foreign Western enterprises according to terms specified by them. In turn, indigenous NGOs would reorient their development objectives more toward those suggested by (Western) international agencies.

Netblocs

Attenuated relations with global development agencies would manifest documentation for this scenario. Support for national ICT infrastructural development would come about through strategic cultural (e.g., linguistic and religious) alliances and networks with other countries. Indigenous NGOs, electronically linked with other like-minded NGOs, would pursue development objectives according to their own distinctive cultural values and traditions.

Networld

Empirical support for this development outcome would be provided by a more equitable partnership of indigenous and global development agencies. As the President of the World Bank (Wolfensohn, 1997) noted in an annual meeting of the Bank, this represents a *Challenge of Inclusion* in which developing countries would be more involved in designing and implementing their own development objectives. As a result of enhanced North-South cooperation and increased access to social and technical information available through the Internet, national governments would be generally supportive of establishing interconnecting infrastructures for development purposes. Indigenous NGOs would show marked improvement in the achievement of their development goals.

The proposed research design is presented below in abbreviated form.

NGO exposure to Internet ➤➤➤➤ NGO achievement of development goals (within the context of the global ICT environment & national responses to it)

Controlling on level of national development (India, Malaysia, Japan)

The relationships found above will be affected by which of the four development scenarios is dominant as a result of the global ICT revolution (see Table 10.3).

Table 10.3   Hypothetical development outcomes

| | *Impact of Information and Communications Technology on:* | | |
Scenario	Global Environment	National Response	NGO Goal Achievement
March of Follies	Benign neglect of developing countries	Low level of support	Little or no improvement
Cargo Cult	Western dominated	Usurped by foreign infrastructure	Westernization of development goals
Netbloc	Fractured along cultural lines	Based on cultural alliances	Reoriented toward indigenous cultural values
Networld	Inclusive, enabling cooperation	Proactive support	Marked improvement

CONCLUSION

The results of this research will only be suggestive, as I am examining NGOs in just three countries. However, given the very substantial differences among these countries, if the same scenario is apparent in each, it should be indicative of larger trends, both globally and nationally. Should the results reveal either a closed and restrictive global environment, or reactive and disengaged national responses, they would signal a call for immediate action. As Nobel laureate Herbert Simon has observed:

> *Technological revolutions are not something that 'happen' to us. We make them, and we make them for better or for worse. Our task is not to peer into the future to see what computers will bring us, but to shape the future we want to have—a future that will create new possibilities for human learning, including, perhaps most important of all, new possibilities for learning to understand ourselves* (Simon, 1987:11).

REFERENCES

Babbie, E. (1998). *The practice of social research*. Belmont, CA: Wadsworth.

Brown, F.B., and Brown, Y. (1994). Distance education around the world. In B. Willis (Ed.), *Distance education: Strategies and tools* (pp. 3-39). Englewood Cliffs, NJ: Educational Technology Publications.

Fisher, J. (1998). *Nongovernments: NGOs and the political development of the Third World*. West Hartford, CT: Kumarian.

Hedley, R.A. (1992). *Making a living: Technology and change*. New York: HarperCollins.

Hedley, R.A. (1999). The information age: Apartheid, cultural imperialism, or global village? *Social Science Computer Review*, 17(1), 78-87.

Howkins, J., and Valantin, R. (Eds.) (1997). *Development and the information age: Four global scenarios for the future of information and communication technology*. Ottawa, ON: IDRC. Accessed on the Internet 9 July, 1999 at *http://www.idrc.ca/books/835/index.html*.

Network Wizards (1999). Internet Domain Survey, January 1999. Accessed on the Internet 27 May, 1999 at *http://www.nw.com/*.

OECD (1997). *Information technology outlook: 1997*. Paris: Organization for Economic Co-operation and Development.

Simon, H.A. (1987). The steam engine and the computer: What makes technology revolutionary? *Computers and People*, 36(11-12), 7-11.

Stavrianos, L.S. (1981). *Global rift: The Third World comes of age*. New York: William Morrow.

United Nations Development Programme (1999). *Human development report*. New York: Oxford University Press.

Wolfensohn, J.D. (1997). *The challenge of inclusion*. Address to the Board of Governors, Hong Kong, China.

World Bank (2000). *World development report 1999/2000*. Oxford: Oxford University Press

The Government's Strategy for Retaining Confidence in Its Exchange Rate: A Game-theoretic Analysis

Shan-non Chin

Associate Professor, Institute of Economics, National Sun Yat-sen University

Recent years have seen growing interest in the causes of speculative pressures on currencies, stimulated by the attack on the exchange rate mechanism of the European Monetary System in September 1992 and by the devaluation and float of the Mexican peso in December 1994. More recently, currency crises occurred in East Asia in 1997. Now, with the benefit of hindsight, it is time to discover what caused the currency depreciation in East Asia? How might macroeconomic policies lead to speculative pressures on a currency? What are the appropriate policy responses? What should we do to prevent another financial crisis—or in the event of another one, what should we do to minimize it? This chapter attempts to provide some perspective on these questions by using a simple game-theoretic analysis on the government's strategy versus the speculators' attack.

FINANCIAL CRISES AND CURRENCY SPECULATION

Beginning in the second half of the 1980s, rapid economic growth was accompanied by sharp increases in stock and land prices. East Asians borrowed against their increased wealth, in some cases rapidly increasing short-term borrowing from abroad. The boom lasted until the mid-1990s, when a series of external shocks—greater competition from China, depreciation of the Japanese yen, and a sharp decline in semiconductor prices—hurt East Asian export revenues, causing slower economic growth and falling asset prices.

In some Asian economies, these events were accompanied by a growing weakness in the financial sector that ultimately triggered a collapse of currencies, starting with Thailand in July 1997. The events in Thailand prompted investors to reassess and test the robustness of currency pegs and financial systems in the region. The result was a wave of currency depreciations (20%-80%) and stock market declines (50% or higher), first affecting Southeast Asia, and then spreading to the rest of the region (Moreno 1998).

Interest in speculative pressures has recently been heightened by concern about the possible reversal of the vast foreign capital inflows that a number of Asian economies have experienced in the last decade. International economists offer at least two general explanations for why an exchange rate may be subject to speculative pressures. First, macroeconomic policies may be inconsistent with a government's exchange rate target; second, even when macroeconomic policies are consistent with an exchange rate peg, the beliefs of speculators or adverse economic conditions may affect the willingness of a government to defend a peg, so that expectations of a currency realignment take on the characteristics of self-fulfilling prophecies; this explanation is offered by Obstfeld (1994) among others.

How might macroeconomic policies lead to speculative pressures on a currency? Suppose there is a country called Latinia, whose currency, the peso, is pegged to the US dollar.[1] Now suppose that Latinia constantly runs budget deficits and that the government pressures the central bank to help finance them. In that case, the central bank expands domestic credit, which creates money for the government to pay its bills, which pumps more pesos into the economy. The excess supply of pesos leads to a depreciation in the peso's value, because people will want to dump pesos from their portfolios and switch to foreign currency instead.

To defend the peso's value and the peg to the dollar, the central bank has to do an about-face: instead of pumping pesos into the economy, it has to take them out of the economy. It does this by buying them with its foreign currency reserves. The peso can be defended only so long as the central bank has foreign currency reserves. Once these are depleted, the peso can no longer be defended.

Currency crises often provoke hysterical reactions in governments. One day your country's economy is humming along nicely, your bonds are triple-A, you have billions of dollars in foreign exchange reserves socked away. Then all of a sudden the reserves are depleted, nobody will buy your paper, and you can only keep money in the country by raising interest rates to recession-inducing levels. How can things go wrong so fast?

Crisis is simply the market's way of telling a government that its policies aren't sustainable.

Imagine a government that is trying to support the dollar value of the ringgit through foreign exchange market "intervention," which basically means selling dollars to keep the ringgit price down. And suppose the government's policies are, for whatever reason, inconsistent with keeping the exchange rate fixed forever.

Speculators will not wait for events to take their course: at some critical moment they will all move in at once, and billions of dollars in reserves may vanish in days, even hours. The abruptness of a currency crisis, then, does not mean that it strikes out of a clear blue sky. In the standard economic model, the real villain is the inconsistency of the government's own policies (Krugman, 1997).

Krugman's analysis shows that in a case like Latinia's, the collapse of the peg will be sudden, as forward-looking speculators who observe the gradual depletion of reserves will attack the peso before reserves are exhausted. At the time of the collapse, Krugman's model predicts that the central bank will be forced to use up all its foreign exchange reserves in a futile attempt to defend the peg. Latinia's example thus illustrates how fiscal deficits tend to produce imbalances in the money market and in the balance payments that are ultimately inconsistent with a pegged exchange rate.

A number of observers point out that the preceding explanation does not seem to describe a couple of recent cases of speculative pressure. For example, in 1992-1993, some European countries faced speculative pressures on their exchange rates pegs to the deutschmark. However at that time, these countries had ample foreign exchange reserves and in some cases at least, such as France, their macroeconomic policies were not obviously inconsistent with the stability of their currencies against the deutschmark. Similarly, after the collapse of the Thailand baht peg in July 1997, the currencies of Hong Kong and other countries were under speculative pressures, despite the fact that they had ample foreign exchange reserves and conservative macroeconomic policies.

These differences have prompted some economists to consider explanations in which the beliefs of speculators may affect the government's incentive to defend or abandon a currency peg, leading to self-fulfilling currency crises (see Obstfeld, 1994). For example, consider another country, Islandia, with a fixed exchange rate and conservative monetary and fiscal policies. Wages there are relatively inflexible, so that the government can increase competitiveness and (temporarily) reduce unemployment by devaluing the currency. (If wages were completely flexible, they would rise immediately in response to the devaluation, and the devaluation would have no effect on employment.) However, the government must weigh the short-term benefits of a devaluation against the higher prices that would result in the long run, which would impose political costs and possibly a loss of the government's credibility as an inflation fighter.

Islandia's government will maintain a stable exchange rate indefinitely, so long as it estimates that the benefits of devaluing are smaller than the costs. However, shifts in market expectations can alter the government's calculations, resulting in a devaluation. For example, if the market for some reason believes that the government intends to devalue the exchange rate, market participants would expect higher inflation to ensue. This would prompt workers to demand higher wages, which would reduce the competitiveness of the economy and increase unemployment. Faced with a rise in unemployment, the government may in fact devalue. Thus, a shift in expectations can lead to an exchange rate crisis and devaluation that otherwise might not have occurred. In this scenario, the shift in expectations may have nothing to do with the soundness of domestic economic policy or other market fundamentals, but may reflect arbitrary and unpredictable factors.

For one thing, markets aren't always cool, calm, and collected. There is abundant evidence that financial markets are subject to occasional bouts of what is known as "herding": everyone sells simply because everyone else is selling. This may happen because individual investors are irrational. It may also happen because fund managers, who control so much of the world's money, will not be blamed if they do what everyone else is doing. One consequence of herding, however, is that a country's currency may be subjected to an unjustified selling frenzy.

It is also true that the long-term sustainability of a country's policies is to some extent a matter of opinion, and that policies that might have worked, given time, may be abandoned in the face of market pressures, which leads to the possibility of self-fulfilling prophecies.

These situations, in turn, create a possible way for private investors with big enough resources to play a nefarious financial game. Here's how it would work, in theory: suppose that a country's currency is in a somewhat ambiguous situation—its current value might be sustainable, or it might not. A big investor quietly takes a short position in that country's currency; that is, he borrows money in pounds, or baht, or ringgits, and invests the money in some other country. Once he has a big enough position, he begins ostentatiously selling the target currency, gives interviews to the *Financial Times* about how he thinks it is vulnerable, and so on. With luck he provokes a run on the currency by other investors, forcing a devaluation that immediately reduces the value of those carefully acquired debts, but not the value of the matching assets, leaving him hundreds of millions of dollars richer.

POLICY RESPONSES TO ASIA'S CRISES

The statistical analysis reveals that episodes of depreciation in East Asia are more associated with larger budget deficits and growth in central bank domestic credit than are episodes of appreciation or periods of tranquility (Moreno, 1998). This is broadly consistent with speculative pressure arising because macroeconomic policies are not consistent with an exchange rate peg. An empirical analysis of episodes of speculative pressure in East Asia suggests that policies designed to prevent imbalances in the balance of payments and money markets may help deter speculation against currencies in the region.

In addition, policymakers in the rest of the Asia region must take into account how business cycle fluctuations or other events may affect market perceptions of the government's ability and willingness to preserve a stable exchange rate. Changes in such perceptions can be very sudden and may require costly adjustments to maintain exchange rate stability.

Here is one way in which a loss of confidence turned into self-reinforcing panic. In 1996, capital was flowing into emerging Asia at the rate of about

$100 billion US a year; by the second half of 1997 it was flowing out at approximately the same rate. Inevitably, with that kind of reversal Asia's asset markets plunged, its economies went into recession, and things only got worse from there.

A loss of confidence by foreign investors can be self-justifying, because capital flight leads to a plunge in the currency, and the balance-sheet effects of this plunge lead to a collapse in domestic investment.

Policy Responses to Currency Speculation
Resulting From Inconsistent Macroeconomic Policies

Observers agree that the key to overcoming East Asia's crises is to restore voluntary financial flows and investment spending to stimulate investor confidence and spending by (i) stabilizing the external payments position of East Asian economies, and (ii) restoring credit flows.

The external payments situation has been stabilized through large IMF-led aid programs (totalling $118 billion for the most affected East Asian economies), the rescheduling of short-term foreign debt, and reductions in foreign borrowing through painful reversals of current account deficits. For example, in South Korea foreign reserves were nearly depleted at the end of 1997. Adjustment efforts strengthened the balance of payments position to such a degree that by the second quarter of 1998 the South Korean won began appreciating, to the discomfort of South Korean exporters.

In practice, efforts at crisis management to restore credit flows seem to have involved at least three types of action.

(i)   IMF financial support

The IMF, together with whatever other sources of funds can be mobilized, provides the troubled country with a credit line. It provides the country with additional funds to intervene in the exchange market—more dollars to support the baht, won, whatever. Leaving aside monetary policy (treated below), this is a sterilized intervention; so it is an attempt to use sterilized intervention to move the exchange rate away from the crisis equilibrium.

The financial rescue packages put together in response to crises in the 1990s are very large by historical standards, and they helped end instability in currency markets relatively quickly. For example, the rescue package for Korea in the last quarter of 1997 totaled $58.4 billion (the IMF share was $21.1 billion), and an additional $22 billion in short-term debt (about 36% of the total short-term debt) was almost immediately rescheduled. While the package did not prevent a painful economic contraction, it stabilized Korea's exchange rate a few months after the crisis broke out and set the stage for the recovery in the Korean economy in 1999.

Large money packages can prevent or end panics in the short run.

(ii)   Fiscal and monetary policies

The government does something—expansionary or contractionary—with its budget or performs a temporary sharp tightening of monetary policy.

(iii)   Structural reform:

When the crisis occurs, the government is urged to announce and implement major structural reforms such as privatization, cleanup of bad banks, etc. Of course, the best answer would be not to get into a crisis in the first place.

Policy Responses to Currency Speculation Resulting From Self-fulfilling Expectations

In fact, there are two very effective ways to prevent runs on currency. One—call it the "benign neglect" strategy—is simply to deny speculators a fixed target. The other—call it the "Caesar's wife" strategy—is to make very sure that the commitment to a particular exchange rate is credible.

(i)   The "benign neglect" strategy

Speculators can't make an easy profit betting against the US dollar, because the US government doesn't try to defend any particular exchange rate—which means that any obvious downside risk is already reflected in the price, and on any given day the dollar is as likely to go up as down.

Australia, in case you didn't know, is the miracle economy of the world financial crisis. Australia has managed to ride out the storm so far without even a serious slowdown. The key to this resilience has been a policy of benign neglect toward the exchange rate: instead of raising interest rates to defend the Aussie dollar, the central bank allowed the currency to slide, from almost 80 US cents in early 1997 to the low 60s by the summer of 1998. As a result, the currency stabilized itself instead of going into free fall.

(ii)   The "Caesar's wife" strategy

The importance of expectations in determining the timing and success of speculation against a currency suggests that a reputation for "toughness" may help policymakers deter such speculation and preserve a peg. Nobody attacks the guilder, because the Dutch clearly have both the capability and the intention of keeping it pegged to the German mark.

What if the exchange rate was completely credible? Suppose that everyone knows that a government will not, under any circumstances, allow the kind of currency depreciation that would lead to a circular process of depreciation and balance-sheet collapse. Then the market will not come to expect the depreciation in the first place, and the crisis will not get started. A truly credible commitment to a fixed exchange rate, in other words, can prevent Asian-type financial crises.

(iii)   The "Exchange Control" strategy

There is also a third option; you can erect elaborate regulations to keep people from moving money out of your country. The term is "exchange controls." Exchange controls used to be the standard response of countries with balance-of-payment crises. The details varied, but usually they worked something like this: exporters were required to sell their foreign-currency earnings to the government at a fixed exchange rate; that currency would in turn be sold at the same rate for approved payments to foreigners, basically for imports and debt service. While some countries tried to make other foreign-exchange transactions illegal, others allowed a parallel market. Either way, once the system was in place, a country didn't have to worry that cutting interest rates would cause the currency to plunge. Maybe the parallel exchange rate would sink, but that wouldn't affect the prices of imports or the balance sheets of companies and banks. This is the obvious alternative to the current wait-and-hope strategy. These controls would allow Asian nations to keep their currencies steady, giving them the breathing room to cut interest rates and get moving again.

Krugman has called for the imposition of capital controls, a step adopted by Malaysia. Under the new rules, central bank approval is needed to convert Malaysian ringgit into foreign exchange, and transactions involving foreign currency or foreign residents are generally restricted. (The government still permits (i) general convertibility of current account transactions, (ii) free flows of direct foreign investment, and (iii) repatriation of interest, profits, and dividends and capital.) This prevents the sudden outflow of capital even if Malaysian interest rates fall below world interest rates. The Malaysian ringgit has been fixed at 3.80 to the US dollar, and the government has adopted a number of stimulating measures.

GAME ANALYSIS

Game theory is concerned with the actions of those decision-makers who are conscious that their actions affect others (Rasmusen, 1989). In the above discussion, besides consistent macroeconomic policies, government has at least three effective strategies to affect the perceptions of the speculators in an attempt to stabilize its currency. In this section, the chapter will try to model these three strategies and the incredible exchange rate strategy as a game and see how they work and how they differ.

The general currency speculation model can be constructed as follows. This is a simultaneous-moves game: all players know that speculative pressures on currencies happen by the possible reversal of the vast foreign capital inflows in Asian economies, and the players do not have a chance to learn others' private information by observing each other. This is also a one-shot game because opportunities like the one George Soros discovered in 1992 are rare, and the game will end in just one period.

Players:

The players are MalayMaha (government officer) and Gesoros (speculator).

Strategies:

Simultaneously, forward-looking speculators will attack the currency until they encounter a big loss or win big money. So the strategy set for speculations is (Attack, Exit). On the other hand, the central bank will try to defend the value of the currency by using one of the above strategies. So the strategy set for the central bank is (Defend, Devalue, Market).

Payoffs:

If the currency depreciates or collapses after the attack, the speculator wins big money (payoffs = 10); otherwise s/he loses her/his interest rate payments (payoffs = -1or –0.5 (depending on if s/he attacks or exits quickly). However, if the exchange rate varies with market conditions, the speculator won't get anything (so payoffs = -1). To preserve a peg, the central bank has to use foreign currency reserves to buy the currency (payoffs = -1 or –0.5). If it lets the market go either way, it costs nothing (payoffs = 0). However, if the government can't (or is unwilling to) defend its currency, the economy might have some negative effects or even lose big money (payoffs = -1 or –10).

Payoffs for both players might vary as the MalayMaha (the central bank's top officer) uses different strategies (see the following tables). The equilibrium strategies are those the players pick in trying to maximize their individual payoffs, as distinct from the many possible strategy profiles obtainable by arbitrarily choosing one strategy per player. These equilibrium outcomes depend on the strategies and payoffs, so there might be different equilibrium strategy profiles in the model.

The next three games (Tables 11.1 to 11.3) illustrate three different strategies that might be used to retain confidence in the exchange rate, so both players will use only that pure strategy. However, the fourth game (Table 11.4) represents a situation in which a country's stable exchange rate policies may be abandoned in the face of market pressures, leading to the possibility of self-fulfilling prophecies and mixed strategies.

Table 11.1   Currency speculation model (1): Benign neglect strategy (pure)

		Gesoros	
		Attack	Exit
MalayMaha	Defend	-1,-1	-0.5,-0.5
	Market	0,-1	0,-0.5

Payoffs to: (MalayMaha, Gesoros)

In the first game (see Table 11.1), MalayMaha uses the benign neglect strategy Market; this leads to the strategy profile (Market, Exit) as a Nash Equilibrium.

Table 11.2   Currency speculation model (2): Caesar's wife strategy (pure)

		Gesoros	
		Attack	Exit
MalayMaha	Defend	-1,-1	-0.5,0
	Devalue	-10,10	-1,-0.5

Payoffs to: (MalayMaha, Gesoros)

In the currency speculation model (2) (in Table 11.2), MalayMaha uses the Caesar's wife strategy to defend the currency peg and the Nash Equilibrium becomes (Defend, Exit).

Table 11.3   Currency speculation model (3): Capital control strategy (pure)

		Gesoros	
		Attack	Exit
MalayMaha	Defend	-1,-1	-0.5,-0.5
	Devalue	-1,-1	-1,-0.5

Payoffs to: (MalayMaha, Gesoros)

If a country's central bank uses a capital control strategy to defend its currency peg (Table 11.3), the currency speculation model (3) shows that the Nash Equilibrium will be (Defend, Exit). Therefore, in equilibrium, all the above three strategies will result in the speculators quickly running away from the attack giving a more stabilized exchange rate.

Table 11.4   Currency speculation model (4): Incredible exchange rate situation (pure and mixed)

		Gesoros	
		Attack (γ)	Exit ($1-\gamma$)
MalayMaha	Defend (θ)	-11,-2	-0.5,-0.5
	Devalue ($1-\theta$)	-10,-10	-1,-0.5

Payoffs to: (MalayMaha, Gesoros)

If a country's currency is in a somewhat ambiguous situation, that is, its current value might or might not be sustainable, then the expectations of the payoffs with defence for MalayMaha will be a more negative value (-11 here) than in the other cases. So we have two pure Nash Equilibrium solutions and one possible mixed-strategy Equilibrium. The two pure Nash Equilibriums are (Defend, Exit) and (Devalue, Attack). This shows that an attack on the currency will be the best strategy for speculators, if the country cannot commit to a particular exchange rate. A mixed strategy equilibrium can be obtained by using the payoff-equating method if MalayMaha plays defend with probability θ, and Gesoros plays attack with probability γ.

Since the payoffs from each of MalayMaha's pure strategies must be equal in a mixed strategy equilibrium, it is true that

$$\prod MalayMaha(Defend) = -11\gamma - 0.5(1-\gamma)$$
$$= -10\gamma - (1-\gamma)$$
$$= \prod MalayMaha(Devalue)$$
$$\Rightarrow -10.5\gamma - 0.5 = -9\gamma - 1$$
$$\Rightarrow \gamma = \frac{1}{3}$$

From the same reasoning, we have

$$\prod Gesoros(Attack) = -2\theta + 10(1-\theta)$$
$$= -0.5\theta - 0.5(1-\theta)$$
$$= \prod Gesoros(Exit)$$
$$\Rightarrow -12\theta + 10 = -0.5$$
$$\Rightarrow \theta = \frac{7}{8}$$

In the mixed-strategy equilibrium, MalayMaha selects to defend 7/8 of the time, while Gesoros sticks in the attack position 1/3 of the time.

CONCLUSION

Although game theory analysis applied to a currency speculation model is quite different from the macroeconomic theory of the exchange rate, it comes up with the same argument. This is, first, speculative sharp practice can play a role in destabilizing currencies. That is, there is a sort of Murphy's Law in these things: if something can go wrong with a currency, it usually will.

Second, the three strategies (1) benign neglect strategy, (2) Caesar's wife strategy, and (3) capital control strategy that have been proposed by Krugman do help policy makers deter speculation against a currency and preserve a peg.

However, the simple one-shot simultaneous game we describe here may not fit well with the real economic world. A more complicated game structure formation, such as sequential (dynamic) games with symmetric (or asymmetric) information should be encouraged. A further empirical study using change in the value of some of the Asian countries' currencies can be used as a reference for this study.

REFERENCES

Drazen, A., and Masson, P.R. (1994). Credibility of policy versus credibility of policymakers. *Quarterly Journal of Economics, 3*, 735-754.

Krugman, P. (2000). I know what the hedges did last summer. *http://web.mit.edu/krugman/www/xfiles.html*.

Krugman, P. (2000). Analytical afterthoughts on the Asian crisis. *http://web.mit.edu/krugman/www/MINICRIS.htm*.

Krugman, P. (1998). Saving Asia: It's time to get radical. *Fortune* (September 7).

Krugman, P. (1997). Bahtulism: Who poisoned Asia's currency markets? *Slate* (August 14).

Krugman, P. (1979). A model of balance of payments crises. *Journal of Money, Credit and Banking, 11*, 311-325.

Moreno, R. (1999). Dealing with currency crises. *FRBSF Economic Letter*, 99-11.

Moreno, R. (1998). Responding to Asia's crises. *FRBSF Economic Letter*, 98-33.

Moreno, R. (1998). What caused East Asia's financial crisis? *FRBSF Economic Letter*, 98-24.

Moreno, R. (1996). Macroeconomic behavior during periods of speculative pressure or realignment: Evidence from Pacific Basin economies. *FRBSF Economic Review*, 1995, No. 3.

Moreno, R. (1996). Models of currency speculation: Implications and East Asian evidence. *FRBSF Economic Letter*, 96-13.

Obstfeld, M. (1994). The logic of currency crises. NBER Working Paper No. 4640.

Rasmusen, E. (1989). *Games and information*. Oxford: Basil Blackwell.

Rose, A. (1996). Are all devaluations alike? *FRBSF Weekly Letter*, 96-06.

ENDNOTES

[1] Moreno (1996) first presents this example in his paper called "Models of Currency Speculation: Implications and East Asian Evidence." *FRBSF Economic Letter*, 96-13.

The Presidential Election in Taiwan and Cross-Strait Relations[1]

Gerard S.H. Chow

Professor and Director, Institute of Mainland China Studies,
National Sun Yat-Sen University

INTRODUCTION

In the year 2000, the people of Taiwan elected Chen Shui-bian as their new president, a leader to take Taiwan into the new millennium. President Lee Teng-hui had completed a political reign that lasted more than 12 years, since he succeeded the late President Chiang Ching-kuo in 1987. In this election, the ruling nationalist party, the Kuomintang (KMT), faced its most difficult mission since the government transferred to Taiwan in 1949. The reason is simple: in May of 2000, the KMT's strong man, President Lee Teng-hui, stepped down and no one else in the KMT holds the same broad powers: it is almost sure that no KMT presidential candidate enjoys the same benefits as President Lee did in the election of 1996. Further, the opposition party, the Democratic Progress Party (DPP), had governed 13 cities and counties that encompass most of the largest rural and urban areas in Taiwan. The DPP controlled three metropolitan areas: Taipei county, and Taichung and Kaohsiung cities; only the city of Taipei remained in the hands of the KMT.

The presidential election was significant for both the ruling and opposition parties. For the former, the election meant defending the continuity of Taiwan's stability and governance: for the latter, the election meant a political rejuvenation and change of governance. On the one hand, there was no reason for the Taiwanese not to change their government; hence, the election offered an opportunity to the opposition parties. On the other hand, under the KMT's governance, Taiwan had enjoyed increased democratization as well as prosperity. Its GNP per capita in 1998 was over US $13,000 and roughly US $15,000 in 2001-2002. Thus, there was also strong reason for the Taiwanese to keep the present ruling party. The election offered a choice to defuse this dilemma for most people on the island.

During the election campaign, the opposition party successfully utilized a slogan on banners highlighting "Anti-Black (Mafia) and Money (Cash)," serious accusations because of the KMT's long-term governance in Taiwan.

Debates on domestic issues varied from pensions for the aged, defense spending, and health care, to budget reallocation for the central and local governments. Besides these domestic issues, there were, of course, external issues for campaign debates. It goes without saying that among these external issues, Taiwan-Mainland China relations should be another focal point for debate. Through the whole period of the presidential election campaign, it was obvious that the China factor played a rather important position that could not be ignored in any analysis of the winner and loser of the election.

This chapter does not examine the factors that helped Chen Shui-bian win the presidential election. It does, however, explore how Beijing's intervention was interpreted in the election. The chapter analyses cross-straits relations before and after the new president was elected.

CROSS-STRAIT POLICY AS CAMPAIGN STRATEGY

During a presidential campaign, it is very unusual for any country to consider the reactions from a neighboring country. Taiwan (ROC), however, is in fact such a country, being covered from the other side of the Taiwan straits by the tremendous shadow of Mainland China. In the 1996 presidential election, thanks to Beijing's threat to resort to force, KMT candidates Lee Teng-hui and Lien Chan won a landslide victory at the last minute, with 54% of the votes, an obvious majority. In 1996 the Taiwanese, for the first time ever in 5,000 years of Chinese history, chose their own president, a prospect seen as indicative of a pro-independent-Taiwan movement by the Chinese government. The Chinese People's Liberation Army (PLA) finally shot two missiles near Taiwan's two harbours, Keelung and Kaohsiung. However, even though China's intention was clear—the missile attack was a signal that the voters who might support Lee Teng-hui should change their minds—the Taiwanese gave the Chinese government a disappointing gift. The candidate that Beijing disliked the most was elected by the Taiwanese voters.

One might agree that it is possibly a myth that presidential elections in Taiwan cannot be fully independent and free until Beijing takes its hands off. In the election of 2000, political parties and independent candidates proposed five tickets. According to their campaign numbers, they were: (i) Soong-Chang, ticket No. 1—this number is generally named "King of the Lot," and is symbolically lucky; (ii) Lien-Shiew, ticket No. 2—this number, according to Lien, would mean victory; (iii) Lee-Fung, ticket No. 3—a presidential candidate supported by the New Party; (iv) Hsu-Chu, ticket No. 4—Hsu Hsin-lian, the ex-chairman of DPP, ran as an independent candidate; (v) Chen-Lu, ticket No. 5—supported by the DPP.

The Lien-Shiew ticket represented the ruling party. Lien Chan, a Chicago PhD was the vice-president, and his partner Shiew the premier. This ticket was generally regarded as having more resources, partially because the back-up party was the KMT, and partially because they were the highest administrative officials, and thus could mobilize more resources—such as manpower, capital, and media—than other candidates. Despite his low popularity, rated in public opinion polls with 20 to 25% support, Lien was considered to have the highest probability of winning the race, according to many surveys.

The weak area for Lien Chan was domestic issues. The KMT was accused of using the "black mafia" and of buying votes in past elections. Surveys even showed that some of the legislators with "black ground" involvement were KMT members. More surprisingly, at local county levels, there were reports that more than a third of council members had black records, and they were KMT members.

Although Lien Chan had weak points on the one hand, he also had superiority on the other. His strong point was his mainland policy, which was basically the legacy of Lee Teng-hui. During his presidential campaign, Lien's mainland policy could be divided into two stages: from July to the end of 1999, Lien insisted that his policy would follow Lee's "special state-to-state" principle.[2] However, he also highlighted a 10-point blueprint for cross-straits relations. In the second stage of the presidential campaign, roughly between January and March of 2000, Lien Chan proposed that the two sides go back to the 1992 principle—one China, respective-interpretation—a consensus of no consensus reached at the talks of the Straits Exchange Foundation (SEF, Taipei) and the Association for Relations Across the Taiwan Straits (ARATS, Beijing).

Lien's retreat from the "Two States Theories" was based on many reasons. Among these reasons, at least two need to be noted. On February 21, 2000, Beijing issued a White Paper entitled "One-China Principle and the Question of Taiwan," emphasizing Beijing's determination to achieve national unification, and setting its own preconditions for using military force if Taiwan should move toward independence. In order to calm tension across the straits, Lien urged the "one-China and respective-interpretation" consensus. His second reason is generally believed to be connected with his presidential campaign: even in the late stages of the campaign, Lien's popularity remained low compared with the popular support for James Soong and Chen Shui-bian. Although Lien wanted to hold support by tilting toward Lee's line, he also wanted to create support via his own political image. To do so, he initiated a little difference with Lee Teng-hui's mainland policy, particularly at a time when the Chinese government was maintaining a tough position toward Taiwan. Thus, Lien Chan retreated.

James Soong, a Berkeley and Georgetown Universities-trained PhD, was the ex-governor of Taiwan Province. His popularity was highest among the five tickets. During his 6 year tenure as governor, Soong was reportedly famous for being "diligent, hard-working and people-loving." Further, during his 6 years in Taiwan Province, he was able to make an excellent distribution of budget resources to the lower level of government. Many county magistrates and city mayors reportedly received generous cash allocations upon request.

At the very beginning of the election, James Soong scored 35 to 40% public support. His potential power to win the election fuelled a KMT split over who should be the right person to represent the ruling party. It is perhaps this split that gave the DPP a good chance to become the first ruling party at the onset of the new century. However, his high popularity did not ensure James Soong's final victory, as in the late period of the campaign, he became involved with the "Hsing-Bill" scandal. A KMT legislator, Yang Chi-Hsiung, revealed that Soong had transferred a million US dollars to the United States while holding his working posts. Since the scandal reached all corners of Taiwan, Soong's popularity dropped to 25 to 30%, with occasional lows of 20 to 22%.

Many analysts saw Soong, a former Nationalist heavyweight running as an independent candidate, as the one most likely to ease tension with Beijing. Mr. Soong was certainly keen to establish his credentials as a peacemaker. However, while Soong's background as a mainland-born immigrant could reassure China that he would seek eventual re-unification, it also meant that he had to fend off accusations that he might "sell out" Taiwan. Soong's vision for cross-strait reconciliation included such Beijing bugbears as involvement by the US and Japan, while it is unclear if his definition of relations as "quasi-international" will be much more welcome in China than Lien's "special state-to-state" principle.[3]

The Chen-Lu ticket, also nicknamed the "Water-Lotus" ticket, was generally regarded as the third potential winner. This combination was supported by the DPP, a Taiwanese party founded almost 10 years previously. The presidential candidate was a former Taipei city mayor, Chen Shui-bian. His partner was a Taoyuan county magistrate, Lu Shiu-lien, a feminist and strong lady. Chen was the defense lawyer in the "Formosa Incident," when Lu and other DPP members were accused of sedition and sentenced to prison.

The DPP's election strategy concentrated on domestic issues. Their main opponents were the pan-KMT candidates. The best strategy for DPP was to play "separated two" rather than "unified one." Attacking the KMT's weakest point, Chen Shui-bian stressed that black gangs and money politics must be cleaned out of Taiwan. In pursuing this policy, Chen Shui-bian's mainland policy seemed to be restricted; nevertheless, Chen had not quit this battlefield. He campaigned that cross-strait relations should be constructed as a "state-to-state special relationship."[4] Founded on the basis of equal statehood, the two sides could be strengthened by mutual cooperation. Chen Shui-bian even urged in his White Paper that direct sea landing between assigned harbours be taken into consideration.[5] He was even more open-minded, saying that if he were elected as president, he wanted to pay a visit to the mainland between March 18 and May 20, 2000 with his official title as President-elect.

China's response to Chen's policy was very negative. China had not had any contact with Chen Shui-bian in the past; confidence between Chen and the Chinese top leaders was almost zero. Further, Beijing calculated that there was little chance for Chen Shui-bian to win the election; Beijing could not perceive that a hundred-year-old party like the KMT could be defeated, and have to step down from Taiwan's political theatre. Therefore, Beijing did not pay too much attention to Chen's theory of "states' special relations," which was somewhat similar to President Lee's "special state-to-state relations." However, the reaction by the Chinese government to the two statements was quite different. Beijing seemed to close its eyes to Chen Shui-bian until March 2000, when he was perceived at last as having possible strength in the election. Beijing reacted very strongly, however, to President Lee Teng-hui when he was interviewed in July 1999 by the Voice of German Radio, and set out his "special state-to-state relations" policy. Beijing's reaction was one of hyper-emotional frustration, even involving the mobilization of military operations. Incidentally, the second half of 1999 saw a high tide in Taiwan's presidential election campaign, and as cross-strait relations were at a low point, tension was very high. Perhaps fortunately, Chen Shui-bian hid behind President Lee Teng-hui, so that his mainland policy attracted little assault from Beijing. Also, Chen probably benefited from his mainland policy, because most of Lee's supporters would accept Chen Shui-bian's stance, and would automatically switch their votes to favour Chen.

CHINA'S REACTION: THREATS AND BLUSTER

Beijing's reactions toward the presidential election in Taiwan can be divided into two phases, one before March 18, 2000, and the second after the election on that date.

Before March 18

The strongest position that Beijing ever took toward Taiwan's presidential election was expressed in the white paper issued on February 21, 2000, entitled "One-China Principle and the Question of Taiwan." In this paper, the Beijing government for the first time presented "three ifs" as preconditions for using force at China's discretion, clearly showing the insecure attitude of the Chinese government. By announcing the preconditions, Beijing tried to restructure and redefine the substance of cross-strait relations in a way that would be regulated unilaterally. China made it clear that, under the "three-ifs" preconditions, it would use all possible means, including force, to protect national sovereignty and territorial integrity and to accomplish Chinese reunification. The "three ifs" read as follows: (a) *if* Taiwan declared independence; (b) *if* Taiwan were invaded by foreign nations; (c) *if* the Taiwan authorities indefinitely delayed negotiations toward a peaceful resolution over the issue of unification.[6]

This tough Chinese bluff shocked the world media. Not only did the Taiwanese people show their anger, but world opinion did not favour Beijing's stance either. For example, on February 22, immediately following the release of Beijing's White Paper, the US government expressed deep concern over the

Chinese statement. In a press conference, government spokesman James Rubin said that the US rejected the use of force, or the threat of the use of force, as a way of resolving the Taiwan question. He warned that the Chinese formula was unhelpful and stressed, "we believe the threat of the use of force is counter-productive to creating an atmosphere for cross-strait talks to go forward."[7]

In Taiwan, the public generally believed the release of the white paper revealed the anxiety in China about the outcome of Taiwan's election,[8] and that China was indicating its concern that whoever won had best stick to the "one-China" principle. Zhu Bang Zao, the Chinese Foreign Ministry spokesperson, went even further by noting that the release of a new white paper on Taiwan policy was an indication that reunification had become urgent.[9]

The 11,000-character document issued by the State Council repeatedly stressed China's ambition for peaceful reunification, while emphasizing Beijing's intention to resort to "drastic measures, including military force" if its overtures were rejected. The document also included another diatribe against Lee Teng-hui, calling him a "saboteur" and a "troublemaker" who was leading Taiwan toward independence. In this regard, analysts had speculated that the white paper could be seen as another response to Lee's "special state-to-state relations" and Chen's "state-to-state special relations" positions.

The Taiwanese government's response to the white paper was cautious and rather low profile. The first response, on February 22, came from the Mainland Affairs Council (MAC), which issued a short statement entitled "How We View Beijing's White Paper" criticizing China's "Three Ifs." In this statement, the ROC government pointed out that: the two sides of the straits have been under separate jurisdictions, neither subject to the other; the PRC has never ruled Taiwan, Pescadores, Kinmen, and Matsu; and Beijing's statement in the white paper that "the ROC already reached its end in history in 1949 and the PRC undoubtedly owns and exercises sovereignty over China, including Taiwan" completely distorts the truth. Further, at the center of cross-strait relations stands the issue of political identity. Before the day of unification arrives, each side should be entitled to different interpretations on "One China." The consensus that "the definition of one China should be subject to respective interpretations" reached by the two sides in 1992 was a consensus circumventing the issue of political states.[10]

Four days later, on February 25, the MAC released an official response entitled "Statement on Mainland China's White Paper," which highlighted the following points:[11]

1. In April 1993, the Koo-Wang talks in Singapore reached four historical agreements on the basis of respecting the reality of separate rule across the straits, but later the PRC government released the so-called "Taiwan Question and China's Unification" White Paper in eight languages to the global community in August 1993. This paper tried to distort the basis of "negotiation on equal footing" and to place the cross-strait relations into the framework of "the principal and the subordinate."

2. It is quite obvious that Beijing intended to influence the ROC's presidential election. Judging from the contents of the white paper, the PRC unilaterally narrows the definition of "one China," trying to impose it on Taiwan, and meanwhile, over-expands the definition of "Taiwan Independence."

3. China is divided. If China is unified, why does the unification issue still exist? If China is one, why bother to mention "one China"?

4. Based on the "special state-to-state relationship," the ROC will negotiate with the PRC on parity conditions, and intensify exchanges.

5. Beijing has repeatedly escalated its military threat targeted at Taiwan, particularly at critical moments when the ROC implements democracy. This shows Beijing's refusal and fear of democracy on the one hand. There is a stark contrast between the two sides of the Straits: democracy and totalitarianism.

Less than three days prior to Taiwan's presidential election, Chinese Premier Zhu Rongji bluntly warned the island's voters against choosing a pro-independence leader, saying, "Let me advise all the people in Taiwan. Do not just act on impulse at this juncture, which will decide the future course that China and Taiwan will follow. Otherwise I'm afraid you won't get another opportunity to regret".[12] With a stern face, Zhu Rongji, in a press conference after the closure of the annual meeting of the National People's Congress, delivered the latest and loudest salvo in an increasingly bellicose rhetorical assault aimed at Taiwan.

Beijing's tough stance resulted in some developments that it seized upon as positive. These included Mr. Chen's more conciliatory statements on cross-strait relations, and the biggest one-day plunge in Taiwan stocks on that day in reaction to the enhanced chances of the pro-independence hopeful.[13] However, many people in Taiwan did not believe Zhu's intimidation would work to push the pro-Chen voters away. Some voters even thought to express their anger by picking the candidate Beijing disliked the most.

Vice-president Lien Chan of the ruling KMT made use of China's threat to prove his point that electing Chen Shui-bian meant choosing war with China. However, he did not carry this tactic too far lest he elicit an outpouring of disgust, which might translate into further support for the DPP. Independent candidate James Soong stressed that neither Lien nor Chen could eliminate the threat from China as Mr. Chen advocated independence, while Lien Chan supported the "two states theory," which Beijing loathes.[14]

After March 18

The Chinese reaction toward the victory of Chen Shui-bian was one of frustration and loss of face. Taiwan's democracy can no longer be dismissed so easily, and Beijing is nervous that people on the mainland may begin to ask, "what about us?" Beijing worries about the precedent that the people of Taiwan have set, because over decades, mainland officials have justified their tyrannical rule by dismissing Taiwan's democracy as a ruse. The KMT held power for 50 years, just as the CCP has held power for 50 years.[15] No wonder Beijing feels so threatened.

Generally speaking, there were varied reactions to Taiwan's presidential election. During an unofficial visit and interviews in China conducted by the author after the election,[16] I found that the Chinese government has toned down the bottom line of its policy. Academic scholars, including one close aide of Wang Dao-han, the chief negotiator and head of the Association for Relations across the Taiwan Straits (ARATS), have shown deep anxiety and worry. They are pessimistic regarding cross-strait relations. Actually, I found a creeping sense of panic, which might not be directly related to the election result; however Chen's victory obviously beat China's Taiwan policy. The Taiwanese elected the person the Chinese government disliked, a strong signal showing the people of Taiwan do not welcome Beijing's hegemony. This could be regarded as one reason that Chinese scholars found that the government policy toward Taiwan was in vain.

Furthermore, Chinese scholars even cast doubts on Chen's attitude toward China. Before Election Day, Chen Shui-bian was interviewed by *Time* magazine, and expressed his position on the issue of "state-to-state special relations." He highlighted three guarantees if he became president, saying, (a) "I absolutely would not put "state-to-state relations" in the constitution; (b) I would not propose a change in the name of the Republic of China; and (c) any change in the status quo would have to be agreed upon by the people in Taiwan."[17] Judging from Chen's low profile before and after the election, there is no reason for mainland scholars to worry too much about his consistency in words and deeds.[18]

However, scholars were worried about the evaporation of power and a creeping vacuum among moderate decision-makers. Due to the serious setbacks of 1996 and 2000, Beijing now faces the issue of how to formulate its Taiwan policy to head toward the goal of reunification. If no solution can be foreseen in the area of peaceful unification, many scholars would not exclude the possibility of using force if that is the way Chinese leaders are forced to go.

For the hardliners in China, Chen's victory was unacceptable. These people are the originators of potential conflicts across the Taiwan Straits. Having been informed that there is no need for any ruling party in Taiwan to provoke the Chinese government (and Taiwan would probably receive more advanced weapons from Washington) they were sternly setting their own bottom line for reunification. These groups warned that the Taiwanese people do have the right to choose their own leader, but the Beijing government also has the power to wage a war for unification. The right of waging a war is in the hands of Beijing.[19] If President Chen Shui-bian has any intention to separate Taiwan from Mainland China, Beijing will consider this action a "vital change," which it could apply as the first "if" laid down in the white paper.

Beijing has the sole power to define whether Taiwan is moving toward national disintegration, so it could immediately resort to the use of force without any warning. Once war is declared, Beijing would determine to destroy Taiwan completely for jeopardizing the nation's integration and sovereignty. Beijing would choose southern Taiwan as the first target, because the voters there most strongly supported Chen Shui-bian. Last but not least, people who work for the Chinese military-based think tank even bluster that the Chinese government is prepared to wage a war with the Americans if Washington duly intervenes.

This position reveals the Chinese fear of Taiwan's democracy, and also indicates that the US has played a key role in how, for better or for worse, the Beijing government would deal with Washington and Taipei. Although the Chinese government has toned down the "wait and see" policy, Beijing will never abandon intimidation by using the threat of force on the people of Taiwan.

THE US ROLE: CAUTIOUS AND PREVENTIVE DIPLOMACY

Although the American role in constructing and framing China and Taiwan into an interacting triangle relationship is clear, U.S. action is rather cautious. Soon after Taiwan's election, President Clinton sent two delegations to Taiwan and China, respectively. The representatives to Taiwan were Lee Hamilton, a former US Congressman, and Richard Bush, Chairman of the Washington-based American Institute in Taiwan (AIT). They were expected to meet the president-elect and to advise him not to undertake any moves that might irritate Beijing amid heightened cross-strait tensions.[20] There are no authorized reports on the talks between the US envoys and Chen Shui-bian; however, the president-elect responded to the media in Taiwan in a restrained and cautious manner.

The other delegation was led by American Ambassador to the United Nations Richard Holbrook, and Stanley Roth, the Assistant Secretary of the State Department. During their 2-day meeting, the US Ambassador testified that Beijing has taken a cautious attitude toward Taiwan. Beijing's new policy is obviously to wait and see, which is quite different than Zhu Rongji's tough position. Ambassador Holbrook had talks with President Jiang Zemin and Vice Premier Chian Chi-chen. He urged Beijing and Taipei to negotiate and repeated US support for Beijing's position that Taiwan and the Mainland China are part of "one China."[21] He also referred to talks with the Chinese top leaders, testifying that, "what is mildly encouraging is that everyone has reacted to the new circumstances with prudence and caution."[22]

High tensions across the Taiwan Straits were escalating, and needed to be reduced. In this regard, the preventive diplomacy of the US scored at least twice, first in July 1999 when the Chinese government threatened to use force against President Lee's "special state-to-state relations." Washington then successfully defused the potential conflict through diplomacy. The second success occurred in 2000 when the two delegations of envoys started mediation. The outcome of the US involvement could change, depending upon how the situation evolves. But certainly, the relationship between China and Taiwan has been controlled; the situation is fairly stable as far as future development is concerned.

Due to the immediate and effective involvement of Washington, a new triangular relationship among Taiwan, China, and the US could be restructured, and therefore the tensions across the Taiwan Straits could be limited. However, potential conflict across the Taiwan Straits still exists, if the Chinese government misjudges President Chen's intention, or the engagement policy of the US appears reactionary. Then the story might be totally different.

CONCLUSION

Newly elected President Chen Shui-bian should be cautious and prudent, *vis à vis* the Chinese "trap." Chen would receive more support from Washington if he displays prudence, and as a result his succession from Lee Teng-hui will be less difficult.

China is presently waiting to see what will happen in Taiwan. It is a policy possibly without any real action other than verbal rhetoric, but it does not mean that China's bluff carries no nationalism and patriotism. Divergent attitudes in China on Taiwan policy are pretty obvious. Those who work for the military and defense sectors are believed to have thought of using force for unification. Other groups, including academic professionals and businessmen, are believed to have a softer policy.

Having undertaken preventive diplomacy, the US government has proven that its indirect or direct engagement was valid and effective. The Chinese government has warned that Washington should not intervene in the Taiwan Straits. The exclusion of Washington from the triangular structure will be China's next step before Beijing takes any bold action toward Taiwan. The firmly structured triangular relationship has been functioning well. Taiwan, living with two giants, has to move toward self-defense rather than provocation. The last important question for the people of Taiwan perhaps is how to persuade the Chinese people what Taiwan and China mean politically!

ENDNOTES

[1] This chapter discusses the Presidential election of March 2000.

[2] Special State-to-State Principle, ROC Policy Document, the Mainland Affairs Council, August 1999.

[3] Taiwanese voters display desire for stability with mainland China, news and analysis, *Financial Times*, March 13, 2000.

[4] *China Policy, in New Century, New Exit—The National Blue Print of Chen Shui-bian*, Chen Shui-bian Presidential Campaign Center, November, 1999, pp.14-17.

[5] *Ibid.*, pp. 30-41.

[6] One-China Principle and the Question of Taiwan, New Chinese News Agency, Beijing, February, 21, 2000.

[7] James P. Rubin, Daily Press Briefing, US Department of State, February, 22, 2000.

[8] *Taipei Times*, February, 24, 2000.

[9] *Taipei Times*, February, 23, 2000.

[10] *How Taipei Views Beijing's White Paper*, Mainland Affairs Council, ROC, April 2000, p. 1.

[11] *Statement on Mainland China's White Paper*, Mainland Affairs Council, February, 25, 2000, pp. 2-3.

[12] Clay Chandler, China Threatens Voters in Taiwan, *Washington Post*, March 16, 2000.

[13] *Hong Kong Standard*, March 16, 2000.

[14] Ching Cheong, Chen May Benefit from Zhu's Warning, *The Straits Times*, March 17, 2000.

[15] Jesse Helms, Two Chinese States, *Washington Post*, March 31, 2000.

[16] The author of this paper visited and conducted interviews in China between 24 March and 2 April, 2000 to solicit opinions from universities, research units, and government officials.

[17] *Time*, March 6, 2000, p. 18.

[18] At the time of writing this paper, Chen Shui-bian urged the Chinese government that a permanent peace between China and Taiwan should be considered. He has shown the will to work out a cooperative strategy with the giant neighbour, which is at least not a provocative stance. Chen is also willing to discuss the issue of "one China." He proposed that "one China" should not be considered as a precondition for talks, but rather as an issue for talks. Further, the DPP has reconsidered the necessity of changing its long-standing position over the clause of "Taiwan Independence," which indicates moderation on the part of the ruling party.

[19] Interviewed opinion from a research fellow in Beijing who works for the Center for Peace and Development.

[20] Jason Blatt, *South China Morning Post*, March 23, 2000, p. 9.

[21] *Ibid.*

[22] *Ibid.*

Economic and Political Interplay Behind Taiwanese Capital Outflow into Mainland China

Jou-juo Chu

Associate Professor, Institute of Interdisciplinary Studies,
School of Social Sciences, National Sun Yat-sen University

INTRODUCTION

The promotion of overseas investment did not become government policy in Taiwan until 1984. Even then, although the government was aware of the maturation of its labour-intensive model of economic development, and the importance of encouraging local enterprises to invest overseas, it took no full-scale action until 2 years later, with the launching of the Caribbean Investment Project. In 1986 capital outflow for the first time exceeded US $50 million. After 1987, the relaxation of foreign exchange controls, the appreciation of the New Taiwan dollar, growing protectionism in US markets, along with the rise of active unionism, environmental consciousness, increased wages and tight labour supply, drove Taiwan's overseas investments up to US $16 billion. From 1986 to 1991, all outward investments from Taiwan, both registered and non-registered, amounted to US $19 billion (Liu, 1993). Approved offshore investments accounted for US $4.52 billion. Of that 43% went to Asian countries, 33% to the US, and 16% to Europe. These figures had yet to include a majority of small- and medium-sized firms that invested in Southeast Asia. According to statistics provided by Southeast Asian governments, Taiwanese investments exceeded US $12 billion, of which 41% was concentrated in Malaysia, 28% in Thailand, and 23% in Indonesia. These extraordinary figures made Taiwan the ninth largest supplier of foreign investment capital in the world.

Although a few large Taiwanese enterprises had invested heavily in the US, the massive outflow of post-1980 Taiwanese capital to Southeast Asian countries mainly came from small- and medium-sized businesses. While Taiwan was suffering a degradation of its domestic investment climate, Thailand, Malaysia, the Philippines, and Indonesia were formulating various incentives to attract Taiwanese capital in an effort to achieve economic prosperity and improve their employment opportunities. In response, the Taiwanese government designated 1989 as the "Action Year for the Development of Trade with Southeast Asia." Taiwanese investments in Southeast Asia were concentrated primarily in labour-intensive industries such as electronics and electrical appliances, textiles, chemicals, basic metals, and metal products.

Although the deteriorating domestic investment environment worked as a push-out factor for Taiwanese capital, there were some draw-in factors in Southeast Asia as well. First, Southeast Asia's low production costs appealed to Taiwanese investors: the cheap labour helped many Taiwanese companies win back original-equipment-manufacturing (OEM) orders from their competitors in, for example, the calculator industry, in which output surged from 58 million units in 1989 to 70 million units in 1990 (Liu, 1993). The second reason for investing in Southeast Asia was that products manufactured there enjoyed Preferential Tariff Treatment (PTT) in the US. Taiwan had been excluded from access to the Generalized System of Preference (GSP) in 1989, so it not only could not enjoy the export quota privileges, but all made-in-Taiwan products faced tariffs of up to 21 to 25% in the US market. To take advantage of GSP and quota privileges given by the US, most of Taiwan's textile producers had expanded into Southeast Asia, including Far Eastern and Carnival in the Philippines, Tab Tong in Indonesia, the Hualon Group in Malaysia, and Tuntex in Thailand. Taiwan's three largest pulp and paper companies also set up mills in Indonesia, Thailand, and Vietnam, while electronics companies such as Chung Hwa Picture Tube, Acer, and Teco Electric had factories in Malaysia (Chin, 1992).

The third reason for investment in Southeast Asia was the unexpected increase in demand for materials, components, and machinery parts from Taiwan. While the growth rate of Taiwan's exports dropped to 2.9% in 1990, its shipments to Malaysia, Indonesia, and Thailand shot up at the rates of 59%, 31%, and 29% respectively (Liu, 1993). In addition, Southeast Asia had an ethnic Chinese population as large as 20 million, a cultural and ethnic affinity that might influence Taiwanese enterprises deciding where to relocate factories or to start new ventures.

This massive outflow of capital to Southeast Asia seemed to spawn an ambition to create a Taiwanese economic empire. To some extent, this intention changed the relationship between the state and the private sector, with significant repercussions. First, out of this economic strength a genuine sense of nationhood gradually materialized, which led to the restoration of lost diplomatic relations Taiwan had once had under the name Republic of China. Secondly, the pressure to stay prosperous and competitive pushed Taiwanese firms to seek new exploitable territories. When Taiwanese capital first started moving to Thailand and Malaysia, the wage rates there were one fifth of those in Taiwan. However, as these economies prospered, wage rates increased rapidly. In these circumstances, China, along with Vietnam, appeared as a better area for investment. In spite of the protracted political confrontation between Taiwan and China and Taiwanese distrust of the Chinese Communist regime, the pressure to remain competitive in export markets did not permit hesitation on the part of Taiwanese businesses.

TAIWAN'S CAPITAL OUTFLOW TO MAINLAND CHINA

In 1987, the Taiwanese government lifted the ban on family visits to relatives in Mainland China, which also provided the opportunity to probe the investment environment there. In that same year, Taiwan opened indirect trade with Mainland China, resulting in a total trade value of US $1.7 billion. The growth was particularly spectacular after 1989. Taking advantage of economic sanctions against China initiated by the US and European countries because of the Chinese crackdown on the democratic movement, Taiwanese firms effectively filled the vacuum. Cross-strait trade increased 28% in 1989: in 1991, shipments to the mainland by way of Hong Kong jumped 42% to US $4.66 billion. Moreover, in the first 8 months of 1992, total indirect exports to the mainland rose another 38% to US $3.9 billion. In addition, it was reported that by the end of 1991, the total of Taiwanese investments was US $3 billion. A Japanese source estimated that more than US $15 billion of Taiwanese capital entered Mainland China via Hong Kong from 1987 to 1991. However, in only the first 4 months of 1992, the Ministry of Economic Affairs received a total of 2,582 registration cases for mainland investment, worth US $837 million.

Generally speaking, two waves of Taiwanese capital outflow to the Chinese mainland have developed. The first wave of Taiwanese companies that swarmed into Mainland China started in 1988 and was comprised mostly of export-oriented, small- and medium-sized family businesses. The majority of their investments were concentrated in manufactured goods such as bicycles, footwear, plastic products, metal products, and electrical appliances. One important organizational characteristic associated with these kinds of businesses was common ownership and management, which required that the business owners participate directly in the organization of the production process. Therefore, "a common medium of communication and a shared system of meaning and values between owners, workers, and potential business clients became an important consideration in selection of location" (Chu, 1999: 174).

For this reason, when these family-owned small- and medium-sized firms were forced to internationalize, they chose to invest in a familiar environment, which resulted in cross-border expansion. This can also explain why the often-mentioned determinants for this rapid growth in cross-strait trade always include geographic proximity, linguistic and cultural similarities, the massive domestic market, and the lower costs of land and labour on the Chinese mainland. Another distinctive characteristic of Taiwan's export-oriented labour-intensive industrial structure was located in an extensive, dense net of sub-contract relationships among mostly small- and medium-sized firms. When a considerable number of firms moved across the Taiwan Strait, this distinctive characteristic of Taiwan's industrial structure soon led to a regiment of connected firms. As a result, between 1988 and 1992, thousands of Taiwanese manufacturers of garments, handbags, sports shoes, toys, bicycles, umbrellas, small consumer electronics, and cameras were established along the coast of Guangdong and Fujian. Within 4 years, Mainland China became Taiwan's fifth largest exporting market and Taiwan was the mainland's second largest investor.

Starting in the mid-1990s, the second wave of Taiwanese capital outflow to the Chinese mainland gradually emerged. However, at this time, the key players were Taiwan's largest business groups. By the end of 1993, only 46 among Taiwan's 350 strong-listed companies had made investments through the official channel. By mid-1996, the figure rose to 83 companies. As a result, by 1995, total cross-strait trade grew about 10 times and exceeded US $20 billion, while Taiwan's total trade with other countries and areas grew only 138.9% in the same period. Total trade between the two regimes exceeded US $5 billion in 1990 and US $11 billion in 1993. In 1995, Taiwan ranked after Japan as Mainland China's second major supplier and became China's seventh largest export market.

The above figures demonstrate that the growth of investment from Taiwan to the mainland was impressive. Prior to 1987, there was actually no Taiwanese investment on the mainland. After the relaxation of foreign exchange controls, Taiwanese companies began to invest in the nearest coastal cities across the Taiwan Strait, with Xiamen attracting the largest investment. After 1990, Taiwanese capital concentrated on land speculation and real estate in the coastal cities of eastern China. According to Taiwan's official statistics, between 1991 and 1995, 11,254 investment applications to the mainland, with a total value over US $56 billion, were approved, while China's statistics showed 31,780 Taiwan investment applications with a total value of more than US $114 billion on the mainland. This accounted for 10% of the mainland's total foreign investment, ranking Taiwan after Hong Kong-Macao the second largest investor in China. Meanwhile, China became the most important outlet for Taiwan's overseas investment, accounting for 66% of the total in 1993. Until 1995, Mainland China accounted for about 50% of the island's total investment abroad, far exceeding Taiwan's investment in the US.

This intensified trade and investment activity between Taiwan and China also reflected in their trading positions with the US. The US has long been the largest market for Taiwanese textile and footwear exports. For example, about 70% of output from factories with Taiwanese equity in the mainland was shipped to the US. Chinese footwear manufacturers with Taiwan investment supplied 200 million pairs of the 500 million pairs of mainland Chinese-made shoes sold in the US in 1991. From 1987 onwards, Mainland China's trade surplus with the US rose dramatically: from US $2.8 billion in 1987, to US $10.4 billion in 1990, to US $12.7 billion in 1991, to US $18.3 billion in 1992. By contrast, during the same period the largest surpluses enjoyed by Taiwan declined. Its trade surplus with the US fell from US $17 billion in 1987 to US $9.6 billion in 1994.

POLITICAL STRUGGLES ALONG WITH RAPID CROSS-STRAIT ECONOMIC INTERACTIONS

The authorities of China and Taiwan have both made active efforts either to facilitate or regulate economic exchanges across the Taiwan Strait. Generally, the Chinese government has been inclined to promote more cross-strait interactions. In contrast, the Taiwanese authority has leaned toward adopting regulatory practices to harness the rapid cross-strait economic exchanges.

Chinese Government Practices to Facilitate Cross-Strait Interactions

On 1 January 1979, the Standing Committee of the National People's Congress (NPC) launched a peaceful reunification offensive, fully elaborated in a nine-point proposal on 30 September 1981 by the vice-chairman of the NPC Standing Committee, Ye Jianying. Ye specifically proposed *santong* (opening three links, i.e., commercial, postal, and travel) and suggested *siliu* (four exchanges, i.e., academic, cultural, economic, and athletic) as the first steps toward gradually eliminating antagonism between the two sides and increasing mutual understanding.

As far as the interests of the Chinese CCP government were concerned, the promotion of cross-strait economic interaction was based on the belief that a deepening of economic interdependence would weaken Taiwan's competence and desire to seek independence. Since the Chinese government regarded Taiwan as a breakaway province, it reckoned that an increase in cross-strait economic exchanges would not only serve to diminish the risk of Taiwan's permanent drifting away from the mainland, but would also contribute to achieving its paramount political objective of national reunification. Hence, it invested a great deal of effort in removing restrictions imposed by the Taiwanese government. The idea of utilizing economic interaction as a means to develop political relations and to promote reunification was first expressed at the 1990 National Work Conference on Taiwan by President Yang Shangkun. He made it clear that political integration via economic exchange should be promoted by manipulating Taiwanese people's opinions, to compel the Taiwan authorities to discuss and lead exchanges between the two sides in a direction favorable to reunification. The same opinion was reiterated by his successor Jiang Zemin.

In concrete practice, the Chinese government provided preferential treatment for Taiwan investment, tolerating a huge trade deficit—approximately US $14.8 billion in 1995—that far exceeded Taiwan's trade surplus with the US. This huge trade deficit was tolerated because, China theorized, a large number of Taiwanese businessmen with vested interests in China would eventually develop into a political group in Taiwan pursuing a China-friendly policy.

Indeed, the positive response by the Taiwanese people toward China's three-links policy clearly offered powerful evidence for this theory. In other words, the Chinese government anticipated that increased cross-strait economic interaction would lead to an interest-based, rather than an ethnic-based pro-China lobby group in Taiwan (Zhang, 1999). For this reason, China offered Taiwanese firms more special concessions than any other foreign businesses. Taiwanese goods faced lower taxes in China, and import controls on Taiwanese goods were less stringent. A 1988 State Council decree gave Taiwanese investors favourable treatment over other foreign investors. Local authorities also tended to give Taiwanese investors more favourable treatment in terms of faster approvals and better support services.

Regulatory Measures Adopted by the Taiwanese Government

Since China unilaterally ended its ban on Taiwanese investment and trade in 1979, various and diverse opinions concerning the pace and scope of economic opening to the mainland have emerged in Taiwan's domestic politics. Initially, Taiwan regarded this peaceful reunification policy with scepticism and responded with a three-no policy. It was not until 1987 that Taiwan began to relax restrictions on trade, investment, and travel to the mainland. Since then, Taiwan's import controls on mainland products have been gradually liberalized, and by the end of 1990, 92 indirect import items were allowed. In July 1987, Taiwan eased its foreign exchange controls, and Taiwanese businesses began to invest indirectly on the mainland via subsidiaries established in Hong Kong and elsewhere. In November of 1987, Taiwan allowed citizens to visit mainland relatives, and the number of Taiwanese visitors to the mainland soared. In June 1989, Taiwan further liberalized indirect imports of mainland goods, and in October 1989, promulgated regulations sanctioning indirect trade, investment, and technical cooperation with China.

Taiwan's policy required that all trade, investment, and visits had to be conducted indirectly—that is, via Hong Kong or elsewhere. In October 1990, official permission for indirect investment and technical cooperation was granted to allow Taiwanese businessmen to register their investment on an approval list. Taiwan still prohibited investment from the mainland, although it was reported that the mainland had invested in Taiwan through its overseas subsidiaries. However, in contrast to the openness of China to Taiwanese goods, the government in Taiwan was less open to the mainland than to other countries (Sung, 1995).

The controversies surrounding the opening of economic interactions with Mainland China carried both political and economic connotations in Taiwan. The most divisive issues pertained to establishing direct transportation links with the mainland and further liberalization of trade, investment, and people flows, including an investment agreement that would provide legal protection to Taiwanese investors. This was particularly true for financial and transportation conglomerates, whose large-scale, long-term investments required greater legal protection that could only be embodied via intergovernmental agreements. The low production costs and large market offered by Chinese mainland attracted large numbers of small- and medium-sized short-term profit-seeking firms and also motivated them to overcome the costs and inconvenience of operating mainland trade and investment through a third party, mainly Hong Kong. Hence they made up the overwhelming bulk of Taiwan's trade and investment in the southern China coastal provinces (see Table 13.1).

In contrast with the enthusiasm of many Taiwanese firms in exploiting the new opportunities provided by Mainland China, Taiwanese authorities feared that overheated cross-strait trade would lead to economic dependency on China, which would eventually threaten its pursuit of a legitimate and autonomous international role. Hence, some government restrictions were created not only to safeguard a hollowing out of Taiwan's industrial activities, but also to prevent the Chinese government using Taiwanese firms with heavy investment in China to extract political benefits. Intergovernmental controversies often occurred among the Ministry of Economic Affairs, the Ministry of Foreign Affairs, and the mainland Affairs Council. The former usually took a more liberal view towards increased linkages with the mainland, while the latter two were more conservative (Yun, 1994).

Taiwan's officials face a complex dilemma. As trade relations between China and Taiwan intensify, and Taiwan's labour-intensive economy gradually diminishes, a large tendency looms toward reliance on Mainland China as a market for its exports as well as a manufacturing base for its products (Chu, 1995). This situation has increased fears that Taiwan might become more vulnerable to political pressures from China. In an effort to steer investments away from excessive concentration in China, Taiwan adopted several measures, including investment seminars on and business tours to Southeast Asia. Taiwan also offered loans to Southeast Asian nations to improve their infrastructure and to establish industrial zones for Taiwanese capital. In 1990, Taiwan's Retired Servicemen Engineering Agency (RSEA) spent US $100 million in Malaysia to turn 82 hectare *Sungai Petani* Industrial Park in Kedah State into an electronics-manufacturing zone, which attracted 30 Taiwanese companies. Further, in 1991, the RSEA built another Free Trade Zone in Malaysia's Ipoh City to house light industries, and Taiwan has agreed to provide up to US $20 million to develop an industrial site at the former US naval base at Subic Bay in the Philippines. In early 1994, President Lee Teng-hui even made a vacation tour to Southeast Asian countries for the purpose of launching a Southward Policy to promote political and economic relations between Taiwan and Southeast Asia. It was expected that alternatives could be created to prevent Taiwan's economy from becoming increasingly dependent on the Chinese mainland. By encouraging Taiwanese firms to relocate to Southeast Asia, the government further internationalized its key industries and created links with growth industries there.

Table 13.1 Taiwan's indirect investments in Mainland China by region: 1991-1998 (unit: US $1,000)

	1991	1992	1993	1994	1995	1996	1997	1998
Shenzhen	43,368 (24.9%)	37,528 (15.2%)	234,852 (7.4%)	33,218 (3.5%)	20,910 (1.9%)	44,775 (3.6%)	79,840 (4.9%)	61,215 (4.0%)
Xiamen	37,528 (21.5%)	19,985 (8.1%)	173,967 (5.5%)	43,516 (4.5%)	31,433 (2.8%)	28,410 (2.3%)	14,304 (1.0%)	44,483 (2.9%)
Guangzhou	8,441 (4.8%)	18,572 (7.5%)	128,259 (4.1%)	48,593 (5.0%)	49,571 (4.5%)	44,504 (3.6%)	67,787 (4.2%)	91,675 (6.0%)
Shanghai	21,393 (12.3%)	17,373 (7.0%)	21,138 (1.0%)	15,596 (1.6%)	410,698 (37.6%)	157,671 (12.8%)	224,160 (13.9%)	243,843 (16.1%)
Beijing	5,975 (3.4%)	5,612 (2.3%)	77,234 (2.4%)	24,622 (2.6%)	19,380 (1.8%)	18,864 (1.5%)	20,361 (1.3%)	44,127 (2.9%)
Fuzhou	10,242 (5.9%)	4,528 (1.8%)	91,439 (2.9%)	24,750 (2.6%)	34,568 (3.2%)	42,513 (3.5%)	19,451 (1.2%)	10,250 (0.7%)
Others	47,211 (27.1%)	143,394 (58.1%)	2,441,522 (77.1%)	787,510 (81.8%)	526,153 (48.2%)	892,504 (72.6%)	1,188,639 (73.6%)	1,023,616 (67.4%)
Total	174,158	246,992	3,168,411	962,209	1,092,713	1,229,241	1,614,542	1,519,209

Source: Statistics on Overseas Chinese & Foreign Investment, Technical Cooperation Outward Technical Cooperation, Indirect Mainland Investment Guide of Mainland Industry Technology, Taipei: Investment Commission, Ministry of Economic Affairs, 1998, pp. 72-73.

CONCLUSION

As the decade ended, capital and other inputs from Taiwan to China created an economic boom that swept across political borders, thoroughly transforming the respective economies in the process. A market of huge proportions has developed without a single meeting, discussion, or negotiation about its growth among officials in these areas. In other words, the dynamic economic growth between Taiwan and China seemingly has given rise to a new type of natural economic territory. Firms from these two countries work together to harness their complementary endowments across political borders. Even so, the question remains: will the emerging breadth and depth of economic interaction between Taiwan and China contribute to the withering away of political confrontation between the two, no matter what they are supposed to be called —two countries or two political entities?

As far as one can see, the answer to this question has been "no." China and Taiwan each have distinct political intentions behind the promotion of cross-strait economic interaction. In China, increased and expanded economic interactions were seen as a way of facilitating eventual political unification. China's political interest in cross-strait trade aimed to weaken Taipei's ability to pursue a flexible foreign policy and to deter Taiwanese independence. The concessions Taiwanese firms enjoyed in China were far better than those other foreign firms received. With this strategy, China sought to make Taiwan sufficiently dependent on China's economy that the potential costs of Chinese economic retaliation would deter any declaration of independence.

In Taiwan, the growth of cross-strait economic interactions was considered as a tool to extract political concessions from China. Of all political concessions, the top three were: to recognize Taiwan as a political entity; to renounce the use of force against the island; and to give Taiwan a larger voice in international affairs (Zhao, 1999b). In other words, cross-strait economic relations served to resist pressure for political reunification and compliance with China's demand that Taiwan should pursue a strict one-China policy.

Meanwhile, Taiwan has sought to use flexible foreign policy to offset its dependence on the Chinese market, and to enhance its security by improving its international political status through expanded participation in international multilateral institutions, as well as a greater political presence in countries through the use of foreign aid. Ironically, the mainland portion of Taiwan's foreign policy has developed faster than its efforts to establish an expanded political role in world affairs. Moreover, China's strategic position in northeast Asia has improved so much that the incentive for Taiwan's neighbouring countries such as Japan and South Korea to risk Chinese opposition to improved ties with Taiwan has significantly declined. As for the US, the instability in its relations with China has prevented it from risking challenges to Chinese interests in Taiwan in case of furthering conflict with China. In addition, China's spectacular economic growth in recent years has increased the interest of all advanced industrial countries in consolidating ties with China. As a result, in the competition between China and Taiwan for international support, Taiwan's position has been deteriorating (Ross, 1995).

Although economic integration does not necessarily reduce political conflict, it should at least increase the potential costs of escalated political conflict. These costs may deter both sides from adopting belligerent policies and possibly further a joint effort to search for mutually satisfactory negotiated solutions. So far, it is too early to conclude that the negative contributions of the massive Taiwanese capital outflow will outweigh the positive ones in terms of improving Taiwan's isolated international position and securing political concessions from China. The dust will settle when major social forces with potential conflicting interests discover a national interest and unite under it.

REFERENCES

Baum, J. (1993). Taipei's offshore empire. *Far Eastern Economic Review,* 18 (March), 44-51.

Chin, J. (1992). Organisations help overseas businessmen cope. *The Free China Journal,* 17, 5.

Chu, J. (1995). Taiwan: A new regional centre in the making. In K. Cao (Ed.), *The changing capital markets of East Asia* (pp. 170-201). London & New York: Routledge.

Chu, Y. (1999). The political economy of Taiwan's mainland policy. In S. Zhao (Ed.), *Across the Taiwan Strait: Mainland China, Taiwan, and the 1995-1996 crisis* (pp. 163-195). New York & London: Routledge.

Clough, R.N. (1992). The Republic of China and the International Community in

the 1990s. *Issues and Studies,* 29(2), 1-18.

Clough, R.N. (1993). *Reaching across the Taiwan Strait: People-to-people's diplomacy.* Boulder, CO: Westview Press.

Khanna, J. (1995). The calculus of interests in the subregional economy of Southern China, Hong Kong, and Taiwan. In J. Khanna (Ed.), *Southern China, Hong Kong, and Taiwan: Evolution of a subregional economy* (pp. 1-13). Washington, DC: The Center for Strategic & International Studies.

Liu, P. (1993). Investing in the neighbourhood. *Free China Review,* 43(2), 28-35.

Ross, R.S. (1995). The politics of economic integration among Taiwan, Hong Kong, and Southern China. In J. Khanna (Ed.), *Southern China, Hong Kong, and Taiwan: Evolution of a subregional economy* (pp. 82-91). Washington, DC: The Center for Strategic & International Studies.

Sung, Y. (1995). Patterns of economic interdependence in the natural economic territory. In J. Khanna (Ed.), *Southern China, Hong Kong, and Taiwan: Evolution of a subregional economy* (pp. 14-41). Washington, DC: The Center for Strategic & International Studies.

Yeh, M.D. (1995). Ask a tiger for its hide? Taiwan's approaches to economic transactions across the Strait. In J. Khanna (Ed.), *Southern China, Hong Kong, and Taiwan: Evolution of a subregional economy* (pp. 61-70). Washington, DC: The Center for Strategic & International Studies.

Yun, E. (1994). The billion NT dollar question. *Free China Review,* 44(1), 16-23.

Zhao, S. (1999a). Introduction: Making sense of the 1995-96 crisis in the Taiwan Strait. In S. Zhao (Ed.), *Across the Taiwan Strait: Mainland China, Taiwan, and the 1995-1996 crisis* (pp. 1-18). New York & London: Routledge.

Zhao, S. (1999b). Economic interdependence and political divergence. In S. Zhao (Ed.), *Across the Taiwan Strait: Mainland China, Taiwan, and the 1995-1996 crisis.* New York & London: Routledge.

The Chinese Role in Asia-Pacific Regional Cooperation

14

Marion Chyun-yang Wang

*Associate Professor, Graduate Institute of Political Science,
College of Social Science, National Sun Yat-Sen University*

INTRODUCTION

In the second half of the twentieth century, four regional projects in Asia, namely the American, the Japanese, the Chinese, and the Asian Projects, provided a regional interface through which internationalization took place and which promoted export-led industrialization in Hong Kong, Singapore, South Korea (ROK), and the Republic of China (ROC) in the 1950s and 1960s. These regions upgraded to NIEs (Newly Industrializing Economies) in the 1970s, diversified their economies in the 1980s, and became economic powerhouses in the 1990s.[1]

China, Japan, and the US now compete for geopolitical and geoeconomic advantages in the Asia-Pacific region. The particular strategies adopted by these three global and/or regional players invoke a wide and often contradictory range of identities and interests in the NIEs. This effect can be readily discerned by the plethora of geoeconomic and geopolitical signifiers deployed by outside forces to identify the NIEs and interpret their interests; these include the Cold War, the New World Order, trade liberalization, economic integration, democratization and nationalism.[2]

OPPORTUNITY AND CHALLENGE IN ASIA-PACIFIC REGIONAL COOPERATION

The Cold War in the Asia-Pacific regional order was marked by contradictions between the claim of the Association of South East Asian Nations (ASEAN) to "autonomy" and the reality of great-power involvement. The onset of the post-Cold-War period in the Asia-Pacific region transformed the security situation into a multipolar game in which the dominant and still emerging regional leaders (Japan and China respectively) have joined the established extra-regional players (US and Russia) in the competition for geopolitical and/or geoeconomic advantages.[3]

The US government is pursuing a three-pronged strategy: multilateralism under the World Trade Organization (WTO), a network of bilateral relationships, and open market-led regionalism under Asia-Pacific Economic Cooperation (APEC). Getting involved with APEC certainly represents a new US strategy for protecting itself in the "Asia-Pacific." To a certain extent, it serves mainly as a tool for prizing open fast-growing Asian markets and for pressing Europe into further trade concessions. The Clinton administration redefined it as an arena for liberalization. It envisaged its own future as "docking on" to APEC by strengthening trans-Pacific links as the North American Free Trade Agreement (NAFTA) is extended.[4] The Asia-Pacific region is America's largest regional trade partner, both as a supplier of US imports and as a market for its exports. Close to 40% of total US trade is now conducted with the East Asia and Pacific region.[5]

The PRC is also entering the struggle for geoeconomic and sociocultural advantages in the Asia-Pacific region by recalling Hong Kong and Taiwan into its economic-cultural orbit. It refers to the idea of growth triangles by proposing "Greater China" as a subregional economic zone. The ROC benefited from the Cold War geopolitical environment: foreign economic assistance helped to alleviate a huge government budget deficit, and carried great weight in financial investment, and paying for imports. Nearly all US aid before 1964 was provided on a grant basis, which made it possible for the ROC to begin its export-led growth in the 1960s without a backlog of debt. The US took an active role in inducing the ROC to adopt an outward-looking economy. Although Hong Kong and Singapore did not receive a large-scale inflow of American aid, the Cold War order also brought a large increase in their exports through the American military and related procurement during the Vietnam War period.[6] In order to maintain stability in the Asia-Pacific region in the post-Cold-War era the US administration's position on Cross-Taiwan-Strait relations is:

1. The US one-China policy is unchanged;

2. The US has an abiding interest in a peaceful approach by Taiwan and China to resolving differences, and supports dialogue as the best way for differences between the two sides to be resolved. The Administration has supported Taiwan's accession to the WTO on its merits. "Bringing China into the WTO is a win-win decision. It will protect our prosperity, and it will promote the right kind of change in China."[7]

Geographically speaking, the Asia-Pacific region can be said to comprise two rather loose groupings with somewhat different positions in the new global economic order, namely APEC and ASEAN. When East Asia faced economic difficulties, countries in the region turned inwards. As their economies have revived, there has been renewed interest in regional institutions, such as APEC and ASEAN. The success of the ASEAN summit in Manila (November, 1999) was the occasion for a "ten plus three" meeting among ASEAN, the PRC,

Japan, and Korea, which offered the opportunity for an unstructured dialogue on both economic and security issues which concern both Northeast and Southeast Asian nations.

For Asian countries, the increasing trade and financial sector integration in the region and in the global economy offers simultaneously enormous potential benefits and new challenges.[8] Besides, East Asia is still under the double pressure of overcoming the negative impact of the financial crisis and meeting new challenges associated with economic globalization. East Asia may become one of the assault targets of international capital in the absence of a rational international financial system and a full-fledged financial supervision and regulation system in regional countries. Financial cooperation should be one focus of the current East Asian Cooperation.[9] Globalization will affect the emerging market economies of Asia and makes imperative not only the maintenance, but also the continued expansion, of a network of well-equipped, first-class regional financial centers.[10]

Excluding Australia, Japan, and New Zealand, Asia now accounts for about one quarter of world GDP on purchasing power parity-adjusted terms. Given this trend, the region could account for one-third of World output by the year 2005. There is an ongoing transformation in the composition of production and trade as the comparative advantages of many Asian economies continues to change. In particular, economies with relatively high wage costs are shifting toward high value-added products, including services.[11]

"GREATER CHINA" IN THE ASIA-PACIFIC REGION

The term "Greater China" subsumes three relatively distinct themes: economic integration, cultural interaction, and political reunification within the international Chinese community. The most common theme in contemporary discussions of "Greater China" is the integration of the world's various Chinese economies, surmounting political boundaries that once divided and isolated them. The varying definitions of the geographical extent of the Greater Chinese economy could be portrayed as five concentric circles, all of which centre on Hong Kong.

These include: Greater Hong Kong (Hong Kong, Macao, and Guangdong), Greater South China (Hong Kong, Macao, Taiwan, and the south-eastern coast of the PRC, extending north perhaps as far as Shanghai), Greater Nanyang (Hong Kong, Macao, south China, Taiwan, Singapore and overseas Chinese entrepreneurs in the rest of south-east Asia), All China (Hong Kong, Macao, Taiwan, and the entire PRC), and Greater China (Hong Kong, Macao, Taiwan, the PRC, Singapore, and overseas Chinese through the world).

The emergence of these variations reflects, to some degree, the changing realities of commercial interaction within the transnational Chinese economy. "Greater China," as the prospective consequence of the "three-way economic integration" of Hong Kong, Taiwan, and Mainland China, seems a more "comfortable" and "apolitical" path to reunification than any formal political settlement.[12] The transnational Chinese economy involves arranging a set of smaller economic circles, integrally connected to larger economic regions, such as the emerging Asia-Pacific economic community, rather than focusing primarily on internal interaction. In addition, it emphasizes relatively spontaneous commercial activity, rather than the negotiation of formal trading arrangements.

"Greater China" involves the increasing cultural interaction of people of Chinese descent across international boundaries. The popular culture of Hong Kong and Taiwan has a growing audience on the mainland. The growth of these kinds of exchanges represents the reintegration of the transnational Chinese society that had been created by the centuries-old Diaspora from the heartland of China to other parts of the world.[13] In the view of a group of ROC and Hong Kong television executives, direct satellite broadcasting of Chinese-language programming will soon create a "Chinese television global village."[14] The creation of a global Chinese culture can exist at precisely the same time as the renaissance of local sub-cultures. Wang Gungwu predicts that the globalization of the world economy and the improvements in communication and transport technology will make it both convenient and imperative for overseas Chinese to maintain at least a partial identity as members of a global Chinese culture.[15]

By taking good care of her own population, the PRC makes a real contribution to regional and world peace. Three international images of the PRC stand out today: a new "yellow Peril," a dynamic economic force with a gigantic market, and a defiant challenger on the world scene. In the international perspective, the key question for the PRC is what role she will play as a political super state.[16]

During the Cold War, the PRC was seen as a swing factor in the tangled web of the US-Soviet Conflict. Since 1979, Beijing has pursued an independent foreign policy and engaged in diplomacy mainly for China's normal national interests, namely modernization. Therefore Beijing sticks to its reforms and opening-up and participates actively in international economic cooperation and exchanges in accordance with the trend towards globalization. China's development strategy stems from a three-step development strategy created at the initiative of Deng Xiaoping in the early 1980s.[17]

The Chinese Communist Party (CCP) developed an open-door policy toward foreign investment through the establishment of Special Economic Zones (SEZs) and the opening of coastal cities and delta areas. The CCP wanted to attract large-scale, high-tech, capital investment from the USA[18] and Japan. The operational vehicle was a "joint venture" between the Mainland Chinese government and the transnational, so that Chinese managers could acquire advanced technology, Western management know-how, and information about world market conditions from their foreign partners.

Since the open-door policy could not achieve its goal, Mainland China proposed a national reunification project to encourage Hong Kong and Taiwanese investment in Guangdong, Fujian, and other coastal provinces. The Chinese open-door-policy-cum-national-unification-project marks a major distinction between Hong Kong (and to a lesser extent Taiwan) and other NIEs. In 1988, the CCP put forward a coastal development strategy, guaranteeing that Hong Kong's and Taiwan's establishments would not be nationalized, that exported goods from them would be free from export tariffs, and that their management would have complete autonomy in running their firms in mainland China. Through the coastal development strategy, Mainland China declared that it was willing to enter the regional production network at the low value-added level.[19]

Post-Tiananmen Chinese foreign policy is susceptible to interpretation as nationalistic and risky. The risks comprise: (1) the nationalistic and assertive character of Chinese strategic culture; (2) the modernization of China's air and naval power; (3) Sino-Russian military technology linkages; (4) the Beijing-Taipei "mini-arms" race; (5) China's claim of a historical burden in the South China Sea; and (6) the promotion of China's diplomatic realignments with its major Asian neighbours—Japan, Singapore, Vietnam, ROK, and India.[20]

The promotion of closer ties with Japan and ASEAN within the region not only boosts China's diplomacy but also strengthens its position as an emerging regional leader. There are signs that China is performing such a role in the Asianization of regional security politics; Hong Kong may become a political lever that can contribute to the growth of a centrifugal subregionalism in China. This tendency for subregionalism is also inherent in the establishment of a Special Economic Zone in Guangdong.

The PRC has developed its own categories to bring certain NIEs into the orbit of an East Asian subregionalism in which it can play a leading role. As an emerging regional leader, China has entered the struggle for geoeconomic and / or sociocultural advantages by creating the concept of "Great China" (or the "China Circle"). This represents an attempt to coordinate and redefine the internal complementarities of evolving subregional arrangements.

It maps China, especial southern China, Taiwan, and Hong Kong–Macao, as a viable growth triangle and thereby assigns to these NIEs an economic and nationalist identity. This imagined subregion of " Greater China" became ever more plausible from 1978 onwards as China created special economic zones and opened its coastal cities. Southern China is now a major production base for its more labour-intensive products. It is estimated that almost 2,000 Hong Kong manufacturing enterprises, mostly in textiles and clothing, toys, and consumer electronics, have moved to this region.[21]

The opening of China made the Chinese market increasingly attractive to Taiwan businesses. The Taiwanese government decided in November 1987 that Taiwanese citizens be allowed to "visit relations" in China. The legalization of travel sharply accelerated the growth in trade. In 1988, the Chinese

State Council promulgated a set of 22 measures to encourage investment from Taiwan. The resulting broad trend is thus toward growing material inter-dependence among Hong Kong, Taiwan, and China. This interdependency is reflected in the crystallization of a subregional division of knowledge, as well as labour, among Hong Kong, Taiwan, and Guangdong and Fujian in China.[22]

Hong Kong and Taiwan are moving up the industrial technology ladder by shifting labour-intensive industries to low-wage regions in southern China. This change has involved economic cooperation across the Taiwan Strait as well as in the Pearl River Delta. Without any direct link between Taiwan and China, most of the flow of people and money targeted in Fujian Province has passed through Hong Kong. The Cross-Taiwan-Strait area has been subordi-nated to development in the Pearl River Delta within the "Greater China" bloc. This delta area (the Hong Kong–Shenzhen-Guangzhou triangle) has been fash-ioned by the Chinese government as an "open district" to pioneer many inno-vations (for example, out-processing and stock trading). After establishing sourcing networks, the Hong Kong/Taiwanese firms then engage in cross-border production management.[23]

Hong Kong is crystallizing its position as a gateway region in providing business and financial services, and Taiwan its position as the source of invest-ment and technology. Ethnic Chinese business people and interested Chinese intellectuals envision a "Greater China" of a much larger, territorial scope and maintain that the formulation of an economic "Greater China" is the first step towards national reunification.

This form of "pragmatic" nationalism is used to redefine and coordinate the internal complementarity of the region in relation to China and its com-petitiveness in the changing global economy. As for Taiwan, the new eco-nomic relation with Mainland China is redefined under the rubrics of "flexible diplomacy" and "economic reunification" in the 1990s. These enable Taiwan to create joint major international/regional organizations (for example, the Olympics and the Asian Development Bank) under the name of "Chinese Taipei" and also to orchestrate unofficial contacts between Taipei and Beijing. Nevertheless, these redefinitions of economic relationships in "Greater China" have assigned an economic-nationalist identity to the subregion.

Confucian Singapore's government is activating the heritage to promote its trade and investment linkages with China through Hong Kong in the name of a shared "Confucian Capitalist" tradition. Hong Kong and Singapore are two of the more liberalized markets. Singapore also promotes its vision of replacing Hong Kong as a gateway to China.[24] Hong Kong's pattern of de-velopment is attributed to its special linkages with Mainland China, or with the Chinese triangle of HK-Mainland-Taiwan.[25] Hong Kong represents the very essence of globalization—open and dynamic,[26] and therefore Hong Kong re-mains the most important region of foreign investment in Mainland China.[27]

Regional or international cooperation depends on stable and sound state relations. The Chinese side stands ready to exchange views on political and security issues of common interest within the framework of East Asian dialogue and cooperation. China's political stability, economic development and social progress constitute China's most important contribution to the development of East Asia.[28]

Faced with the adverse effects of the Asian financial crisis, the Chinese government has implemented a series of measures to expand and keep stable the growth of China's economy, and has worked hard to defend the value of its currency, *Renminbi*. China has also taken part in the aid program of the International Monetary Fund, provided assistance in capital and materials to some Asian countries, and made its own contribution to stabilizing the economic situation of Asia and the World at large.

China is also moving toward greater openness; the *Renminbi* now trades on a market basis in the country, and exchange controls on current transactions have been eliminated.[29] However, in order to overcome the challenge of the Asian financial crisis, China needs two important conditions: a stable and developing domestic economy, and a favourable external stance in today's world. The processes of regional economic globalization and development of regional economic blocs have markedly accelerated the realization of both of these conditions. In particular, the development of transformation, telecommunication, and electronic information technologies has brought international exchange and cooperation in economic science and technology areas ever closer.[30] Multinational Corporations (MNCs) have become an important force in the allocation of global resources.

The ASEAN-China, Japan and ROK Dialogue of Finance and Central Bank Deputies, which was proposed by the Chinese side (March, 1998), was launched successfully under the auspices of ASEAN. The group has had useful discussions on how to monitor and regulate short-term capital flows and to reform the international financial system. In order to become more open to the outside world and increase the level of utilization of foreign funds, China will continue to focus on Foreign Direct Investment (FDI). The role of FDI and MNCs in China is indeed an issue of national and international importance.

CONCLUSION

With the diversity in the Asia-Pacific region, regional cooperation is based on open regionalism. The "Chinese" actors play different roles in Asia-Pacific regional cooperation. There are powerful integrative forces in play, that is, a natural economic complementarity among the three economies (Hong Kong, the ROC and the PRC), a common cultural and ethnic background among the world's Chinese communities, family ties linking various segments of the Chinese diaspora, and the age-old sense that a powerful China should be a unified China. However, there are also significant disintegrative factors, including differences in levels of economic development, in political and economic systems, and in cultural identities.[31] As a middle power in the Asia-Pacific region the ROC's influence is determined by whether she will accept "three links" with the PRC or not. As a potential leading economic power in the world, the PRC struggles for the central role in the process of Asia-Pacific regional cooperation through a three-pronged strategy:

1. Domestic economic reform and opening up China's economy through the establishment of Special Economic Zones (SEZs) and opening of coastal cities and delta areas.

2. Integrating geoeconomic and sociocultural advantages of "Greater China" as a subregional economic zone to influence decision-making in APEC and ASEAN.

3. Actively engaging neighbouring states in Asia-Pacific regional cooperation.

By and large, China will be the world's largest economy in this century and at least a strong regional power. Official contact between Mainland China and Taiwan will be a plus in China's struggle for the leading role in Asia-Pacific regional cooperation.

ENDNOTES

[1] The achievements of the successful Asian economies are largely due to market-oriented, outward-looking growth strategies, plus the high value these societies traditionally place on education and hard work. There are three general explanations for East Asian NIEs.

First, culturalists contend that Confucianism provides the key to understanding the economic success of East Asia.

Second, from the neoclassical viewpoint, economists argue that limited government intervention and reliance on the private sector accounts for the high GDP growth rates of the East Asia States.

Third, the East Asian states experienced both bureaucratic autonomy and public-private cooperation, so that the strong states in East Asia not only were able to formulate strategic developmental goals, but also were able to put them into effective policy action to promote rapid industrialization.

Lai, O.K., and So, A.Y. (1997). Hong Kong and newly industrializing economies: From Americanization to Asianization. In G.A. Postiglione and J.T.H. Tang (Eds.), *Hong Kong's reunion with China* (pp. 102-122). New York, M.E. Sharpe.

[2] Sum, N-L. (1996). The NICs and competing strategies of East Asian regionalism. In A. Gamble and A. Payne (Eds.), *Regionalism and world order* (pp. 207-245). New York: St. Martin's Press.

[3] *Ibid.*, pp. 213-214, p. 221.

[4] Sum, *op. cit.*, p. 223.

[5] Bureau of East Asian and Pacific Affairs, US Department of State, US Economic Relations with East Asia and the Pacific. August 13, 1999 (*http://www.state.gov*).

[6] Lai and So, *op. cit.*, p. 106.

7 Roth, S.O. *East Asia in the year 2000: Problems and prospects in the year of the Dragon*, Washington, DC. February 22, 2000 (*http:/www.state.gov*).

8 There are two reasons for it: 1) As these economies develop, their comparative advantages will continue to change. Therefore efficiency and flexibility will become all the more important for continued economic success; 2) As trade and financial links within Asia intensify, developments in one economy will have a larger impact on the others. The challenges are in three related areas: trade, financial flows, and regional cooperation.

First—On Trade. To sustain growth, a number of countries will need to improve their infrastructure, especially in transportation, telecommunications, and power supply. Regional trade initiatives must be compatible with further global trade liberalization. Asian emphasis on a cooperative approach to trade matters will complement and enhance the global framework being developed through the WTO.

Second—Challenges in the financial area. Asia needs a stronger, more dynamic financial infrastructure that can handle the increasingly complex intermediation requirements of the region. The 'swap' arrangements among a member of Asian central banks are a good example of constructive cooperation to maintain regional stability.

Third—The challenges for regional policy cooperation.

See T. Hannah, *The Role of APEC in the Asia–Pacific Region*, Lecture at Foreign Affairs College, Beijing, 21 June, 1999 (*http://www.apecsec.org.sg*).

9 Address by Premier Zhu Rongji of the People's Republic of China at the Third ASEAN+3 Informal Summit, 28 November, 1999 (*http://www.asean.or.id*).

10 M. Camdessus, *Globalization and Asia: The challenge for regional cooperation and the implications for Hong Kong*, address at the conference, 'Financial Integration in Asia and the Role of Hong Kong,' Hong Kong, 7 March, 1999 (*http://www.imf.org/external/np/speeches*).

11 *Ibid.*

12 Harding, H. (1993). The concept of "Greater China:" Themes, variations and reservations. *The China Quarterly*, 136, 661-664.

13 *Ibid.*, p. 672.

14 *Ibid.*, pp. 674-675.

15 *Ibid.*, p. 677.

16 Weng, B.S.J. (1997). Mainland China, Taiwan, and Hong Kong as international actors. In G.A. Postiglione and J.T.H. Tang (Eds.), *Hong Kong's reunion with China* (pp. 42-43). New York: M.E. Sharpe.

17 First step—to double the 1980 GNP by 1990 and to meet the people's basic needs for food and clothing; second step—to double the 1996 figure by the end of the 20th century and ensure the people a more comfortable life; third step—to raise the per capita GNP to the level of moderately developed countries, to achieve modernization by and large, and to build China into a strong, prosperous, democratic, and culturally advanced socialist country by the middle of this century. China's strategic priorities:

1. To conduct strategy economic restructuring China will promote industrial optimization and upgrading by relying on scientific and technological progress and technical innovations.

2. To continue the construction of infrastructure.

3. To develop rural industries and small cities and towns.

4. To implement the strategy of vigorously developing the western part of China, or developing the west strategy.

See Wu, B., 'On China's economic prospects in the 21st century' (*http://www.China.org.cn*).

[18] China has worked slowly to change its economic isolation, encouraged by a consistently bipartisan US trade policy. Some of the principle goals of this trade policy have been to support Chinese domestic economic reform, improve market access of US business to the Chinese market, and integrate China more fully into the Pacific regional economy. With the passage of PNTR and China WTO membership, the US gains in four distinct ways.

First, WTO accession commits China to the rules of the international economy.

Second, the agreement obligates China to undertake internal reform.

Third, by opening up China's economy and accelerating the process of economic reform, the agreement has the potential to open China's society beyond just trade.

Fourth, China's WTO membership will finally allow American business—most importantly small and medium-sized businesses—greater access to the world's largest emerging market.

See, Shi Guang Sheng: Speech delivered at the Press Conference of the First Session of the 9th National People's Congress, 9 March, 1998 (*http://www.moftec.gov.cn/moftec/official/html*).

[19] The coastal development strategy had the following characteristics.

First, the strategy was targeted at investors from Taiwan and Hong Kong.

Second, it was specifically targeted at small investment projects from small and medium-sized firms in Taiwan and Hong Kong.

Third, it allowed investment in labour-intensive industries, which relied solely on raw material imports.

Fourth, instead of encouraging joint-venture contracts, the present strategy preferred wholly-owned foreign investment because of capital shortages.

Lai and So, *op. cit.*, p. 110.

[20] Sum, *op. cit.*, p. 215.

[21] Sum, *op. cit.*, pp. 231-232.

[22] *Ibid.*, p. 232.

[23] *Ibid.*, pp. 232-233.

[24] D. Beveridge, *Hong Kong group wins Telecom battle*, 29 February, 2000, (*http://www.washington post.com*); *Ibid.*, pp. 234-236.

[25] Lai and So, *op. cit.*, p. 103.

[26] Camdessus, *loc. cit.*

[27] Shi Guang Sheng, speech delivered at the Press Conference of the First Session of the 9th National People's Congress, 9 March, 1998 (*http://www.oftee.gov.cn/moftec/official/html*).

[28] The Chinese side wishes to advance the following proposals.

First: To institutionalize meetings of Finance and Central Bank Deputies, and convene meetings of finance and central bank governors based on the deputy meetings.

Second: To share information and experience on financial reforms and readjustments internationally with their respective countries by means of this mechanism.

Third: To coordinate the positions of East Asian countries on major international financial and economic issues through this mechanism, so that East Asia may do its part in the reform of the international financial system. East Asia should also seek closer international cooperation in the high-tech area.

Address by premier Zhu Rongji of the People's Republic of China at the Third ASEAN+3 Informal Summit, 28 November, 1999 (*http://www.asean.or.id*).

[29] Camdessus, *loc. cit.*

[30] The effects will be strengthened in the following aspects:

1. Further optimizing the industrial structure of foreign investment.

2. Further enlarging the fields open to foreign investment.

3. Further improving the geographical distribution of foreign investment. China will actively support the development of capital-and technology-intensive industries in the coastal areas. But foreign investment is actively encouraged and guided into central and western China.

4. Foreign investment will be attracted through multiple channels and forms with a view to diversifying sources of foreign investment.

Investment by transnational corporations will be actively introduced and guided. Cooperation between large state-owned enterprises and transnational corporations will be promoted with priorities attached so as to facilitate the development of emerging and pillar industries.

Shi, *loc. cit.*

[31] Harding, *op. cit.*, p. 684.